Leaving Certificate
Higher Level

Accounting

Martina Rodgers

The Educational Company of Ireland

Edco

The Educational Company of Ireland
Ballymount Road
Walkinstown
Dublin 12

www.edco.ie

A member of the Smurfit Kappa Group plc

ISBN: 978-1-84536-619-3

Design and layout: Liz White Designs

Cover design: Identikit

Cover photograph: Shutterstock

Editor: Alicia McAuley

Proofreaders: Alicia McAuley, Dog's-ear

The paper used in this book comes from Managed Forests in Northern Europe. For every tree felled, at least one new tree is planted

CONTENTS

Revised

Introduction

- You will have spent two years working towards the Leaving Cert Accounting exam and will have only three hours to demonstrate all of your knowledge. **Good preparation is essential so that you will be able to answer the questions that appear on the exam paper**. This book is designed to help you with this preparation.

- There are three sections in the exam. Be familiar with the topics that appear in each section; these are listed in the table on p.viii. Rather than answering extra questions from a section, it would be advisable to spend any extra time *re-reading your completed questions* so as to gain as many marks as possible in these questions.

- The table on p.viii shows the topics that have been examined in previous years. This should be useful in anticipating questions that may appear on the exam. It would be unwise to try to predict the paper; be familiar with all topics and prepare a number of topics really well.

- Note carefully the important points listed at the end of each chapter in this book.

- Learn the layouts needed, using the templates included in this book.

- Stick to the timing. All sections must be attempted and it is important to complete questions to get the highest marks possible.

Good luck!

Exam Section

Layout of the exam

Section 1 – 120 marks

Do Question 1 for 120 marks.

Final accounts with adjustments of one of the following:

- Company
- Manufacturing
- Sole trader
- Departmental

OR Do **two** 60-mark questions from a choice of three.

Questions asked previously:

- Depreciation of fixed assets
- Revaluation of fixed assets
- Debtors'/creditors' control account
- Published accounts
- Tabular statement
- Service firm
- Cash-flow statement
- Correction of errors (suspense accounts)
- Club accounts
- Incomplete records

Section 2 – 200 marks

Do **two** 100-mark questions from a choice of three. Questions asked previously:

- Interpretation of accounts (every year)
- Incomplete records
- Service firm
- Correction of errors (suspense accounts)
- Published accounts
- Tabular statement
- Club accounts
- Cash-flow statement

Section 3 – 80 marks

Do the costing question.

Questions asked previously:

- Overhead apportionment and reapportionment
- Product costing
- Stock valuation
- Under-/over-absorption of overheads
- Marginal costing
- Marginal costing with absorption costing
- Marginal costing with flexible budget

OR Do the budgeting question.

Questions asked previously:

- Production budget
- Cash budget
- Production and cash budget combined
- Flexible budget

General advice

Read each question carefully. Any information needed for calculations **will be given** in the questions – you may just need to look hard to find it. All information is included for a reason, so use it! Always check what is being asked in the actual question in the exam – **do not presume that the exam questions will be exactly the same as ones you have practised.**

If anything unusual appears, do not panic. Use your knowledge of the topic to attempt an answer; be sure to apply the rules that you are familiar with:

- For every debit there must be a credit.
- If one asset increases, another asset must decrease or a liability must increase.
- The accruals concept: all expenses/gains that relate to the current year must be included in the profit and loss account for that year, regardless of whether they have been paid or not.
- The balance sheet must show all assets and liabilities on the last day of the trading year.

Top Tip!

Rather than answering extra questions from a section, it would be advisable to spend any extra time re-reading your completed questions so as to gain as many marks as possible in these questions.

Practise, practise, practise. Use a question for which you have the solution. Put the solution away and attempt the question on your own from the beginning to the end. Practising without looking at notes is the **only way** to test if you know the required layouts. When you have finished, correct your work using the solution, highlight problem areas and revise these.

Each time you do this you should time how long it takes you to complete the question; try to get quicker and more accurate with each attempt.

Layouts and Ratios

- Learn the layouts needed using the templates in this book, e.g. layout of published accounts, cash-flow forecast, manufacturing account. Practise writing them out from memory on a blank sheet of paper.
- Learn all the ratios and practise writing them out on a regular basis. Pay particular attention to the investment ratios of EPS, DPS, dividend yield, dividend cover, price earnings and price dividend. Be sure that you know what profit to use when calculating the different ratios, e.g. ROCE and ROSF.

Top Tip!

The following topics have previously appeared as 60-mark **and** 100-mark questions: tabular statement, cash-flow statement, published accounts, service firm, correction of errors, and club accounts. Check the following table carefully to see where these questions appeared on the past exam papers.

Theory

The theory section in any question is always worth a considerable number of marks. To avoid losing these marks, you must learn the theory. The relevant theory for each topic is included in the chapters of this book.

Questions on Past Leaving Cert Exam Papers

	'13	'12	'11	'10	'09	'08	'07	'06	'05	'04	'03	'02	'01
Section 1 Do Question 1 **or** *two* other questions from Questions 2, 3 and 4													
Question 1													
Company		Q1					Q1			Q1		Q1	
Manufacturing	Q1		Q1		Q1				Q1				Q1
Sole trader				Q1		Q1		Q1			Q1		
Questions 2, 3, 4													
Debtors' control			Q2				Q2				Q3		
Creditors' control			Q4			Q2			Q2				
Revaluation		Q3			Q3		Q3			Q3	Q4		Q3
Depreciation	Q2			Q3					Q3			Q2	
Tabular statement	Q3				Q2		Q4			Q2		Q4	Q2
Farm accounts		Q4			Q4			Q2					
Cash-flow statement				Q2				Q3	Q4				Q4
Published accounts			Q3			Q4		Q4			Q2		
Service firm										Q4			
Correction of errors		Q2										Q3	
Club accounts	Q4					Q3							
Incomplete records				Q4									
Section 2 Do **two** questions from Questions 5, 6 and 7													
Interpretation of accounts (ratios)	Q5	Q5	Q5	Q5	Q5	Q5	Q5	Q5	Q5	Q5	Q5	Q5	Q5
Service firm		Q6		Q6			Q6				Q6		Q6
Incomplete records	Q7				Q7		Q7		Q7		Q7		Q7
Tabular statement			Q7					Q6					
Correction of errors				Q7		Q7		Q7		Q7			
Published accounts	Q6					Q6			Q6			Q6	
Club accounts			Q6							Q6		Q7	
Cash-flow statement		Q7			Q6								
Section 3 Do **one** question from Questions 8 and 9													
Overhead apportionment and product costing						Q8			Q8			Q8	
Product costing	Q8b			Q8b							Q8b		
Overhead apportionment/reapportionment		Q8a					Q8a						
Stock valuation	Q8a			Q8a		Q8b					Q8a		
Under-/Over-absorption of overheads	Q8c			Q8c									
Marginal costing			Q8			Q8a				Q8			Q8
Marginal and absorption costing								Q8					
Production budget			Q9			Q9			Q9				Q9
Cash budgeting		Q9		Q9			Q9			Q9		Q9	
Production and cash budgeting combined	Q9				Q9								
Flexible budgeting		Q8b				Q8b		Q9			Q9		

Final Accounts

1

Learning objectives

In this chapter you will learn about:

1. The layout of a trading, profit and loss and appropriation account and a balance sheet of a company
2. The layout of a manufacturing account
3. The layout of sole trader and departmental final accounts
4. The types of adjustments that can occur in final accounts
5. The preparation of company, manufacturing, sole trader and departmental final accounts with adjustments

Final accounts are prepared on the last day of the trading year and are made up of a **trading, profit and loss and appropriation** account and a **balance sheet**. A **manufacturing** account is included for manufacturing firms.

Company Final Accounts

The following tables show **sample layouts** for company final accounts.

Top Tip!

> Familiarity with the sample layouts will be of great help for final accounts and also published accounts, cash-flow statements and questions on ratio analysis.

Sample layout of a trading, profit and loss account

Trading, Profit and Loss Account for Year Ended 31/12/-9			
	€	€	€
Sales			X
Less Cost of sales			
Opening stock		X	
Purchases		X	
Carriage in/import duty		X	
		X	
Less Closing stock		(X)	
Cost of sales			(X)
Gross profit			X

contd →

Trading, Profit and Loss Account for Year Ended 31/12/-9 (continued)	€	€	€
Less Expenses			
Administration			
Insurance, rent and rates, depreciation of buildings, general expenses, wages and salaries, directors' fees	X	X	
Selling and distribution			
Advertising, discount, bad debts, loss on sale of delivery van, carriage out	X	X	(X)
			X
Add Income			
Rent receivable, profit on sale of machine, investment income			X
Operating profit			X
Less Debenture interest			(X)
Profit before taxation			X
Less Taxation			(X)
Profit after taxation			X
Less Appropriation			
Preference dividend paid		X	
Ordinary dividend paid		X	
Preference dividend due		X	
Ordinary dividend due		X	(X)
Retained profit			X
P+L balance 1/1/-9			X
P+L balance 31/12/-9			X

Sample layout of a balance sheet

Balance Sheet as on 31/12/-9	Cost €	Depr. €	Net €
Tangible fixed assets			
Buildings	X	X	X
Delivery vans	X	X	X
	X	X	X
Intangible fixed assets			
Patents			X
Financial assets			
Investments			X
			X
Current assets			
Debtors	X		
Less Bad debt provision	(X)	X	
Closing stock		X	
Bank		X	
Investment income due		X	
		X	

Balance Sheet as on 31/12/-9 (continued)			
	€	€	€
Less **Creditors: amounts falling due within 1 year**			
Creditors	X		
Debenture interest due	X		
Preference dividend due	X		
Ordinary dividend due	X	(X)	
Working capital			X
Total net assets			X
Financed by:			
Creditors: amounts falling due after 1 year			
Debentures			X
Capital and reserves	Authorised	Issued	
Ordinary shares @ €1	X	X	
Preference shares @ €1	X	X	
	X	X	
Revaluation reserve		X	
P+L balance 31/12/-9		X	
Shareholders' funds			X
Capital employed			X

Manufacturing Account

When preparing the final accounts of a manufacturing firm, a manufacturing account has to be supplied with the other accounts. It is prepared before the trading, profit and loss account and the balance sheet. (See p.4.)

Top Tip!

The layout of the manufacturing account is also used in the **costing** and **budgeting** questions of management accounting.

The **main headings** in the manufacturing account are:

- Direct materials
- Direct costs
- Factory overheads

The **purpose** of the manufacturing account is **to calculate the cost of manufacture**. All items are added together to calculate this cost except the following, which are subtracted, as they reduce cost:

- Closing stock of raw materials
- Closing stock of work in progress
- Sale of scrap materials

Point to note

If **machinery is disposed of** then a:
- **Profit** made **reduces costs** and is **subtracted**
- **Loss** made **increases costs** and is **included with factory overheads**

Sample layout of a manufacturing account

Manufacturing Account for Year Ended 31/12/-9			
		€	€
Direct materials			
Opening stock of raw materials			X
Purchases of raw materials			X
Add Carriage in/custom duty			X
			X
Less Closing stock of raw materials			(X)
Cost of raw materials used			X
Add **Direct costs**			
Manufacturing wages		X	
Hire of special equipment		X	
Royalty fees		X	X
Prime cost			X
Add **Factory overheads**			
General factory expenses		X	
Factory light and heat		X	
Supervisor's salary		X	
Factory insurance		X	
Depreciation of plant and machinery		X	
Depreciation of factory buildings		X	X
			X
Add Opening stock of work in progress			X
Less Closing stock of work in progress			(X)
Less Sale of scrap materials			(X)
Cost of manufacture			X
Manufacturing profit			X
Market value of manufactured goods			X

> **Top Tip!**
>
> Direct costs and factory overheads must be shown separately. It is essential that the correct layout is followed and that the correct costs are included under the appropriate headings. For example, manufacturing wages are a direct cost and must be shown as such; depreciation of machinery is a factory overhead and must be placed in the correct position.

Current market value

- If goods have to be transferred from the factory at **current market value**, then the **current market value is included** at the bottom of the manufacturing account.

- If the current market value is **greater than** the cost of manufacture, then a **manufacturing profit** has been made, and the factory has produced the goods more cheaply than they could have purchased them.

> **Point to note**
>
> The cost of manufacture figure replaces the purchases figure in the trading account.

- If the current market value is **less than** the cost of manufacture, then a **manufacturing loss** has been made, and it has cost the factory more to make the goods than it would have to purchase them.

- The **current market value** becomes the **purchases figure** and the manufacturing profit/loss is added/subtracted to the gross profit to calculate the total gross profit (see Question 3, p.22).

Sole Trader Account

The layout of a sole trader account varies slightly from that of a company account:

- The money invested in the business by the owner is the capital. There are no shareholders and thus no dividends to be paid out of profits, the profits belong solely to the owner. The profits are added to the capital in the **financed by** section.
- Amounts taken from the business by the owner are called **drawings**. They are deducted from the capital in the **financed by** section. All amounts attributable to personal premises or taken for personal use must be included in the drawings figure.
- The long-term loan is usually a mortgage rather than a debenture.

Departmental Account

This is a company account for a business consisting of several departments. It is necessary to prepare a **trading, profit and loss account** for each department **and** for the business as a whole.

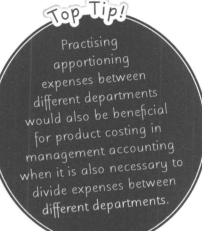

Top Tip!

Practising apportioning expenses between different departments would also be beneficial for product costing in management accounting when it is also necessary to divide expenses between different departments.

- Expenses and gains are divided between departments, using the most suitable basis (usually either floor space or sales).
- Expenses that can be directly associated with buildings, e.g. insurance, light and heat, and loan interest, are split based on floor space.
- Other expenses are usually allocated on the basis of sales.
- Expenses specific to one department are charged to that department only.

Adjustments

The following is a checklist of adjustments that have been examined in previous years. All of these adjustments are covered in the sample questions in this chapter.

Top Tip!

Practising these adjustments will give you the knowledge you need to tackle a new or altered adjustment.

- Closing stock with a net realisable value of less than the value included in the accounts
- Goods on a sale-or-return basis treated incorrectly as a credit sale
- Goods on a sale-or-return basis treated incorrectly as a credit purchase
- Goods in transit not entered in the books
- Goods withdrawn by a sole trader for personal use not entered in the accounts
- Disposal of a fixed asset during the year; purchase of replacement; monies received from a sale treated incorrectly
- Revaluation of a fixed asset at the end or at the beginning of the current year
- Addition to a fixed asset, e.g. an extension carried out by own workers using own materials
- Reconciliation of a bank statement with a cashbook figure and inclusion of new information in the accounts
- An asset destroyed and compensation claimed from insurance
- Intangible assets, e.g. patents; goodwill incorporating a gain, e.g. investment income or an expense, e.g. debenture interest, to be written off over a number of years
- A suspense figure arising from an error or a number of errors in the accounts and incorporated with another figure, e.g. general expenses
- Purchase of a fixed asset including VAT and no entry of the VAT in the VAT account   *contd →*

- Calculation of debenture interest payable and provision for amounts due
- Calculation of investment interest receivable and provision for amounts due
- Provision for corporation tax
- Calculation of preference and ordinary dividends paid and due
- Provision for depreciation on fixed assets
- Creation of bad debt provision
- Increase in bad debt provision
- Decrease in bad debt provision

Top Tip!

You need to be confident in working out how each adjustment affects the figures in the trial balance. All relevant figures must be included in the accounts.

Points to note

Note carefully the following tips to avoid common errors that lead to marks being lost.

Trial balance

- **Expenses** appear on the debit side of the trial balance and **gains** on the credit side. Check items such as discount and commission to determine if they are gains or expenses.
- **Assets** appear on the debit side of the trial balance. To increase an asset, debit; to decrease, credit.
  Liabilities appear on the credit side of the trial balance. To increase a liability, credit; to decrease, debit.
- Always check items such as VAT, bank, etc. to decide if they are assets or liabilities.
- **Reserves** belong to the owners of the business in the same way that capital does and thus appear on the credit side of the trial balance. If the **profit and loss balance** from the previous year is on the **debit side of the trial balance**, then it is a **loss** carried forward from the previous year and must be **deducted** from any retained profit.

Adjustments

- The **double entry rule** 'For each and every debit there must be a credit and vice versa' applies for all adjustments and should be followed. Note this rule well as it will help you deal with all adjustments.
- **Any deduction from stock during the year means a deduction from the purchases figure.** The **closing stock figure** is a valuation of the stock on hand on the last day of the trading year. Any materials taken during the year are not taken from this end-of-year figure but from purchases made during the year.
- Follow the procedure given in the sample questions when dealing with **suspense**.

Question layout

- Include with the date the headings for both the trading, profit and loss account and the balance sheet.
- Include the headings **'Administration'** and **'Selling and distribution'** in the profit and loss account.
- Total the **cost and accumulated depreciation columns** in the balance sheet.
- Check for **common current assets**, e.g. debtors, closing stock, investment interest due.
- Check for **common current liabilities**, e.g. creditors, dividends due, debenture interest due.
- Use the correct layout for **Financed by: 'Creditors: amounts falling due in more than 1 year'**, then **'Capital and reserves'**.

Sample questions and solutions

Question 1 – Company

Byrne Ltd has an authorised capital of €1,100,000 divided into 800,000 ordinary shares at €1 each and 300,000 8% preference shares at €1 each. The following trial balance was extracted from its books on 31/12/2009.

	€	€
Land and buildings at cost	820,000	
Accumulated depreciation – land and buildings		65,600
Patents (incorporating 3 months' investment interest)	57,000	
6% investments 1/4/2009	200,000	
Delivery vans at cost	166,000	
Accumulated depreciation – delivery vans		49,950
Stocks 1/1/2009	72,200	
Purchases and sales	550,000	970,000
Directors' fees	80,000	
Salaries and general expenses	194,300	
Debenture interest paid	1,250	
Profit and loss balance 1/1/2009		66,040
Debtors and creditors	64,000	43,300
Provision for bad debts		2,560
Interim dividends for first 6 months	36,000	
10% debentures (including €100,000 9% debentures issued at par on 1/4/2009)		150,000
VAT		3,800
Bank	10,500	
Issued share capital – Ordinary shares		700,000
– Preference shares		200,000
	2,251,250	2,251,250

The following information and instructions are to be taken into account:
  (i) Stock at 31/12/2009 at cost was €78,000 – this figure includes old stock, which cost €7,000 but has a net realisable value of 40% of cost.
 (ii) Patents, which incorporate 3 months' investment income, are to be written off over a 6-year period commencing in 2009.
(iii) Provide for depreciation on delivery vans at the annual rate of 15% of cost from the date of purchase to the date of sale.

   NOTE: On 31/3/2009 a delivery van, which had cost €50,000 on 1/7/2006, was traded in against a new van, which cost €70,000. An allowance of €31,000 was given on the old van. The cheque for the net amount of this transaction was incorrectly treated as a purchase of trading stock. This was the only entry made in the books in respect of this transaction.
 (iv) Buildings are to be depreciated at the rate of 2% of cost per annum (land at cost was €120,000). At the end of 2009 the company revalued the land and buildings at €990,000.
  (v) The figure for the trial balance has been taken from the firm's bank account. However, a bank statement dated 31/12/2009 has arrived, showing a credit balance of €13,260. A comparison of the bank account and the bank statement has revealed the following discrepancies:

   1 Investment income of €5,000 has been paid direct into the firm's bank account.
   2 A cheque for €540 received from a customer has been entered into the books (cashbook and ledger) as €390.
   3 A direct debit to ESB of €910 has not been recorded in the firm's books.
   4 A credit transfer of €720 has been paid direct to the firm's bank account on behalf of a bankrupt debtor. This represents a first and final payment of 20 cent in the euro.
   5 Lodgements not yet cleared amount to €2,200.
 (vi) The directors recommend that:
   1 The preference dividend due be paid
   2 A final dividend on ordinary shares be provided, bringing the total dividend up to 9c per share
   3 Provision be made for both investment income and debenture interest due
   4 Provision for bad debts be adjusted to 4% of debtors

You are required to prepare a:
 (a) Trading, profit and loss account for the year ended 31/12/2009   (75)
 (b) Balance sheet as at 31/12/2009   (45)
                                                                                          (120 marks)

Solution

Note 1   Closing stock contains old stock worth €7,000 that has a net realisable value of 40%
   Stock has lost 60% of value.
   Loss incurred: 60% of 7,000 = 4,200
   Closing stock: 78,000 – 4,200 = 73,800 **T** and **BS**

Note 2   Removal of investment interest and writing off of patents over 6 years

   Three months' investment interest has been entered incorrectly into the patents accounts and needs to be removed.

Step 1   Calculate the investment interest for the year.
   6% investments 1/4/2009: 200,000
   Investment was purchased on 1/4/2009, thus only 9 months' interest is receivable.
   6% of 200,000 = 12,000 ÷ 12 = 1,000 × 9 = 9,000   **P+L**
   3 months: 1,000 × 3 = 3,000

Step 2   Remove the €3,000 from the patents account – but first you must understand the error.

		€	€
What should have happened	Debit bank	3,000	
	Credit investment income		3,000
What did happen	Debit bank	3,000	
	Credit patents		3,000
To correct the error	Debit patents	3,000	
	Credit investment income		3,000

The investment income was entered into the credit side of the patents account in error and therefore must be entered on the debit side to reverse this error.
When the patents account is corrected, the balance is €60,000.

Step 3   Patents are to be written off over 6 years.
60,000 ÷ 6 = 10,000   **P+L**
The remaining balance, 60,000 – 10,000 = 50,000, is included in the balance sheet.

Patents Account				
	€		€	
Balance	57,000	**P+L**	10,000	
Investment income	3,000	Balance c/d	50,000	
	60,000		60,000	
Balance b/d	50,000 **BS**			

Note 3   **Investment income**

Two figures are needed for the accounts: (1) the investment income receivable for the year for the profit and loss account (in this case 9 months); and (2) the amount due for the balance sheet.

	€	
Interest for year	9,000	
Less Paid (into patents)	3,000	**P+L income**
Less Paid (paid directly)	5,000	(part v)
Due	1,000	**BS current asset**

Investment Income Account			
	€		€
P+L	9,000	Patents	3,000
		Bank	5,000
	9,000	Balance c/d	1,000
Balance b/d	1,000		9,000

Point to note

- The **total amount of interest receivable** for the year must be included in the profit and loss account as income.
- The profit and loss account **must show all interest** for the year.

Note 4   **Depreciation of delivery vans including the disposal of an old van and purchase of a new van treated as the purchase of trading stock**

Step 1   Open the 3 accounts and enter the balances given in the trial balance.

Van Account				
	€		€	
Balance (1)	166,000	Disposal (2)	50,000	
Allowance (4)	31,000	Balance c/d	186,000	
Bank (5)	39,000			
	236,000		236,000	
Balance b/d	186,000 **BS**			

Step 2 Transfer the old van from the van account to the disposal account.

	€	€
Debit disposal	50,000	
Credit vans		50,000

Step 3 Calculate the total depreciation charged on the old van from the date of purchase to the date of sale. Bought 1/7/2006 and sold 31/3/2009 = 2 years and 9 months in total

	€
15% of 50,000 = 7,500 × 2 =	15,000
7,500 ÷ 12 × 9 =	5,625
Total	20,625

Provision for Depreciation Account

	€		€
Disposal (3)	20,625	Balance (1)	49,950
Balance c/d	56,475	P+L (6)	27,150
	77,100		77,100
		Balance b/d	56,475 **BS**

Transfer the total depreciation from the depreciation account to the disposal account:

	€	€
Debit depreciation	20,625	
Credit disposal		20,625

Disposal Account

	€		€
Vans (2)	50,000	Depreciation (3)	20,625
Profit (4) **P+L**	1,625	Allowance (4)	31,000
	51,625		51,625

Step 4 The trade-in allowance of €31,000 is the amount received for the old van. Record as follows:

	€	€
Debit vans	31,000	
Credit disposal		31,000

OR

	€
Cost of van	50,000
Depr. of van	20,625
Net book value	29,375
Allowance	31,000
Allowance > NBV = Profit of 1,625	

Calculate the profit/loss by calculating the missing figure required to balance the disposal account. In this case, enter €1,625 on the debit side, thus there is a profit on disposal.

Step 5 The amount paid for the new van has been incorrectly treated as the purchase of trading stock. It has been entered in the credit of the bank but debited to the purchases account instead of the van account. To correct this:

	€	€
Debit vans	39,000	
Credit purchases		39,000

Balance the van account and correct the purchases figure:

Step 6 Calculate the depreciation to be charged to the profit and loss account for the year 2009. Enter into the provision for depreciation account and balance this account.

	€
Purchases	550,000
Less Error	39,000
	511,000 **T**

Point to note

- When calculating the depreciation, use the **original cost figure** for the months **up to the date of the sale**.

- Then use the **new cost figure** for the months **after the sale**.

- The depreciation charge is for the year and thus should cover the full 12 months.

NOTE: The sale of the old van took place on 31/3/2009.

	€
15% of 166,000 ÷ 12 × 3 months =	6,225
15% of 186,000 ÷ 12 × 9 months =	20,925
12 months =	27,150

Note 5   **Depreciation of buildings including the revaluation of land and building at year end**

Step 1   Calculate the depreciation on the buildings for the year.

	€
Land and buildings at cost	820,000
Less Land	120,000
Buildings at cost	700,000

2% of 700,000 = 14,000   **P+L**

Step 2   Revalue land and buildings to €990,000.

There is an increase of €170,000 in value (from €820,000 to €990,000).

Buildings Account

	€		€
Balance	820,000		
Revaluation	170,000	Balance c/d	990,000
	990,000		990,000
Balance b/d	990,000 **BS**		

Land and buildings (820,000 + 170,000)   990,000   **BS**

Step 3   Transfer all depreciation charged on land and buildings at 31/12/2008 to the revaluation reserve account.

Provision for Depreciation Account

	€		€
Revaluation	79,600	Balance b/d	65,600
Balance c/d	0	**P+L**	14,000
	79,600		79,600

Accumulated depreciation (65,600 + 14,000 − 79,600)   0   **BS**

Step 4   The balance on the revaluation reserve is included with the other reserves in the Financed by section in the balance sheet.

Revaluation Reserve Account

	€		€
Balance c/d	249,600	Buildings	170,000
		Depr.	79,600
	249,600		249,600
		Balance b/d	249,600

Revaluation reserve (170,000 + 79,600)   249,600   **BS**

Points to note

- When buildings are revalued at the **end of the year**, the **depreciation** for the year is calculated on the **original valuation**.
- When buildings are revalued at the **beginning of the year, depreciation** is charged on the **new valuation**.
- Either way, make sure to include the depreciation for the year in the **P+L**.

Note 6 **Reconciliation of the bank figure in the trial balance with the bank statement received**

	€	
Balance as cashbook (taken from trial balance)	10,500	
Add Investment income received	5,000	
Add Cheque understated	150	
Less ESB	(910)	
Add Payment by debtor	720	
Corrected bank figure	15,460	**BS**

	€
Balance as bank statement	13,260
Add Lodgements not yet cleared	2,200
	15,460

Points to note
- The figure for **bank** in the trial balance comes from the firm's own cashbook. If the balance is in the credit column of the trial balance, then it is a **bank overdraft**.
- A **bank overdraft on the bank statement** is described as a debit balance. A credit balance means there is money in the account. From the bank's point of view they owe you.
- Identify the changes that affect the cashbook figure and those that affect the bank statement figure.

Top Tip!

It is always possible to check that the cashbook figure is correct by calculating the correct bank statement figure, as both should be the same after the reconciliation.

Points to note
- Any adjustment that affects the firm's cashbook figure also affects other figures in the trial balance and these must be altered accordingly.
- Any adjustment that affects the bank statement only has no effect on other figures.

Note 7 **Correction of debtors and writing off of bankrupt debtor**

A debtor made a payment of €540 but this was recorded incorrectly as €390: reduce debtors by the difference of €150.

A bankrupt debtor has paid €720 directly into the bank, reducing debtors further. This was 20 cent in the euro of the amount owed: calculate the full amount of the debt (20% = 720; 1% = 36; 100% = 3,600).

	€	
Amount of debt	3,600	
Less Paid	(720)	
Bad debts	2,880	**P+L**

	€	
Debtors	64,000	
Less Cheque	(150)	
Less Total debt	(3,600)	
	60,250	**BS**

Note 8 **Payment of ESB by direct debit to be included in the accounts**

	€	
Salaries and general expenses	194,300	
Add ESB	910	
	195,210	**P+L**

Note 9 Calculation of dividends

The information given is as follows:

	€
8% preference shares (issued)	200,000
Ordinary shares (issued)	700,000
Interim dividends for first 6 months	36,000

Final dividend on ordinary shares **to bring the total dividend** up to 9c per share

Step 1 Calculate the preference dividend.

	€	
8% of 200,000 =	16,000	
6 months paid	8,000	**Appropriation**
Due	8,000	**Appropriation** and **BS**

Step 2 Calculate the ordinary dividend paid.

	€	
Interim dividends	36,000	
Preference shares paid	8,000	
Ordinary shares paid	28,000	**Appropriation**

Step 3 Calculate the ordinary dividend due.

	€	
9% of 700,000 =	63,000	
Paid	28,000	
Due	35,000	**Appropriation** and **BS**

Note 10 Calculation of debenture interest

10% debentures (including 100,000 9% debentures issued at par on 1/4/2009) €150,000

	€	
10% of 50,000	5,000	
9% of 100,000 ÷ 12 × 9	6,750	
	11,750	**P+L**
	1,250	Paid
	10,500	Due **BS**

Note 11 Adjust bad debt provision to 4%

4% of 60,250	=	2,410	new provision for bad debts: **subtract from debtors in BS**
		2,560	old provision for bad debts: **not entered in the accounts**
		150	decrease in bad debt provision: **P+L account, other income**

Top Tips!

- It is the **new provision** that is **deducted from debtors** in the balance sheet; the old provision is only used to calculate whether there has been an increase or decrease.

- An **increase in the provision** is **recorded as an expense**, as it is believed that the risk of bad debts has increased.

- A **decrease in the provision** is **treated as income**, as it is believed that the risk of bad debts has been reduced.

Trading, Profit and Loss Account for Year Ended 31/12/09		€	€	€
Sales				970,000
Less Cost of sales				
Opening stock			72,200	
Purchases	N4		511,000	
			583,200	
Less Closing stock	N1		(73,800)	
Cost of sales				(509,400)
Gross profit				460,600
Less Expenses				
Administration				
Patents written off	N2	10,000		
Depreciation of buildings	N5	14,000		
Salaries and general expenses	N8	195,210		
Directors' fees		80,000	299,210	
Selling and distribution				
Bad debts written off	N7	2,880		
Depreciation of delivery vans	N4	27,150	30,030	(329,240)
				131,360
Add **Other income**				
Reduction in bad debt provision	N11			150
Profit on sale of delivery van	N4			1,625
Investment income	N3			9,000
				142,135
Less Debenture interest	N10			(11,750)
Profit before taxation				130,385
Less Appropriation				
Preference dividend paid	N9		8,000	
Ordinary dividend paid	N9		28,000	
Preference dividend due	N9		8,000	
Ordinary dividend due	N9		35,000	(79,000)
Retained profit				51,385
P+L balance 1/1/2009				66,040
P+L balance 31/12/2009				117,425

Balance Sheet as on 31/12/09

		Cost €	Acc. Depr. €	NBV €
Tangible fixed assets				
Land and buildings	N5	990,000		990,000
Delivery vans	N4	186,000	56,475	129,525
		1,176,000	56,475	1,119,525
Intangible fixed assets				
Patents	N2			50,000
Financial assets				
6% investments				200,000
				1,369,525
Current assets				
Debtors	N7	60,250		
Less Bad debt provision	N11	(2,410)	57,840	
Closing stock			73,800	
Bank	N6		15,460	
Investment income due	N3		1,000	
			148,100	
Less **Creditors: amounts falling due within 1 year**				
Creditors		43,300		
VAT		3,800		
Ordinary dividend due	N9	35,000		
Preference dividend due	N9	8,000		
Debenture interest due	N10	10,500	100,600	
Note capital				47,500
				1,417,025
Financed by				
Creditors: amounts falling due after more than 1 year				
Debentures				150,000
Capital and reserves		Auth.	Issued	
Ordinary shares at €1 each		800,000	700,000	
8% preference shares at €1 each		300,000	200,000	
		1,100,000	900,000	
Revaluation reserve	N5		249,600	
P+L balance 31/12/2009			117,425	
Shareholders' funds				1,267,025
Capital employed				1,417,025

Question 2 – Company

Carey Ltd has an authorised capital of €1,200,000 divided into 800,000 ordinary shares at €1 each and 400,000 9% preference shares at €1 each. The following trial balance was extracted from its books on 31/12/2010.

	€	€
Land and buildings	770,000	
Accumulated depreciation – buildings		46,200
Discount (net)		10,100
Patents (incorporating 4 months' investment interest)	50,500	
9% investments 1/5/2010	150,000	
Delivery vans	183,000	
Accumulated depreciation – delivery vans		54,900
Stocks 1/1/2010	52,900	
Purchases and sales	474,000	723,000
Directors' fees	71,200	
Salaries and general expenses	137,700	
Debenture interest paid for first 3 months	4,500	
Profit and loss balance 1/1/2010		93,000
Debtors and creditors	51,300	46,800
Insurance (including suspense)	6,750	
Provision for bad debts		2,250
Dividends paid	30,000	
8% debentures issued 1/4/2010		200,000
Commission on sales	5,000	
VAT		7,400
Bank		3,200
Issued share capital – Ordinary shares		600,000
– Preference shares		200,000
	1,986,850	1,986,850

The following information and instructions are to be taken into account:

(i) Stock at 31/12/2010 at cost was €63,700. No record has been made in the books for goods in transit on 31/12/2010. The invoice for these goods has been received, showing a recommended selling price of €15,000, which is cost plus 20%.

(ii) It was discovered that goods which had cost the firm €8,500 were sent to a customer on a sale-or-return basis. These goods were charged in error to the customer at cost plus 25%.

(iii) A new warehouse was purchased during the year for €300,000 plus VAT @ 13.5%. The amount paid to the seller was entered in the buildings account. No entry was made in the VAT account.

(iv) Patents, which incorporate 4 months' investment income, are to be written off over a 5-year period, commencing in 2010.

(v) During 2010 stock which cost €5,000 was destroyed by fire. The insurance company has agreed to contribute €4,500 towards the fire damage. No adjustment has been made in the books and the cheque has not yet been received.

(vi) The suspense figure arises as a result of the posting of an incorrect figure for debenture interest to the debenture interest account (the correct figure had been entered in the bank) and discount received €400 entered only in the creditors' account.

(vii) During 2010 an extension to the main building was built by the firm's own workers. The cost of their labour, €29,000, is included in salaries and general expenses. The materials, costing €41,500, were taken from stocks. No entry has been made in the books in respect of this extension.

(viii) Depreciation is to be provided on fixed assets as follows:

Land and buildings: 2% of cost per annum for a full year (land at cost on 1/1/2010 was €100,000)

Delivery vans: 20% of book value

(ix) The directors are proposing that:

1 Provision should be made for both investment interest and debenture interest due

2 Provision for bad debts to be adjusted to 4% of debtors

You are required to prepare a:

(a) Trading, profit and loss account for the year ended 31/12/2010   (75)

(b) Balance sheet as at 31/12/2010   (45)

(120 marks)

Solution

Note 1   **No record made of goods in transit, but the invoice has been received**

These goods have been purchased by the firm and need to be included in the accounts at cost price.

		€	
Selling price is 120%	=	15,000	
Cost price = €15,000 ÷ 120 × 100	=	12,500	
Add Purchases 474,000 + 12,500	=	486,500	**T**
Add Creditors 46,800 + 12,500	=	59,300	**BS**
Add Closing stock 63,700 + 12,500	=	76,200	**T, BS**

Note 2   **Goods sent to a customer on a sale-or-return basis have been charged in error to the customer's account**

Goods have been charged in error as a credit sale at the selling price and this needs to be reversed.

Point to note
Stock is always shown at cost price.

		€	
Cost price	=	8,500	
Selling price = cost price + 25% = 8,500 + 2,125	=	10,625	
Less Sales 723,000 – 10,625	=	712,375	**T**
Less Debtors 51,300 – 10,625	=	40,675	**BS**
Add Closing stock 76,200 (**N1**) + 8,500	=	84,700	**T, BS**

Note 3   **Fixed assets purchased including VAT; no entry in the VAT account**

Calculate the amount of the VAT: 13.5% of 300,000 = 40,500

Remove the VAT from the buildings account and transfer it to the VAT account.

	€	€
Debit VAT	40,500	
Credit buildings		40,500

Buildings 770,000 – 40,500 = 729,500 **BS**

The credit balance of €7,400 in the VAT account becomes a debit balance of €33,100. This debit balance is recorded as a current asset in the balance sheet.

Land and Buildings Account				
	€			€
Balance	770,000	VAT		40,500
		Balance c/d		729,500
	770,000			770,000
Balance b/d	729,500			

VAT Account				
	€			€
Buildings	40,500	Balance		7,400
		Balance c/d		33,100
	40,500			40,500
Balance b/d **BS**	33,100			

Note 4 **Removal of investment interest and writing off of patents over 5 years**

Patents Account			
	€		€
Balance	50,500	P+L	11,000
Investment income	4,500	Balance c/d	44,000
	55,000		55,000
Balance b/d	44,000		

9% investments 1/5/2010: €150,000
Investment purchased on 1/5/2010 =   8 months
9% of 150,000 = 13,500 ÷ 12 × 8   =   9,000   **P+L**
13,500 ÷ 12 × 4   =   4,500   Paid
                                        4,500   Due **BS**

Remove €4,500 from patents: 50,500 + 4,500 = €55,000
55,000 ÷ 5 = 10,000   **P+L**
55,000 – 11,000 = 44,000   **BS**

Note 5 **Stock destroyed by fire; compensation agreed but not yet received**

Stock was destroyed during 2010. Any damage to stock during the year affects the **purchases figure** (remember, the closing stock figure is simply the stock actually on hand on the last day of the year). Thus purchases are reduced by the amount of the loss. The cheque due is included as a current asset and any loss recorded in the P+L account as an expense.

Purchases (**N1**)   486,500 – 5,000 = 481,500   **T**
Compensation due   4,500   **BS Current asset**
Loss due to fire   5,000 – 4,500 = 500   **P+L**

Note 6 **Suspense figure included with insurance**

Errors with debenture interest and discount received have resulted in a suspense figure that has been included with insurance. This involves:

1 Calculating the correct debenture interest
2 Entering the discount received
3 Finding the correct figure for insurance

	€
1 8% of 200,000 = 16,000 ÷ 12 × 9 = 12,000	**P+L**
16,000 ÷ 12 × 3 =	4,000 Paid
	8,000 Due **BS**

Debenture Interest			
	€		€
Bank	4,500	Insurance	500
Balance c/d	8,000	P+L	12,000
	12,500		12,500

The trial balance shows that debenture interest paid for 3 months is €4,500. The correct figure is €4,000. €500 too much has been debited to the debenture interest account and needs to be removed.

Debit insurance
Credit debenture interest

2 Discount received of €400 entered only in the creditors' account; enter discount into the discount account.

Debit insurance

Credit discount

Calculate the new discount figure

3 Calculate the new insurance figure.

Discount			
	€		€
P+L	10,500	Balance	10,100
		Insurance	400
	10,500		10,500

Insurance			
	€		€
TB	6,750	P+L	7,650
Debenture interest	500		
Discount	400		
	7,650		7,650

Note 7 No entry made for extension built using firm's materials and staff

Record the extension, capital expenditure, correctly in the books.

Note that any deductions from stock during the year affect the purchases figure, **not** closing stock.

Add Buildings with the materials and wages used	729,500 (**N3**) + 41,500 + 29,000 = 800,000	**BS**
Less Salaries with the amount of wages incurred	137,700 − 29,000 = 108,700	**P+L**
Less Purchases with the materials used	481,500 (**N5**) − 41,500 = 440,000	**T**

Note 8 Depreciation of delivery vans

20% of book value

	€
Cost	183,000
Less Accumulated depreciation	54,900
Book value	128,100

20% of 128,100 = 25,620   **P+L**

Accumulated depreciation 54,900 + 25,620 = 80,520   **BS**

Note 9 Depreciation of building

	€
Land and buildings at cost	800,000
Less Land	100,000
Building at cost	700,000

2% of 700,000 = 14,000   **P+L**

Note 10 Adjust the provision for bad debts to 4% of debtors

4% of 40,675 (**N2**) = 1,627   New provision for bad debts   **BS**

2,250   Old provision for bad debts

623   Decrease in bad debt provision   **P+L Income**

Trading, Profit and Loss Account for Year Ended 31/12/10		€	€	€
Sales	N2			712,375
Less Cost of sales				
Opening stock			52,900	
Purchases	N1,5,7		440,000	
			492,900	
Less Closing stock	N1,2		(84,700)	
Cost of sales				(408,200)
Gross profit				304,175
Less Expenses				
Administration				
Patents written off	N4	11,000		
Insurance	N6	7,650		
Depreciation of buildings	N9	14,000		
Salaries and general expenses	N7	108,700		
Loss due to fire	N5	500		
Directors' fees		71,200	213,050	
Selling and distribution				
Commission on sales		5,000		
Depreciation of delivery vans	N8	25,620	30,620	(243,670)
				60,505
Add **Other income**				
Reduction in bad debt provision				623
Discount	N6			10,500
Investment income	N4			9,000
				80,628
Less Debenture interest	N6			(12,000)
Profit before taxation				68,628
Less Appropriation				
Dividend paid				(30,000)
Retained profit				38,628
P+L balance 1/1/2008				
P+L balance 31/12/2008				131,628

Balance Sheet as on 31/12/10

		Cost €	Acc. Depr. €	NBV €
Tangible fixed assets				
Land and buildings	N3,7	800,000	60,200	739,800
Delivery vans		183,000	80,520	102,480
		983,000	140,720	842,280
Intangible fixed assets				
Patents	N4			44,000
Financial assets				
6% investments				150,000
				1,036,280
Current assets				
Debtors	N2,10	40,675		
Less Bad debt provision		(1,627)	39,048	
Closing stock			84,700	
Compensation due	N5		4,500	
VAT	N3		33,100	
Investment income due			4,500	
			165,848	
Less **Creditors: amounts falling due within 1 year**				
Creditors	N1	59,300		
Bank		3,200		
Debenture interest due		8,000	(70,500)	
Working capital				93,348
Financed by				
Creditors: amounts falling due after more than 1 year				
Debentures				200,000
Capital and reserves		Auth.	Issued	
Ordinary shares at €1 each		800,000	600,000	
8% preference shares at €1 each		400,000	200,000	
		1,200,000	800,000	
P+L balance 31/12/2008			1,131,628	
Shareholders' funds				931,628
Capital employed				1,131,628

Question 3 – Manufacturing

Baker Ltd, a manufacturing firm, has an authorised capital of €1,000,000 divided into 750,000 ordinary shares at €1 each and 250,000 12% preference shares at €1 each.

The following trial balance was extracted from its books at 31/12/2011:

	€	€
Factory land and buildings (cost €660,000)	615,000	
Plant and machinery (cost €366,000)	222,000	
Discount (net)		5,400
Stock on hand 1/1/2011		
Finished goods	67,300	
Raw materials	52,000	
Work in progress	48,000	
Sales		953,000
Patents	80,000	
General factory overheads	75,200	
Purchase of raw materials	465,700	
Sale of scrap materials		6,200
Hire of special equipment	15,000	
Profit and loss balance 1/1/2011		38,600
Carriage on raw materials	4,100	
Debtors and creditors	51,630	45,850
Interim dividends (3 months)	23,500	
9% debentures (including €40,000 issued at par on 1/9/2011)		190,000
VAT		15,520
Direct factory wages	206,550	
Bank		12,810
Issued share capital – Ordinary shares		600,000
– Preference shares		150,000
Selling and distribution expenses	56,900	
Administration expenses (including suspense)	34,500	
	2,017,380	2,017,380

The following information and instructions are to be taken into account:

(i) Stock on hand at 31/12/2011:

	€
Finished goods	75,400
Raw materials	59,600
Work in progress	35,800

The figure for finished goods included items which cost €8,500 to produce but now have a sales value of 40% of cost.

(ii) It was discovered that goods, which had cost the firm €3,500 to produce, were sent to a customer on a sale-or-return basis. These goods were charged in error to the customer at cost plus 20%.

(iii) Included in the figure for sale of scrap materials is €2,100 received from the sale of an old machine on 1/5/2011. This machine had cost €24,000 on 1/8/2006. The cheque received had been entered in the bank account. These were the only entries in the books.

(iv) The suspense figure arises as a result of discount allowed €500 entered in the discount account only.

(v) During 2011 an extension was built to the factory. The work was carried out by the firm's own employees. The cost of their labour, €32,000, was included in factory wages. The cost of materials used, €42,000, was included in purchases. No entry has been made in the books in respect of this extension.

(vi) Depreciation is to be provided on fixed assets as follows:
Buildings: 2% of cost per annum for a full year
Land at cost on 1/1/2011 was €130,000
Plant and machinery: 20% of cost per annum from date of purchase to date of sale
At the end of 2011 the company revalued the land and buildings at €850,000.

(vii) The directors are proposing:
1 The preference dividend due be paid
2 The total ordinary dividend for the year should be 8c per share
3 Provision should be made for debenture interest
4 Corporation tax of €12,000

(viii) Goods should be transferred from factory at current market value of €850,000.

You are required to prepare a:

(a) Manufacturing, trading, profit and loss account for the year ended 31/12/2011   (75)

(b) Balance sheet as at 31/12/2011   (45)

(120 marks)

Solution

Note 1   **Decrease in value of closing stock**

60% of 8,500 = 5,100

75,400 − 5,100 = 70,300   Closing stock of finished goods   **T** and **BS**

Note 2   **Sale-or-return goods incorrectly charged to the customer**

Cost price	=	€3,500
Selling price	=	Cost price + 20% = 3,500 + 700 = 4,200
Less Sales		953,000 − 4,200 = 948,800 **T**
Less Debtors		51,630 − 4,200 = 47,430 **BS**
Add Closing stock of finished goods		70,300 (**N1**) + 3,500 = 73,800 **T, BS**

NOTE: Stock is always shown at cost price.

Note 3   **Disposal of old machine, amount received incorrectly treated as sale of scrap materials**

	€
Sale of scrap materials	6,200
Less Amount received from sale of machine	2,100
Sale of scrap materials	4,100 **M**

Accumulated depreciation on the old machine

Machine bought 1/8/2006 and sold 1/5/2011 = 4 years and 9 months in total

		€
20% of 24,000 = 4,800 × 4	=	19,200
4,800 ÷ 12 × 9	=	3,600
		22,800

Depreciation charge for 2011 (P+L figure)

NOTE: The sale of the old machine took place on 1/5/2011.

		€
20% of 366,000 ÷ 12 × 4 months	=	24,400
20% of 342,000 ÷ 12 × 8 months	=	45,600
12 months	=	70,000

Plant and Machinery Account			
	€		€
Balance	366,000	Disposal	24,000
		Balance c/d	342,000
	366,000		366,000
Balance b/d	342,000 **BS**		

Provision for Depreciation Account			
	€		€
Disposal	22,800	Balance	144,000
Balance c/d	191,200	**Manf.**	70,000
	214,000		214,000
		Balance b/d	191,200 **BS**

or

Disposal Account			
	€		€
Machinery	24,000	Depreciation	22,800
Profit on disposal **M**	900	Bank	2,100
	24,900		24,900

Cost of machine	24,000
Depr. of machine	22,800
Net book value	1,200
Bank	2,100
Bank > NBV = Profit of 900	

Note 4 Suspense

1 Enter discount allowed into debtors' account and calculate new debtors' figure
2 Find the correct figure for administration expenses

Debtors' Account			
	€		€
Balance (**N2**)	47,430	Discount	500
		Balance c/d	46,930
	47,430		47,430

Administration Expenses Account			
	€		€
TB	34,500	P+L	35,000
Discount	500		
	35,000		35,000

Note 5 Extension built using the firm's workers and materials

Add Buildings	660,000	+	32,000	+	42,000	=	734,000	**BS**
Less Factory wages	206,550	–	32,000			=	174,550	**M**
Less Purchases	465,700	–	42,000			=	423,700	**M**

Note 6 Depreciation and revaluation of buildings

	€
Land and buildings at cost	734,000
Less Land	130,000
Building at cost	604,000 × 2% = 12,080 **M**

Revalue land and buildings from 734,000 to 850,000, an increase of 116,000
Accumulated depreciation 660,000 (cost) – 615,000 (book value) = 45,000 + 12,080 = 57,080

Land and Building	734,000 + 116,000		=	850,000 **BS**
Depreciation	57,080 – 57,080		=	0 **BS**
Revaluation reserve	116,000 + 57,080		=	173,080 **BS**

Note 7   Dividends

1

		€	
Preference dividend 12% of 150,000	=	18,000	
18,000 ÷ 12 × 3	=	4,500	Paid **Appropriation**
		13,500	Due **Appropriation** and **BS**

2

	€
Interim dividends	23,500
Preference dividend paid	4,500
Ordinary dividend paid	19,000

3

		€	
Ordinary dividend 8% of 600,000	=	48,000	
Paid		19,000	**Appropriation**
Due		29,000	**Appropriation** and **BS**

Note 8   Debenture interest

		€	
9% of 150,000	=	13,500	
9% of 40,000 ÷ 12 × 4	=	1,200	
		14,700	**P+L** and **BS**

> **Point to note**
>
> Goods are to be transferred from factory at €850,000. If cost of manufacture is less than this amount then a manufacturing profit has been made. The market value of goods replaces the purchases figure in the trading account and the manufacturing profit is added to gross profit to get the total gross profit.

Manufacturing Account of Baker Ltd for Year Ended 31/12/11		€	€
Raw materials			
Opening stock of raw materials			52,000
Purchases of raw materials	N5		423,700
Carriage in			4,100
			479,800
Less Closing stock of raw materials			(59,600)
Cost of raw materials used			420,200
Add **Direct costs**			
Factory wages	N5	174,550	
Hire of special equipment		15,000	189,550
Prime cost			609,750
Factory overheads			
General factory overheads		75,200	
Depreciation on plant and machinery	N3	70,000	
Depreciation on factory land and buildings	N6	12,080	157,280
			767,030
Work in progress 1/1/2011			48,000
			815,030
Less Work in progress 31/12/2011			(35,800)
			779,230
Less Sale of scrap materials	N3	4,100	
Profit on sale of machine	N3	900	(5,000)
Cost of manufacture			774,230
Gross profit on manufacture			75,770
Goods transferred from factory at current market value			850,000

Trading, Profit and Loss Account for Year Ended 31/12/11

		€	€
Sales	N2		948,800
Less Cost of sales			
Opening stock of finished goods		67,300	
Goods transferred from factory at current market value		850,000	
		917,300	
Less Closing stock of finished goods	N1,2	(73,800)	
Cost of sales			843,500
Gross profit on trading			105,300
Gross profit on manufacture			75,770
			181,070
Less Expenses			
Administration	N4	35,000	
Selling and distribution		56,900	(91,900)
			89,170
Add **Other income**			
Discount			5,400
			94,570
Less Debenture interest	N8		(14,700)
Profit before taxation			79,870
Less Taxation			12,000
Profit after taxation			67,870
Less Appropriation			
Preference dividend paid	N7	4,500	
Ordinary dividend paid	N7	19,000	
Preference dividend due	N7	13,500	
Ordinary dividend due	N7	29,000	(66,000)
Retained profit			1,870
P+L balance 1/1/2011			38,600
P+L balance 31/12/2011			40,470

Balance Sheet as on 31/12/11		Cost €	Acc. Depr. €	NBV €
Tangible fixed assets				
Land and buildings	N5,6	850,000	0	850,000
Delivery vans	N3	342,000	191,200	150,800
		1,192,000	191,200	1,000,800
Intangible fixed assets				
Patents				80,000
				1,080,800
Current assets				
Stocks Raw materials		59,600		
Work in progress		35,800		
Finished goods		73,800	169,200	
Debtors	N4		46,930	
			216,130	
Less **Creditors: amounts falling due within 1 year**				
Creditors		45,850		
Bank		12,810		
VAT		15,520		
Corporation tax due		12,000		
Ordinary dividend due		29,000		
Preference dividend due		13,500		
Debenture interest due		14,700	(143,380)	
Working capital				72,750
				1,153,550
Financed by				
Creditors: amounts falling due after more than 1 year				
Debentures				190,000
Capital and reserves		Auth.	Issued	
Ordinary shares at €1 each		750,000	600,000	
8% preference shares at €1 each		250,000	150,000	
		1,000,000	750,000	
Revaluation reserve	N6		173,080	
P+L balance 31/12/2011			40,470	
Shareholders' funds				963,550
Capital employed				1,153,550

Question 4 – Manufacturing

Smith Ltd, a manufacturing firm, has an authorised capital of €850,000 divided into 650,000 ordinary shares at €1 each and 200,000 9% preference shares at €1 each.

The following trial balance was extracted from its books at 31/12/2009:

	€	€
Factory buildings (cost €550,000)	495,000	
Plant and machinery (cost €240,000)	198,000	
12% investments 1/2/2009	120,000	
PAYE/PRSI		6,000
Discount (net)		3,200
Selling and distribution expenses	32,150	
Administration expenses	41,600	
Stock on hand 1/1/2009		
Finished goods	71,500	
Raw materials	52,900	
Work in progress	31,800	
Sales		897,000
Goodwill (incorporating 3 months' investment interest received)	91,400	
General factory overheads (including suspense)	62,300	
Purchase of raw materials	412,600	
Sale of scrap materials		7,250
Hire of special equipment	16,200	
Profit and loss balance 1/1/2009		70,355
Debtors and creditors	62,500	58,200
Dividends paid	31,250	
7% debentures (including €60,000 issued at par on 1/11/2009)		210,000
VAT		12,350
Direct factory wages	211,400	
Bank		15,620
Issued share capital – Ordinary shares		550,000
– Preference shares		100,000
Debenture interest paid for first 3 months	2,500	
Provision for bad debts		3,125
	1,933,100	1,933,100

The following information and instructions are to be taken into account:

(i)   Stock on hand at 31/12/2009:

	€
Finished goods	82,500
Raw materials	56,200
Work in progress	29,500

(ii)   It was discovered that goods, which had cost the firm €5,200 to produce, were sent to a customer on a sale-or-return basis. These goods were charged in error to the customer at cost plus 25%.

(iii)   Included in the figure for sale of scrap materials is €3,520 received from the sale of an old machine on 1/7/2009. This machine had cost €18,000 on 1/9/2006. The cheque received had been entered in the bank account. These were the only entries in the books.

(iv)   Goodwill, which incorporates 3 months' investment income, is to be written off over a 5-year period, commencing in 2009.

(v) The suspense figure arises as a result of the posting of an incorrect figure for debenture interest to the debenture interest account (the correct figure had been entered in the bank) and discount received €350 was entered in the discount account only.

(vi) During 2009 a warehouse was built by the firm's own employees. The cost of their labour, €28,620, was included in factory wages. The cost of materials used, €71,380, is included in purchases. No entry has been made in the books in respect of this extension.

(vii) Depreciation is to be provided on fixed assets as follows:
Buildings: 2% of cost per annum for a full year
Land at cost on 1/1/2009 was €150,000
Plant and machinery: 20% of cost per annum from date of purchase to date of sale

(viii) The directors are proposing:
1 Provision should be made for both investment income and debenture interest due
2 Corporation tax of €15,000

You are required to prepare a:

(a) Manufacturing, trading, profit and loss account for the year ended 31/12/2009   (75)
(b) Balance sheet as at 31/12/2009   (45)

(120 marks)

Solution

Note 1   **Sale-or-return goods incorrectly charged to the customer**

Cost price = €5,200; Selling price = €5,200 + €1,300 (25%) = €6,500

Less Sales	897,000 – 6,500 =	890,500 **T**
Less Debtors	62,500 – 6,500 =	56,000 **BS**
Add Closing stock of finished goods	82,500 + 5,200 =	87,700 **T, BS**

Note 2   **Disposal of old machine, amount received incorrectly treated as sale of scrap materials**

Sale of scrap materials: 7,250 – 3,520 = 3,730   **M**

Accumulated depreciation on the old machine
Machine bought 1/9/2006 and sold 1/7/2009 = 2 yrs 10 months

$$€$$

$$20\% \text{ of } 18{,}000 = 3{,}600 \times 2 \;=\; 7{,}200$$
$$3{,}600 \div 12 \times 10 \;=\; \underline{3{,}000}$$
$$10{,}200$$

Depreciation charge for 2009 (P+L figure)

NOTE: The sale of the old machine took place on 1/7/2009.

$$€$$

$$20\% \text{ of } 240{,}000 \div 12 \times 6 \text{ months} \;=\; 24{,}000$$
$$20\% \text{ of } 222{,}000 \div 12 \times 6 \text{ months} \;=\; 22{,}200$$
$$12 \text{ months} \;=\; 46{,}200 \quad \textbf{M}$$

Plant and Machinery Account					
	€			**€**	
Balance	240,000		Disposal	18,000	
			Balance c/d	222,000	
	_____			_____	
	240,000			240,000	
Balance b/d	222,000	**BS**			

Provision for Depreciation Account

	€		€
Disposal	10,200	Balance	42,000
Balance c/d	78,000	M	46,200
	88,200		88,200
		Balance b/d	78,000 **BS**

Disposal Account

	€		€
Machinery	18,000	Depreciation	10,200
		Bank	3,520
		Loss M	4,280
	18,000		18,000

OR

	€
Cost of machine	18,000
Depr. of machine	10,200
Net book value	7,800
Bank	3,520
Bank < NBV = Loss of 4,280	

Note 3   Investment income

Investment income for 11 months:

$120,000 \times 12\%$ = $14,400 \div 12 \times 11$ = 13,200 **P+L**

$14,400 \div 12 \times 3$ = 3,600 Paid included with goodwill

9,600 Due **BS**

Note 4   Removal of 3 months' investment income and writing-off of goodwill

Goodwill Account

	€		€
Balance	91,400	P+L	19,000
Investment income	3,600	Balance c/d	76,000
	95,000		95,000
Balance b/d **BS**	76,000		

OR $91,400 + 3,600 = 95,000 \div 5$

= 19,000 **P+L**

$95,000 - 19,000$ = 76,000 **BS**

Note 5   Suspense

1 Calculate the correct figure for debenture interest

2 Enter discount received into creditors' account and calculate new creditors' figure

3 Find the correct figure for factory overheads

Debentures: 150,000 for 1 year; 60,000 for 2 months

7% of 150,000 = 10,500; 7% of $60,000 \div 12 \times 2$ = 700; 10,500 + 700 = 11,200   **P+L**

First 3 months paid $10,500 \div 12 \times 3$ = 2,625 Paid

11,200 – 2,625 = 8,575 Due   **BS**

Incorrect figure in debenture interest account of €2,500 needs to be corrected:

Debenture Interest Account					
	€			**€**	
TB	2,500	P+L		11,200	
Factory O/H	125				
Balance c/d	8,575				
	11,200			11,200	
		Balance b/d		8,575	**BS**

Creditors' Account					Factory Overheads Account				
	€		**€**			**€**			**€**
Discount	350	Balance	58,200		TB	62,300	Debenture interest		125
Balance BS	57,850						Discount		350
	58,200		58,200		P+L				61,825
						62,300			62,300

Note 6 **Warehouse built using the firm's workers and materials**

Add Buildings	550,000	+	28,620	+ 71,380	=	650,000	**BS**
Less Factory wages	211,400	−	28,620		=	182,780	**P+L**
Less Purchases	412,600	−	71,380		=	341,220	**M**

Note 7 **Depreciation of buildings**

Buildings 650,000 − 150,000 (land) = 500,000 × 2% = 10,000 **P+L**
Accumulated depreciation 55,000 + 10,000 = 65,000 **BS**

Note 8 **Corporation tax**

Corporation tax: €15,000 in the P+L account and in the BS as a current liability

Manufacturing Account of Smith Ltd for Year Ended 31/12/09			
		€	**€**
Direct materials			
Raw materials			
Opening stock of raw materials			52,900
Purchases of raw materials	N6		341,220
			394,120
Less Closing stock of raw materials			(56,200)
Cost of raw materials used			337,920
Add **Direct costs**			
Factory wages	N6	182,780	
Hire of special equipment		16,200	198,980
Prime cost			536,900

contd →

Manufacturing Account of Smith Ltd for Year Ended 31/12/09 (continued)

		€	€
Add **Factory overheads**			
General factory overheads	N5	61,825	
Loss on sale of machine	N2	4,280	
Depreciation on plant and machinery	N2	46,200	
Depreciation on factory land and buildings	N6	10,000	122,305
			659,205
Work in progress 1/1/2009			31,800
			691,005
Less Work in progress 31/12/2009			(29,500)
			661,505
Less Sale of scrap materials	N2		(3,730)
Cost of manufacture			657,775

Trading, Profit and Loss Account for Year Ended 31/12/09

		€	€	€
Sales	N1			890,500
Less Cost of sales				
Opening stock of finished goods			71,500	
Cost of manufacture			657,775	
			729,275	
Less Closing stock of finished goods	N1		(87,700)	
Cost of sales				(641,575)
Gross profit				248,925
Less Expenses				
Administration				
Administration expenses		41,600		
Goodwill w/o	N4	19,000	60,600	
Selling and distribution			32,150	(92,750)
				156,175
Add **Other income**				
Investment income	N3			13,200
Discount				3,200
				172,575
Less Debenture interest	N5			(11,200)
Profit before taxation				161,375
Less Taxation	N9			(15,000)
Profit after taxation				146,375
Less Appropriation				
Dividend paid	N8			(31,250)
Retained profit				115,125
P+L balance 1/1/2009				70,355
P+L balance 31/12/2009				185,480

		Cost €	Acc. Depr. €	NBV €
Tangible fixed assets				
Land and buildings	N6,7	650,000	65,000	585,000
Plant and machinery	N2	222,000	78,000	144,000
		872,000	143,000	729,000
Intangible fixed assets				
Goodwill				76,000
Financial assets				
12% investments				120,000
				925,000
Current assets				
Stocks Raw materials		56,200		
Work in progress		29,500		
Finished goods		87,700	173,400	
Investment income due			9,600	
Debtors	N1	56,000		
Less Bad debt provision		(3,125)	52,875	
			235,875	
Less **Creditors: amounts falling due within 1 year**				
Creditors	N5	57,850		
Bank		15,620		
VAT		12,350		
PAYE/PRSI		6,000		
Corporation tax due		15,000		
Debenture interest due		8,575	(115,395)	
Working capital				120,480
				1,045,480
Financed by				
Creditors: amounts falling due after more than 1 year				
Debentures				210,000
Capital and reserves		Auth.	Issued	
Ordinary shares at €1 each		650,000	550,000	
8% preference shares at €1 each		200,000	100,000	
		850,000	650,000	
P+L balance 31/12/2009			185,480	
Shareholders' funds				835,480
Capital employed				1,045,480

Question 5 – Sole trader

The following trial balance was extracted from the books of J. O'Sullivan on 31/12/2010.

	€	€
Buildings (cost €850,000)	833,000	
Fixtures and fittings (cost €55,000)	49,000	
Delivery vans (cost €60,000)	48,000	
12% investments 1/3/2010	90,000	
Salaries and general expenses (incorporating suspense)	53,120	
Debtors and creditors	71,400	89,200
Stocks 1/1/2010	52,870	
Purchases and sales	623,500	849,130
Provision for bad debts		3,570
Discount (net)	1,200	
6% fixed mortgage (including increase of €50,000 received on 1/9/2010)		200,000
Commission	15,000	
Rent		24,000
Insurance	8,800	
USC		1,150
Drawings	26,000	
VAT		6,670
Bank	1,830	
Capital		700,000
	1,873,720	1,873,720

The following information and instructions are to be taken into account:

(i) Stock at 31/12/2010 at cost was €61,520. It was discovered that goods, received from a supplier on 31/12/2010 on a sale-or-return basis, were treated incorrectly as a credit purchase. The recommended retail selling price of these goods was €12,000, which was purchase price plus 25%.

(ii) Buildings were revalued to €1,100,000 on 1/1/2010.

(iii) The suspense figure arises as a result of discount received €425 entered in the creditors' account only.

(iv) During 2010 new fixtures were fitted by the firm's own employees. The cost of their labour, €12,900, was treated as a business expense and the cost of materials used, €21,500, was taken from stocks. No entry was made in the books in respect of the new fittings.

(v) The figure for the trial balance has been taken from the business bank account. However, a bank statement dated 31/12/2010 has arrived, showing a debit balance of €120. A comparison between the bank account and the bank statement has revealed the following discrepancies:

    1 Mortgage interest paid, €4,500, through internet banking

    2 A credit transfer of €550 was paid into the bank account on behalf of a debtor who had previously been written off as a bad debt and who now wishes to trade again with O'Sullivan. This amount represents full settlement of the old debt

    3 A cheque issued for €2,000 for rates has not yet been presented for payment

(vi) Depreciation is to be provided on fixed assets as follows:

    Buildings: 2% of cost per annum for a full year

    Fixtures and fittings: 15% of cost per annum for a full year

    Delivery vans: 20% of book value

(vii) Provision is to be made for mortgage interest due and investment income due.

(viii) Provision for bad debts is to be adjusted to 4% of debtors.

You are required to prepare a:

(a) Trading, profit and loss account for the year ended 31/12/2010 (75)

(b) Balance sheet as at 31/12/2010 (45)

(120 marks)

Solution

Note 1   Sale-or-return goods incorrectly recorded as a credit purchase

Selling price = €12,000 = 125%; Cost price = 100% = €9,600

Less Purchases	623,500	– 9,600	=	613,900	**T**
Less Creditors	89,200	– 9,600	=	79,600	**BS**
Less Closing stock	61,520	– 9,600	=	51,920	**T, BS**

Note 2   Revaluation of building at the beginning of the year

Buildings at cost: €850,000; Accumulated depreciation: €17,000

Revalue buildings to €1,100,000 on 1/1/2010:

Revaluation reserve 250,000 + 17,000 = 267,000   **BS**

Depreciation for year: buildings 2% of 1,100,000 = 22,000   **P+L**

Note 3   Suspense

1 Enter the discount received in the discount account

2 Find the correct figure for salaries and general expenses

Discount Account			
	€		**€**
TB	1,200	Discount	425
		P+L	775
	1,200		1,200

Salaries and General Expense Account			
	€		**€**
TB	53,120		
Discount	425	P+L	53,545
	53,545		53,545

Note 4   Fixtures fitted by the firm's workers using the firm's materials

Add Fixtures and fittings	55,000 + 21,500 + 12,900	=	89,400	**BS**
Less Salaries and general expenses	53,545 (**N3**) – 12,900	=	40,645	**P+L**
Less Purchases	613,900 (**N1**) – 21,500	=	592,400	**T**

Note 5   Bank reconciliation statement

	€		**€**
Balance as cashbook	1,830	Balance as per bank statement	(120)
Less Mortgage interest paid	(4,500)	*Less* Cheques not yet presented	2,000
Add Payment by debtor	550		
Corrected bank figure	(2,120) **BS**		(2,120)

NOTE: Bad debt recovered was €550.   **P+L Income**

Note 6   Depreciation

Fixtures and fittings	15% of 89,400 = 13,410	Acc. depr. 13,410 + 6,000 = 19,410 **BS**
Delivery vans	20% of 48,000 = 9,600	Acc. depr. 9,600 + 12,000 = 21,600 **BS**

Note 7 **Mortgage interest**

6% of 150,000 = 9,000

6% of 50,000 for 4 months = 1,000

	9,000	4,500 Paid
	1,000	5,500 Due
P+L	10,000	

Note 8 **Investment income**

12% of 90,000 for 10 months = 9,000 **P+L** and Due **BS CA**

Note 9 **Adjust the provision for bad debts to 4% of debtors**

No change to debtors' figure

4% of	71,400 =	2,856	New bad debt provision **BS**
		3,570	Old bad debt provision
		714	Decrease in BDP **P+L Income**

Trading, Profit and Loss Account for Year Ended 31/12/10			€	€	€
Sales					849,130
Less Cost of sales					
Opening stock				52,870	
Purchases	N1,4			592,400	
				645,270	
Less Closing stock	N1			51,920	
Cost of sales					593,350
Gross profit					255,780
Less Expenses					
Administration					
Depreciation of fixtures and fittings	N6		13,410		
Depreciation of buildings	N2		22,000		
Salaries and general expenses	N3,4		40,645		
Insurance			8,800	84,855	
Selling and distribution					
Discount	N3		775		
Commission			15,000		
Depreciation of delivery vans	N6		9,600	25,375	110,230
					145,550
Add **Other income**					
Reduction in bad debt provision					714
Bad debt recovered	N5				550
Rent					24,000
Investment income	N8				9,000
					179,814
Less Mortgage interest	N7				10,000
Net profit for the year					169,814

		Cost €	Acc. Depr. €	NBV €
Tangible fixed assets				
Land and buildings	N2	1,100,000	22,000	1,078,000
Fixtures and fittings	N4,6	89,400	19,410	69,990
Delivery vans	N6	60,000	21,600	38,400
		1,249,400	21,600	1,186,390
Financial assets				
12% investments				90,000
				1,276,390
Current assets				
Debtors		71,400		
Less Bad debt provision	N9	(2,856)	68,544	
Closing stock			51,920	
Investment income due	N7		9,000	
			129,464	
Less **Creditors: amounts falling due within 1 year**				
Bank	N5	2,120		
Creditors	N1	79,600		
VAT		6,670		
PRSI		1,150		
Mortgage interest due		5,500	95,040	
Working capital				34,424
				1,310,814
Financed by				
Creditors: amounts falling due after more than 1 year				
Mortgage				200,000
Capital and reserves				
Capital 1/1/2007			700,000	
Add Net profit			169,814	
			869,814	
Less Drawings			26,000	
			843,814	
Revaluation reserve	N2		267,000	
				1,110,814
				1,310,814

Question 6 – Sole trader

The following trial balance was extracted from the books of P. Carr on 31/12/2011.

	€	€
Capital		880,000
Drawings	41,500	
Buildings at cost	870,000	
Equipment	90,000	
Delivery vans (cost €144,000)	67,200	
8% investments 1/7/2011	100,000	
6% fixed mortgage (including increase of €30,000 received on 1/4/2011)		160,000
Carriage in	6,330	
Debtors and creditors	52,900	67,500
Purchases and sales	631,000	877,440
Stocks 1/1/2011	72,300	
VAT		2,200
PRSI and USC		1,400
Bank		8,750
Discount (net)		7,360
Salaries and general expenses	63,890	
Mortgage interest paid for first 3 months	1,025	
Provision for bad debts		2,645
Insurance (incorporating suspense)	11,150	
	2,007,295	2,007,295

The following information and instructions are to be taken into account:

(i) Stock at 31/12/2011 at cost was €56,230. No record had been made in the books for goods in transit on 31/12/2011. The invoice for these goods had been received, showing the recommended retail price of €8,700, which is cost plus 20%.

(ii) There are wages outstanding of €3,400 plus 12.5% employer's PRSI.

(iii) Provide for depreciation on delivery vans at the annual rate of 20% of cost from the date of purchase to the date of sale.

NOTE: On 1/4/2011 a delivery van, which had cost €60,000 on 1/11/2007, was traded in against a new van, which cost €90,000. An allowance of €21,000 was made on the old van. The cheque for the net amount of this transaction was entered in the bank account but was incorrectly treated as purchase of trading stock.

(iv) During the year a warehouse costing €55,000 and stock costing €10,000 were destroyed by fire. The employees of the business rebuilt the warehouse. Their labour, costing €25,000, was treated as a business expense and the cost of materials used, €35,000, was taken from stocks. The insurance company has agreed to pay compensation of €60,000. No entry has been made in the books in respect of the destruction and subsequent rebuilding of the warehouse.

(v) The suspense figure arises as a result of the posting of an incorrect figure for mortgage interest to the interest account and discount allowed of €660 entered only in the discount account. The correct interest was entered in the bank account.

(vi) New equipment was purchased during the year for €80,000 plus 12.5% VAT. The amount paid to the vendor was entered in the equipment account. No entry was made in the VAT account.

(vii) Goods taken by Carr for personal use have been omitted from the books. These goods had a retail value of €13,500, which is cost plus 20%.

(viii) Depreciation is to be provided on the remaining fixed assets as follows:
   Buildings: 2% of cost per annum for a full year
   Equipment: 20% of cost per annum for a full year
(ix) Provision is to be made for mortgage interest due and investment income due.
(x) Provision for bad debts is to be adjusted to 5% of debtors.

You are required to prepare a:

(a) Trading, profit and loss account for the year ended 31/12/2011 (75)
(b) Balance sheet as at 31/12/2011 (45)

(120 marks)

Solution

Note 1   No record made of goods in transit, but the invoice has been received

Selling price = €8,700 = 120%; Cost price = 100% = €7,250

Add Purchases	631,000	+ 7,250	= 638,250	**T**
Add Creditors	67,500	+ 7,250	= 74,750	**BS**
Add Closing stock	56,230	+ 7,250	= 63,480	**T**

Note 2   Wages and employer's PRSI due

Calculate the PRSI: 12.5% of 3,400 = 425; the total cost of the workers, i.e. their gross wages, plus the employer's PRSI, must be included in the accounts as an expense.

Salaries and general expenses 63,890 + 3,400 + 425 = 67,715   **P+L**
The amount owed in respect of PRSI increases to 1,825 (1,400 + 425).   **BS**
Wages due 3,400   **BS**

Note 3   Disposal of an old van with the purchase of a new van treated as the purchase of trading stock

Corrected purchases figure
Net amount of the transaction =
   90,000 – 21,000 = 69,000
Purchases 638,250 (**N1**) – 69,000 =
   569,250 **T**

Delivery Vans Account			
	€		€
Balance	144,000	Disposal	60,000
Bank	69,000	Balance c/d	174,000
Allowance	21,000		
	234,000		234,000
Balance b/d	174,000 **BS**		

Accumulated depreciation on the old van
Van bought 1/11/2007 and sold 1/4/2011
   = 3 yrs 5 mths
Total depreciation = 41,000

Depreciation charge for 2011 (P+L figure)
NOTE: The old van was sold on 1/4/2011.

Provision for Depreciation Account			
	€		€
Disposal	41,000	Balance	76,800
Balance c/d	69,100	**P+L**	33,300
	110,100		110,100
		Balance b/d	69,100 **BS**

	€
20% of 144,000 ÷ 12 × 3 months =	7,200
20% of 174,000 ÷ 12 × 9 months =	26,100
12 months =	33,300

Disposal Account			
	€		€
Van	60,000	Depreciation	41,000
Profit **P+L**	2,000	Allowance	21,000
	62,000		62,000

Note 4 **Buildings destroyed by fire and subsequently rebuilt using the firm's employees and materials, compensation not yet received**

Buildings 870,000 – 55,000 + 35,000 + 25,000 = 875,000   **BS**

Purchases 569,250 (**N3**) – 10,000 (stock destroyed) – 35,000 (materials for rebuild) = 524,250 **T**

Salaries and general expenses 67,715 (**N2**) – 25,000 = 42,715   **P+L**

Total cost of fire = 55,000 + 10,000 = 65,000

Compensation **due** 60,000 **(include as current asset)**   **BS**

Loss due to fire 5,000 (include as administration expense)   **P+L**

Note 5 **Suspense**
1 Calculate the correct figure for mortgage interest
2 Enter discount allowed into debtors' account
3 Find the correct figure for insurance

Mortgage interest

                                    €

6% of 130,000 = 7,800 ÷ 12 × 3 = 1,950 Paid

6% of 160,000 = 9,600 ÷ 12 × 9 = 7,200 Due   **BS**

                                  9,150 **P+L**

Incorrect figure in debenture interest account of €1,025 needs to be corrected:

Debenture Interest Account

	€		€
TB	1,025	P+L	9,150
Insurance	925		
Balance c/d	7,200		
	9,150		9,150
		Balance b/d	7,200 **BS**

Debtors' Account

	€		€
Balance	52,900	Discount	660
		Balance	52,240 **BS**
	52,900		52,900

Insurance Account

	€		€
TB	11,150	Debenture interest	925
Discount	660	P+L	10,885
	11,810		11,810

Bad debt provision 5% of 52,240 = 2,612   **BS**

Old provision = 2,645

Decrease in BDP = 33   **P+L Income**

Note 6 **Equipment purchased including VAT; no entry in the VAT account**

Calculate the VAT: 12.5% of 80,000 = 10,000

Equipment Account

	€		€
Balance	90,000	VAT	10,000
		Balance c/d	80,000 **BS**
	90,000		90,000
Balance b/d	80,000		

VAT Account

	€		€
Equipment	10,000	Balance	2,200
		Balance c/d	7,800 **BS**
	10,000		10,000
Balance b/d	7,800		

Depreciation of equipment 80,000 × 20% = 16,000 **P+L**

Note 7 **Drawings taken from purchases not recorded in the books**

Selling price = €13,500 = 120%; Cost price = 100% = €11,250

Purchases (**N4**)   524,250 – 11,250 = 513,000   **T**

Drawings   41,500 + 11,250 = 52,750   **BS**

Note 8 **Depreciation of buildings**

875,000 × 2% = 17,500   **P+L**

Accumulated depreciation 17,500   **BS**

Note 9 **Investment income for 6 months**

100,000 × 8% = 8,000 ÷ 12 × 6 = 4,000 **P+L** and   **BS CA**

Trading, Profit and Loss Account for Year Ended 31/12/11		€	€	€
Sales				877,440
Less Cost of sales				
Opening stock			72,300	
Purchases	N1,3,4,7		513,000	
			585,300	
Less Closing stock	N1		(63,480)	
Cost of sales				(521,820)
Gross profit				355,620
Less Expenses				
Administration				
Depreciation of equipment	N6	16,000		
Depreciation of buildings	N8	17,500		
Salaries and general expenses	N2	42,715		
Loss due to fire	N4	5,000		
Insurance	N5	10,885	92,100	
Selling and distribution				
Carriage out		6,330		
Depreciation of delivery vans	N3	33,300	39,630	(131,730)
				223,890
Add **Other income**				
Discount				7,360
Reduction in bad debt provision				33
Profit from sale of van	N3			2,000
Investment income	N9			4,000
				237,283
Less Mortgage interest	N5			(9,150)
Net profit for the year				228,133

Balance Sheet as on 31/12/11		Cost €	Acc. Depr. €	NBV €
Tangible fixed assets				
Land and buildings	N4	875,000	17,500	857,500
Equipment	N6	80,000	16,000	64,000
Delivery vans	N3	174,000	69,100	104,900
		1,129,000	102,600	1,026,400
Financial assets				
8% investments				100,000
				1,126,400
Current assets				
Debtors	N5	52,240		
Less Bad debt provision		(2,612)	49,628	
Closing stock			63,480	
Compensation due			60,000	
VAT	N6		7,800	
Investment income due			4,000	
			184,908	
Less **Creditors: amounts falling due within 1 year**				
Wages due	N2	3,400		
Bank		8,750		
Creditors	N1	74,750		
PRSI	N2	1,825		
Mortgage interest due		7,200	95,925	
Working capital				88,983
				1,215,383
Financed by				
Creditors: amounts falling due after more than 1 year				
Mortgage				160,000
Capital and reserves				
Capital 1/1/2011			880,000	
Add Net profit			228,133	
			1,108,133	
Less Drawings	N7		52,750	
				1,055,383
				1,215,383

Question 7 – Departmental

Brooks Ltd has an authorised capital of €850,000 divided into 600,000 ordinary shares at €1 each and 250,000 6% preference shares at €1 each. The following trial balance was extracted from its books on 31/12/2009.

	€	€
Land and buildings at cost	550,000	
Accumulated depreciation – land and buildings		26,000
11% investments 1/5/2009	75,000	
Fixtures and fittings	80,000	
Accumulated depreciation – fixtures and fittings		12,000
Grocery department		
Sales		589,200
Purchases	409,215	
Carriage in	5,425	
Stock 1/1/2009	47,890	
Hardware department		
Sales		392,800
Purchases	298,760	
Carriage in	6,160	
Stock 1/1/2009	39,520	
Advertising	61,200	
Salaries and general expenses	54,200	
Profit and loss balance 1/1/2009	21,000	
Debtors and creditors	71,200	56,700
Insurance	28,400	
Light and heat	24,800	
Provision for bad debts		1,830
Dividend paid	20,250	
9% debentures		120,000
PAYE and PRSI		1,770
Bank	7,280	
Issued capital – 400,000 ordinary shares at €1 each		400,000
– 200,000 6% preference shares at €1 each		200,000
	1,800,300	1,800,300

The following information and instructions are to be taken into account:

(i) Stocks at 31/12/2009 at cost were grocery €63,100, hardware €46,700. The figure for grocery stock includes old stock, which cost €6,300 but now has a net realisable value of 60% of cost.

(ii) It was discovered that hardware goods, received from a supplier on 31/12/2009 on a sale-or-return basis, were treated incorrectly as a credit purchase. The recommended retail selling price of these goods was €16,000, which was cost price plus 25%.

(iii) The figure for the trial balance was taken from the firm's bank account. However, a bank statement dated 31/12/2009 has arrived, showing a credit balance of €15,400. A comparison of the bank account and the bank statement has revealed the following discrepancies:

1 Investment income of €2,500 has been paid directly into the firm's bank account

2 A cheque issued for insurance of €5,200 has not yet been presented for payment

3 A credit transfer of €420 has been paid directly to the firm's bank account on behalf of a bankrupt debtor. This represents a first and final payment of 30 cent in the euro

(iv) It was decided on 1/1/2009 to revalue the land and buildings at €700,000. The value of land is €150,000.

Provide for depreciation as follows:

Buildings are to be depreciated at the rate of 2% of cost per annum.
Fixtures and fittings are to be depreciated at 15% of book value per annum.

(v) Advertising includes payment of an annual contract worth €3,600 for the year ending 31/3/2010.

(vi) Expenses are to be allocated to each department using the most appropriate basis. The floor space of the store is divided as follows: Grocery ¾   Hardware ¼

(vii) The directors recommend that:

1 Provision be made for both investment income and debenture interest due
2 Provision for bad debts be adjusted to 5% of debtors

You are required to prepare a:

(a) Trading, profit and loss account for each department as well as for the entire firm for the year ended 31/12/2009   (75)

(b) Balance sheet as at 31/12/2009   (45)

(120 marks)

Solution

Note 1   Decrease in value of closing stock

40% of 6,300 = 2,520
Grocery closing stock: 63,100 – 2,520 = 60,580   **T, BS**

Note 2   Sale-or-return goods incorrectly recorded as a credit purchase

		€	
Selling price = €16,000 = 125%; Cost price = 100%	=	12,800	
Less Hardware purchases	298,760 – 12,800 =	285,960	**T**
Less Creditors	56,700 – 12,800 =	43,900	**BS**
Less Hardware closing stock	46,700 – 12,800 =	33,900	**T, BS**

Note 3   Bank reconciliation statement

	€		€
Balance as cashbook	7,280	Balance as per bank statement	15,400
Add Investment income received	2,500	*Less* Cheque not yet presented	5,200
Add Payment by debtor	420		
Corrected bank figure	10,200 **BS**		10,200

Note 4   Investment income for 8 months

	€	
75,000 @ 11% = 8,250 ÷12 × 8 =	5,500	**P+L**
	2,500	Paid
	3,000	Due **BS**

Note 5 **Writing-off of bad debt and adjustment of bad debt provision**

Debtor paid 420 = 30%; 100% = 1,400

Bad debt 1,400 – 420 = 980   **P+L**

Debtors 71,200 – 1,400 = 69,800   **BS**

New bad debt provision 5% of 69,800	= 3,490	**BS**
Less Old provision	= 1,830	
Increase in bad debt provision	1,660	**P+L**

Note 6 **Revaluation of buildings at the beginning of the year**

Land and buildings at cost 550,000; Accumulated depreciation 26,000

Revalue land and buildings to 700,000 on **1/1/2009**:

Revaluation reserve 150,000 + 26,000 = 176,000 **BS FB**

Depreciation for year

Land and buildings   2% of 700,000 – 150,000 land = 11,000 **P+L**

Fixtures and fittings   15% of 68,000 = 10,200   **P+L**

Note 7 **Advertising prepaid**

Advertising prepaid   3,600 ÷ 12 × 3 = 900   **BS**

Advertising   61,200 – 900 = 60,300   **P+L**

Note 8 **Debenture interest**

9% of 120,000 = 10,800   **P+L, BS**

Note 9 **Apportionment of expenses between departments**

Divide the expenses between the departments using the most suitable basis.

	Grocery	Hardware	Total
Floor space	¾	¼	
Sales	60%	40%	
Total	589,200	392,800	982,000

Expense	Basis	Grocery	Hardware	Total
Depr. of fixtures and fittings	Floor space	7,650	2,550	10,200
Depr. of buildings	Floor space	8,250	2,750	11,000
Salaries and general expenses	Sales	32,520	21,680	54,200
Insurance	Floor space	21,300	7,100	28,400
Light and heat	Floor space	18,600	6,200	24,800
Advertising	Sales	36,180	24,120	60,300
Bad debts	Sales	588	392	980
Increase in BDP	Sales	996	664	1,660
Debenture interest	Floor space	8,100	2,700	10,800

Top Tip!

These calculations can be carried out on the face of the **P+L account**, as under exam conditions there are severe time restrictions; the table has been used here to clearly illustrate **the basis used** and the **division of the expenses**.

Trading, Profit and Loss Account for Year Ended 31/12/09		Grocery €	Hardware €	Total €	Grocery €	Hardware €	Total €
Sales					589,200	392,800	982,000
Less Cost of sales							
Opening stock		47,890	39,520	87,410			
Purchases	N2	409,215	285,960	695,175			
Carriage in		5,425	6,160	11,585			
		462,530	331,640	794,170			
Less Closing stock	N1,2	60,580	33,900	94,480			
Cost of sales					401,950	297,740	699,690
Gross profit					187,250	95,060	282,310
Less Expenses							
Administration							
Depreciation of fixtures and fittings	N6	7,650	2,550	10,200			
Depreciation of buildings	N6	8,250	2,750	11,000			
Salaries and general expenses		32,520	21,680	54,200			
Insurance		21,300	7,100	28,400			
Light and heat		18,600	6,200	24,800			
Selling and distribution							
Advertising	N7	36,180	24,120	60,300			
Bad debts written off		588	392	980			
Increase in bad debt provision	N5	996	664	1,660			
					(126,084)	(65,456)	(191,540)
					61,166	29,604	90,770
Add **Other income**							
Investment income *(floor space)*	N4				4,125	1,375	5,500
					65,291	30,979	96,270
Less Debenture interest	N8				(8,100)	(2,700)	(10,800)
Profit before taxation					57,191	28,279	85,470
Less Appropriation							
Dividends paid							20,250
Retained profit							65,220
P+L balance 1/1/2009							(21,000)
P+L balance 31/12/2009							44,220

Balance Sheet as on 31/12/09		Cost €	Acc. Depr. €	NBV €
Tangible fixed assets				
Land and buildings		700,000	11,000	689,000
Fixtures and fittings		80,000	22,200	57,800
		780,000	33,200	746,800
Financial assets				
6% investments				75,000
				821,800
Current assets				
Debtors	N5	69,800		
Less Bad debt provision		(3,490)	66,310	
Advertising prepaid	N7		900	
Closing stock grocery			60,580	
Hardware			33,900	
Bank	N3		10,200	
Investment income due			3,000	
			174,890	
Less **Creditors: amounts falling due within 1 year**				
Creditors	N2	43,900		
PAYE and PRSI		1,770		
Debenture interest due	N9	10,800	56,470	
Working capital				118,420
				940,220
Financed by				
Creditors: amounts falling due after more than 1 year				
Debentures				120,000
Capital and reserves		Auth.	Issued	
Ordinary shares at €1 each		600,000	400,000	
8% preference shares at €1 each		250,000	200,000	
		850,000	600,000	
Revaluation reserve	N6		176,000	
P+L balance 31/12/2009			44,220	
Shareholders' funds				820,220
Capital employed				940,220

Question 8 – Sole trader (2010, HL, Section 1, Q1)

The following trial balance was extracted from the books of Nora O'Connell on 31/12/2009.

	€	€
Buildings (cost €620,000)	515,000	
Delivery vans (cost €90,000)	80,000	
4% investments (01/7/2009)	120,000	
Patents	60,400	
6% fixed mortgage (including increase of €80,000 received on 01/4/2009)		180,000
Debtors and creditors	50,000	120,000
Purchases and sales	465,200	659,650
Stock 01/1/2009	63,200	
Commission		5,550
Salaries and general expenses (incorporating suspense)	75,000	
Provision for bad debts		1,800
Discount (net)	1,600	
Rent	8,000	
Mortgage interest paid for the first three months	1,400	
Advertising	2,400	
VAT		4,600
Bank		13,300
PAYE and PRSI		5,400
Drawings	32,000	
Capital		495,000
	1,479,750	1,479,750

The following information and instructions are to be taken into account:

(i) Stock at 31/12/2009 at cost was €75,400. This figure includes damaged stock, which cost €8,200 but which now has a net realisable value of €3,400.

(ii) Patents, which incorporate 3 months' investment income received, are to be written off over a 5-year period commencing in 2009.

(iii) Provide for depreciation on vans at the annual rate of 12½% of cost from the date of purchase to the date of sale.

NOTE: On 31/3/2009 a van, which cost €24,000 on 30/9/2006, was traded in against a new van, which cost €48,000. An allowance of €12,000 was given on the old van. The cheque for the net amount of this transaction was incorrectly treated as a purchase of trading stock. This was the only entry made in the books in respect of this transaction.

(iv) The suspense arises as a result of the incorrect figure for mortgage interest (although the correct entry had been made in the bank account) and from €1,000 paid towards PAYE and PRSI entered only in the bank account.

(v) Goods with a retail selling price of €8,400 were returned to a supplier. The selling price was cost plus 20%. The supplier issued a credit note showing a restocking charge of 10% of the cost price. No entry has been made in respect of this restocking charge.

(vi) Provision is to be made for mortgage interest due. 10% of the mortgage interest for the year refers to the private section of the building.

(vii) Provide for depreciation on buildings at a rate of 3% of cost per annum. It was decided to revalue the buildings at €850,000 on 31/12/2009.

(viii) The advertising payment is towards a 24-month campaign which began on 01/10/2009.

(ix) A cheque for €400 had been received on 31/12/2009 in respect of a debt of €900 previously written off as bad. The debtor has agreed to pay the remainder within one month. No entry was made in the books to record this transaction.

You are required to prepare a:

(a) Trading, profit and loss account for the year ended 31/12/2009 (75)

(b) Balance sheet as at 31/12/2009 (45)

(120 marks)

Solution

(a) Trading, Profit and Loss Account for Year Ended 31/12/09 (1)			€		€		€	
Sales							659,650	(3)
Less Cost of Sales								
Stock 1/1/2009					63,200	(3)		
Add Purchases	**W1**				429,900	(6)		
					493,100			
Less Stock 31/12/2009	**W2**				(70,600)	(5)	(422,500)	
Gross profit							237,150	
Less Expenses								
Administration								
Salaries and general expenses	**W3**	73,900	(7)					
Rent		8,000	(3)					
Patents written off	**W4**	12,320	(5)					
Depreciation – Buildings		18,600	(3)	112,820				
Selling and distribution								
Commission		5,550	(3)					
Discount		1,600	(3)					
Advertising	**W5**	300	(5)					
Loss on sale of van	**W6**	4,500	(6)					
Depreciation on vans	**W7**	13,500	(5)	25,450			(138,270)	
							98,880	
Add Operating income								
Bad debt recovered							900	(2)
Operating profit							99,780	
Investment interest	**W8**						2,400	(4)
							102,180	
Less Mortgage interest	**W9**						(8,640)	(5)
Net profit for the year							**93,540**	(6)

Penalties: Deduction of 1 mark each for the omission of 2 expense headings in the profit and loss account.

(b) Balance Sheet as on 31/12/09		Cost €	Acc. Depr. €	Net €	Total €
Intangible fixed assets					
Patents					49,280 (4)
Tangible fixed assets					
Buildings		850,000 (1)		850,000	
Delivery vans	W10,W11	114,000 (2)	16,000 (3)	98,000	
		964,000	16,000	948,000	948,000
Financial assets					
4% investments					120,000 (2)
					1,117,280
Current assets					
Stock			70,600 (2)		
Debtors	W12	50,500			
Less Provision for bad debts		(1,800)	48,700 (3)		
Investment interest due			1,200 (2)		
Advertising prepaid			2,100 (2)	122,600	
Less **Creditors: amounts falling due within one year**					
Creditors	W13		120,700 (4)		
Mortgage interest due			8,100 (2)		
PAYE & PRSI	W14		4,400 (3)		
VAT			4,600 (2)		
Bank overdraft	W15		12,900 (3)	(150,700)	(28,100)
					1,089,180
Financed by					
Creditors: amounts falling due after more than one year (1)					
6% fixed mortgage					180,000 (2)
Capital and reserves					
Capital				495,000 (1)	
Add Revaluation reserve	W16			353,600 (3)	
Add Net profit				93,540	
				942,140	
Less Drawings	W17			(32,960) (3)	909,180
					1,089,180

Workings

1	Purchases	465,200 – 36,000 + 700	429,900
2	Closing stock	75,400 – 4,800	70,600
3	Salaries and general expenses	75,000 – 1,000 – 100	73,900
4	Patents	60,400 + 1,200 ÷ 5	12,320
5	Advertising	2,400 – 2,100	300
6	Loss on sale of van	24,000 – 12,000 – 7,500	4,500
7	Depreciation – delivery vans	8,250 + 750 + 4,500	13,500
		11,250 + 2,250	
		2,812.50 + 10,687.50	
8	Investment interest	1,200 + 1,200	2,400
9	Mortgage interest	6,000 + 3,600 – 960	8,640
10	Delivery vans	90,000 – 24,000 + 48,000	114,000
11	Accumulated depr. – vans	10,000 + 13,500 – 7,500	16,000
12	Debtors	50,000 + 500	50,500
13	Creditors	120,000 + 700	120,700
14	PAYE and PRSI	5,400 – 1,000	4,400
15	Bank overdraft	13,300 – 400	12,900
16	Revaluation reserve	230,000 + 123,600	353,600
	Depreciation – buildings	105,000 + 18,600	123,600
17	Drawings	32,000 + 960	32,960

2 Depreciation and Revaluation of Fixed Assets

Learning objectives

In this chapter you will learn about:

1 The term depreciation, the factors to be taken into account when calculating depreciation and the methods by which it is calculated

2 The depreciation of fixed assets

3 The disposal of fixed assets

4 The revaluation of fixed assets

5 The transfer to the revenue reserve upon disposal of an item that has been revalued

Depreciation of Fixed Assets

Fixed assets are items of value that a business will have in its possession for a number of years; they include items such as buildings, machinery, equipment and vehicles.

The balance in a **fixed asset account** appears on the **debit side** and is always the original **cost** of the asset. When an asset is purchased, the double entry is:

Debit   Fixed asset a/c

Credit   Bank a/c

Fixed assets lose value over time due to age, use, etc. This loss in value is recorded in the accounts as **depreciation**, a non-cash expense charged to the **profit and loss account** each year. If depreciation was not charged, then profits would be overstated, which is against the prudence concept, and the net assets in the balance sheet would not show the true value. Thus:

Debit   Profit and loss a/c

Credit   Provision for depreciation a/c

> **Point to note**
>
> The **provision for depreciation account** shows the **depreciation** charged to the profit and loss account for the asset each year. The **balance** on this account is always on the **credit side** and is the **total depreciation charged on the asset to date**.

The balance sheet must show what you believe the assets to be worth at the end of each year:

Cost of asset –	Accumulated depr. =	Net book value (NBV) of asset
(balance from fixed asset a/c)	(total depr. on the asset to date; balance from depr. a/c)	(the actual value of the asset)

The two main methods of calculating depreciation are:

1 Straight-line method

The depreciation is calculated as a percentage of the cost price. The same amount of depreciation is charged each year over the useful life of the asset. This method is suitable for assets such as buildings. Profit is gained from these assets over a long period of time and they depreciate slowly.

2 Reducing-balance method

The depreciation is charged as a percentage of the cost price in year 1 and as a percentage of the book value of the asset in all other years. The depreciation charge for each year changes. A larger amount is written off at the beginning and each year a smaller amount is charged to the profit and loss account. This method is suitable for items that lose value quickly, e.g. computers.

Disposal of Fixed Assets

When a firm decides to dispose of a fixed asset, 3 accounts are affected:

- Fixed asset a/c   (Existing)
- Provision for depreciation account   (Existing)
- Disposal account   (New)

The factors to be taken into account when arriving at the annual depreciation charge are:

1 Cost of asset
2 Scrap value of asset
3 Estimated life of asset
4 Method of depreciation

The rules for the disposal of a fixed asset are as follows:

Debit	Disposal a/c	with the **cost** of the asset
Credit	Fixed asset a/c	
Debit	Provision for depreciation a/c	with the **total depreciation** charged on the asset to date
Credit	Disposal a/c	
Debit	Bank a/c	with the **amount of money received** from selling the asset
Credit	Disposal a/c	

In the event of a trade-in:

Debit	Fixed asset a/c	with cost price of new asset
Credit	Disposal a/c	with the **allowance** given for the the old asset
Credit	Bank a/c	with the **amount actually paid** for the new asset

- The **disposal account** is opened to establish whether a profit or loss has been made on the disposal of the asset.
- If the **credit side is greater than the debit side**, then a **profit** has been made on the disposal; essentially, the asset has been over-depreciated in the books.
- If the **debit side is greater than the credit side**, then a **loss** has been made on the disposal; essentially, the asset has been under-depreciated in the books.
- There is **never** a balance b/d on the disposal account; the balancing figure is the profit or loss figure which is charged to the profit and loss account appropriately.

Revaluation of Fixed Assets

Over time **certain fixed assets may increase in value**, most usually land and buildings. Any increase in value is recorded in the accounts so that the accounts will give a true and fair view of the firm.

When **revaluation** takes place, a new account called the **revaluation reserve account** is opened. **All increases in value are shown in this account.** The revaluation reserve is included with the other reserves in the balance sheet.

The rules for revaluation of fixed assets are as follows:

Debit   Fixed asset a/c   with the **increase** in value

Credit   Revaluation reserve a/c

Debit   Provision for depreciation a/c   with the **total depreciation** charged on the asset to date

Credit   Revaluation reserve a/c

If the revalued item is sold:

Debit   Revaluation reserve a/c   with the capital gain from revaluation of the asset

Credit   Revenue reserve a/c

Study Tips

- Depreciation, disposal and revaluation of fixed assets are very important topics, each of which can appear in the exam in a number of places: as a complete **60-mark question** in **Section 1** or as **an adjustment**.
- In the past they have appeared as adjustments in the following questions:
  - Final accounts of sole trader, company and manufacturing
  - Published accounts
  - Cash-flow forecast
  - Tabular statement
  - Service firm
- If the rules are well understood and practised, then it will be possible to deal with these adjustments in any type of question. Good knowledge of these topics is essential.

Sample questions and solutions

Question 1

Euro Express Ltd prepares its final accounts to 31 December each year. The company's policy is to depreciate its vehicles at the rate of 15% of cost per annum, calculated from the date of purchase to the date of disposal, and to accumulate this depreciation in a provision for depreciation account.

On 1/1/2008, Euro Express Ltd owned the following vehicles:

    No. 1, purchased on 1/1/2005 for €90,000
    No. 2, purchased on 1/9/2006 for €100,000
    No. 3, purchased on 1/5/2007 for €96,000

On 1/3/2008, Vehicle No. 2 was crashed and traded in against a new vehicle costing €110,000. The company received compensation to the value of €50,000 and the cheque paid for the new vehicle was €85,000. On 1/8/2009, Vehicle No. 1 was traded in for €35,000 against a new vehicle costing €88,000. Vehicle No. 1 had a refrigeration unit fitted on 1/1/2006, costing €30,000. This refrigeration unit was depreciated at the rate of 30% of cost for the first 2 years and thereafter at the rate of 15% of cost per annum.

You are required to show, with workings, for each of the 2 years 2008 and 2009:

(a) The vehicles account (6)

(b) The vehicle disposal account (16)

(c) The provision for depreciation account (32)

(d) One method used for calculating depreciation (6)

(60 marks)

Procedure

1 Calculate the total cost of vehicles on the given date, 1/1/2008, and enter this figure as the opening balance in the vehicles account.

2 Calculate the total depreciation accumulated on the vehicles up to the given date, 1/1/2008, and enter this as the opening balance in the depreciation account.

Top Tip!

It is vital to read the question through carefully. Look out for any additions made to the vehicles, such as the fitting of a refrigeration unit. These additions must be included in all calculations.

- Additions to vehicles, e.g. refrigeration unit, may have a **different depreciation rate** for a number of years; take note and calculate accordingly.
- The **date of purchase and sale** is important. Depreciation is usually calculated from the date of purchase to the date of sale. Always check that depreciation is calculated for the **correct number of months**, e.g. a vehicle purchased on 1/9/2005 accrues **4 months'** depreciation in 2005.

3 Follow the rules for the disposal of vehicles.

4 Calculate the depreciation charge for the year, enter it into the provision for depreciation account and balance all the accounts.

Top Tip!

For the yearly depreciation charge, calculate the percentage on the original vehicles for the months before the disposal, then calculate the percentage on the new total for vehicles for the months after the disposal. Add these together for the total yearly depreciation to be charged to the profit and loss account.

Solution

Note 1

Vehicles on 1/1/2008	€
No. 1	90,000
No. 2	100,000
No. 3	96,000
Refrigeration unit	30,000
Total to vehicles a/c	316,000

Note 2

Total Depr. on 1/1/2008	€
No. 1	58,500
No. 2	20,000
No. 3	9,600
Total to depr. a/c	88,100

Note 4 Date of trade-in 1/3/2008

P+L 2008	€
316,000 × 15% for 2 months	7,900
326,000 × 15% for 10 months	40,750
	48,650

Note 6 Date of trade-in 1/9/2009

P+L 2009	€
326,000 × 15% for 7 months	28,525
294,000 × 15% for 5 months	18,375
	46,900

Vehicle	Purchased	Annual charge €	Depr. to 1/1/2008		2008	2009
No. 1 €90,000 Refrigeration unit 30,000 (30% depr. for first 2 yrs)	1/1/05 1/1/06	13,500 9,000	3 yrs 2 yrs	€40,500 €18,000	€18,000 (€120,000 × 15%)	Traded in 1/8/2009 7 mths' depr. €10,500 Total = €87,000 **(N5)** (40,500 + 18,000 + 18,000 + 10,500)
No. 2 €100,000	1/9/06	15,000	1 yr 4 mths	€20,000	Crashed on 1/3/08 2 mths' depr. €2,500 Total = €22,500 **(N3)** (20,000 + 2,500)	
No. 3 €96,000	1/5/07	14,400	8 mths	€9,600	€14,400	€14,400

Vehicles Account

			€				€
01/01/2008	Balance b/d	N1	316,000	01/03/2008	Disposal		100,000
01/03/2008	Purchases		110,000	31/12/2008	Balance c/d [BS Cost]		326,000
			426,000				426,000
01/01/2009	Balance b/d		326,000	01/08/2009	Disposal		120,000
01/08/2009	Purchases		88,000	31/12/2009	Balance c/d [BS Cost]		294,000
			414,000				414,000
01/01/2010	Balance b/d		294,000				

Provision for Depreciation on Vehicles Account

			€				€
01/03/2008	Disposal	N3	22,500	01/01/2008	Balance b/d	N2	88,100
31/12/2008	Balance c/d [BS Depr.]		114,250	31/12/2003	P+L [for the year]	N4	48,650
			136,750				136,750
01/08/2008	Disposal	N5	87,000	01/01/2009	Balance b/d		114,250
31/12/2009	Balance c/d [BS Depr.]		74,150	31/12/2004	P+L [for the year]	N6	46,900
			161,150				161,150
				01/01/2010	Balance b/d		74,150

Disposal of Vehicles Account

		€				€
01/03/2008	Vehicles	100,000	01/03/2008	Depreciation	N3	22,500
			01/03/2008	Compensation		50,000
			01/03/2008	Allowance (trade in)		25,000
			01/03/2008	Loss [P+L Expense]		2,500
		100,000				100,000
01/08/2009	Vehicles	120,000	01/08/2009	Depreciation	N5	87,000
01/08/2009	Profit [P+L Gain]	2,000	01/08/2009	Allowance (trade in)		35,000
		122,000				122,000

Top Tip!

If extracts from the profit and loss account and balance sheet for 2008 and 2009 were required they would appear as below.

Profit and Loss Account for Year Ended 31/12/08

Less **Expenses**	
Depreciation of delivery vans	48,650
Loss on sales of van	2,500

Balance Sheet as on 31/12/08

Tangible fixed assets	Cost	Acc. Depr.	NBV
Delivery vans	326,000	114,250	211,750

Profit and Loss Account for Year Ended 31/12/09	
Less **Expenses**	
Depreciation of delivery vans	46,900
Add **Income**	
Profit on sale of van	2,000

Balance Sheet as on 31/12/09			
Tangible fixed assets	**Cost**	**Acc. Depr.**	**NBV**
Delivery vans	294,000	74,150	219,850

Straight-line method

The depreciation is calculated as a percentage of the cost price; the same amount of depreciation is charged each year over the useful life of the asset.

Question 2

On 1 January 2003 Murphy Ltd owned freehold property and land which cost €610,000, including land worth €200,000. The company depreciates its buildings at the rate of 2% per annum using the straight-line method. It is the company's policy to apply a full year's depreciation in the year of acquisition and no depreciation in the year of disposal. This property had been purchased 5 years earlier and depreciation had been charged against profits in each of these 5 years (land is not depreciated).

The following details were taken from the firm's books:

Jan 1 2003   Revalued property at €900,000. Of this revaluation €310,000 was attributable to land.

Jan 1 2004   Purchased buildings for €320,000. During the year 2004, €120,000 was paid to a building contractor for an extension to these recently purchased buildings. Materials to the value of €20,000 were taken from the firm's stock for use in the extension.

Jan 1 2005   Sold for €380,000 land which cost €200,000 but was revalued on 1/1/2003.

Jan 1 2006   Revalued buildings owned at €1,260,000 (a 20% increase in respect of each building).

Jan 1 2007   Sold for €750,000 the buildings owned on 1/1/2003. The remaining buildings were revalued at €660,000.

You are required to:

(a)   Prepare the relevant ledger accounts in respect of the above transactions for the years ended 31 December 2003 to 31 December 2007
(Bank account and profit and loss account **not** required)   **(60 marks)**

Solution

The workings that follow have been carried out in order of how the question should be completed. It is essential to read the question carefully and lay out work well to avoid errors in the figures.

Note 1   **Depreciation at 1/1/2003** (NOTE: land is not depreciated)

$610,000 - 200,000 = 410,000 \times 2\% = 8,200 \times 5 = 41,000$

Subtract the land to find the cost of the buildings and calculate the depreciation; there has been 5 years' depreciation on the buildings to date.

Note 2   **Revaluation of property on 1/1/2003 to €900,000**
Increase the value of property by 290,000.
Transfer all depreciation to date to the revaluation reserve account.

Note 3   **Depreciation for the year ended 31/12/2003** (NOTE: land is not depreciated)
$900,000 - 310,000 = 590,000 \times 2\% = 11,800$
Enter as the profit and loss figure in the provision for depreciation account.

Note 4   **Purchase of buildings on 1/1/2004**
Increase the value of property with the new addition.
$320,000 + 120,000 + 20,000 = 460,000$

Note 5   **Depreciation for the year ended 31/12/2004** (NOTE: land is not depreciated)
$590,000 + 460,000 = 1050,000 \times 2\% = 21,000$
Enter as the profit and loss figure in the provision for depreciation account.

Note 6   **Disposal of land on 1/1/2005** (NOTE: land is not depreciated)
Land is recorded in the books at a value of 310,000 (originally 200,000 but revalued on 1/1/2003).
Transfer the land at its recorded value from the buildings account to the disposal account, enter the amount received from the sale into the disposal account and calculate the profit.

Note 7   **Transfer to revenue reserve for disposed of land**
The land has been disposed of; thus all amounts relating to the land in the revaluation reserve account are now transferred to the revenue reserve account.
Land was revalued on 1/1/2003; this led to an increase in the value of 110,000.
Therefore 110,000 is transferred from the revaluation reserve account to the revenue reserve account.

Note 8   **Depreciation for the year ended 31/12/2005**
$1,050,000 \times 2\% = 21,000$

Note 9   **Revaluation of buildings on 1/1/2006 to 1,260,000 (20% per building)**
Increase in the value of buildings: 210,000
Transfer all depreciation to date to the revaluation reserve: 53,800

Note 10   **Depreciation for the year ended 31/12/2006**
$1,260,000 \times 2\% = 25,200$

Note 11   **Disposal of buildings on 1/1/2007**
Disposal of buildings owned on 1/1/2003
These buildings were revalued twice – on 1/1/2003 (to €590,000) and on 1/1/2006 (gaining a further 20%).
Recorded value: $590,000 \times 20\% = 118,000$; $590,000 + 118,000 = 709,000$
Transfer value of building from buildings account to disposal account.
The last revaluation took place on 1/1/2006; the buildings are being sold on 1/1/2007; therefore only 1 year's depreciation needs to be transferred from the depreciation account to the disposal account.
Depreciation: $708,000 \times 2\% = 14,160$
Enter the amount received from the sale into the disposal account and calculate the profit.

Note 12   **Transfer to revenue reserve for disposal of buildings**
The building has been disposed of; thus all amounts relating to the building in the revaluation reserve account are now transferred to the revenue reserve account.

	€
Revalued on 1/01/03	180,000
Depreciation	41,000
Revalued on 1/01/06 (590,000 × 20%)	118,000
Depreciation (03, 04, 05 €11,800 × 3)	35,400
Transfer	374,400

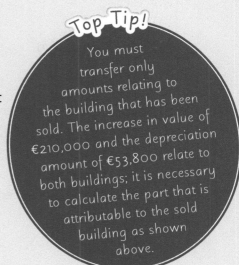

Top Tip!
You must transfer only amounts relating to the building that has been sold. The increase in value of €210,000 and the depreciation amount of €53,800 relate to both buildings; it is necessary to calculate the part that is attributable to the sold building as shown above.

Note 13 Revaluation of buildings on 1/1/2007 to €660,000

1,260,000 − 708,000 = 552,000: value of remaining building

Increase value by 108,000.

Transfer the depreciation that remains after the disposal to the revaluation reserve (this amounts to the depreciation on the remaining building for 2006: 552,000 × 2% = 11,040).

Note 14 Depreciation for the year ended 31/12/2007

660,000 × 2% = 13,200

			€				€
Land and Buildings Account							
01/01/2003	Balance b/d		610,000	31/12/2003	Balance b/d		900,000
01/01/2003	Revaluation reserve	N2	290,000				
			900,000				900,000
01/01/2004	Balance b/d		900,000	31/12/2004	Balance b/d		1,360,000
	Bank	N4	320,000				
	Bank	N4	120,000				
	Purchases	N4	20,000				
			1,360,000				1,360,000
01/01/2005	Balance b/d		1,360,000	01/01/2005	Disposal	N6	310,000
				31/12/2005	Balance c/d		1,050,000
			1,360,000				1,360,000
01/01/2006	Balance b/d		1,050,000	31/12/2006	Balance c/d		1,260,000
01/01/2006	Revaluation reserve	N9	210,000				
			1,260,000				1,260,000
01/01/2007	Balance b/d		1,260,000	01/01/2007	Disposal	N11	708,000
01/01/2007	Revaluation reserve	N13	108,000	31/12/2007	Balance c/d		660,000
			1,368,000				1,368,000
01/01/2007	Balance b/d		660,000				

			€				€
Provision for Depreciation on Buildings Account							
01/01/2003	Revaluation reserve	N2	41,000	01/01/2003	Balance b/d	N1	41,000
31/12/2003	Balance c/d		11,800	31/12/2003	Profit and loss	N3	11,800
			52,800				52,800
31/12/2004	Balance c/d		32,800	01/01/2004	Balance b/d		11,800
				31/12/2004	Profit and loss	N5	21,000
			32,800				32,800
31/12/2005	Balance c/d		53,800	01/01/2005	Balance b/d		32,800
				31/12/2005	Profit and loss	N8	21,000
			53,800				53,800
01/01/2006	Revaluation reserve	N9	53,800	01/01/2006	Balance b/d		53,800
31/12/2006	Balance c/d		25,200	31/12/2006	Profit and loss	N10	25,200
			79,000				79,000
01/01/2007	Disposal	N11	14,160	01/01/2007	Balance b/d		25,200
01/01/2007	Revaluation reserve	N13	11,040	31/12/2007	Profit and loss	N14	13,200
31/12/2007	Balance c/d		13,200				
			38,400				38,400
				01/01/2008	Balance b/d		13,200

Disposal of Land Account							
			€				**€**
01/01/2005	Buildings	N6	310,000	01/01/2005	Bank	N6	380,000
01/01/2005	Profit		70,000				
			380,000				380,000

Disposal of Buildings Account							
			€				**€**
01/01/2007	Buildings	N11	708,000	01/01/2007	Depreciation	N11	14,160
01/01/2007	Profit		56,160	01/01/2007	Bank	N11	750,000
			764,160				764,160

Revaluation Reserve Account							
			€				**€**
01/01/2005	Revenue reserve	N7	110,000	01/01/2003	Land and buildings	N2	290,000
01/01/2007	Revenue reserve	N12	374,400		Depreciation	N2	41,000
	Balance c /d		229,440	01/01/2006	Land and buildings	N9	210,000
					Depreciation	N9	53,800
				01/01/2007	Land and buildings	N13	108,000
					Depreciation	N13	11,040
			713,840				713,840

Question 3 – Revaluation of fixed assets (2007, HL, Section 1, Q3)

On 1 January 2002 McGrath Ltd owned freehold property and land which cost €670,000, consisting of land €240,000 and buildings €430,000. The company depreciates its buildings at the rate of 2% per annum using the straight-line method. It is the company's policy to apply a full year's depreciation in the year of acquisition and no depreciation in the year of disposal. This property had been purchased 8 years earlier and depreciation had been charged against profits in each of these 8 years (land is not depreciated).

The following details were taken from the firm's books:

Jan 1 2002   Revalued property at €810,000. Of this revaluation €290,000 was attributable to land.

Jan 1 2003   Sold for €340,000 land which cost €240,000 but was revalued on 1/1/2002.

Jan 1 2004   Purchased buildings for €470,000. During the year 2004, €150,000 was paid to a building contractor for an extension to these recently purchased buildings. The company's own employees also worked on the extension and they were paid wages amounting to €80,000 by McGrath Ltd for this work.

Jan 1 2005   Revalued buildings owned at €1,403,000 (a 15% increase in respect of each building).

Jan 1 2006   Sold for €660,000 the buildings owned on 1/1/2002. The remaining buildings were revalued at €860,000.

You are required to:

(a) Prepare the relevant ledger accounts in respect of the above transactions for the years ended 31 December 2002 to 31 December 2006
(Bank account and profit and loss account **not** required)   (55)

(b) Show relevant extract from balance sheet as at 31/12/2006   (5)

(60 marks)

Solution

(a)

Land and Buildings Account					(15)
	€			€	
01/01/02 Balance b/d	670,000	(1)			
01/01/02 Revaluation reserve	140,000	(1)	31/12/02 Balance c/d	810,000	
	810,000			810,000	
01/01/03 Balance b/d	810,000		01/01/03 Disposal	290,000	(1)
	810,000			810,000	
01/01/04 Balance b/d	520,000	(1)	31/12/04 Balance c/d	1,220,000	
Bank	470,000	(1)			
Bank	150,000	(1)			
Wages	80,000	(1)			
	1,220,000			1,220,000	
01/01/05 Balance b/d	1,220,000		31/12/05 Balance c/d	1,403,000	
01/01/05 Revaluation reserve	183,000	(2)			
	1,403,000			1,403,000	
01/01/06 Balance b/d	1,403,000		01/01/06 Disposal	598,000	(3)
01/01/06 Revaluation reserve	55,000		31/12/06 Balance c/d	860,000	
	1,458,000			1,458,000	

Provision for Depreciation on Buildings Account					(21)
	€			€	
01/01/02 Revaluation reserve	68,800	(2)	01/01/02 Balance b/d	68,800	(2)
31/12/02 Balance c/d	10,400		31/12/02 Profit and loss	10,400	(2)
	79,200			79,200	
31/12/03 Balance c/d	20,800		01/01/03 Balance b/d	10,400	
			31/12/03 Profit and loss	10,400	(2)
	20,800			20,800	
31/12/04 Balance c/d	45,200		01/01/04 Balance b/d	20,800	
			31/12/04 Profit and loss	24,400	(2)
	45,200			45,200	
01/01/05 Revaluation reserve	45,200	(2)	01/01/05 Balance c/d	45,200	
31/12/05 Balance c/d	28,060		31/12/05 Profit and loss	28,060	(2)
	73,260			73,260	
01/01/06 Disposal	11,960	(2)	01/01/06 Balance b/d	28,060	
01/01/06 Revaluation reserve	16,100	(3)	31/12/06 Profit and loss	17,200	(2)
31/12/06 Balance c/d	17,200				
	42,400			42,400	
			01/01/07 Balance b/d	17,200	

Disposal of Land Account (3)

	€			€	
1/1/2003 Land and buildings	290,000	(1)	01/01/03 Bank	340,000	(1)
31/12/2003 Profit and loss (profit)	50,000	(1)			
	340,000			340,000	

Disposal of Buildings Account (4)

	€			€	
01/01/06 Land and buildings	598,000	(1)	01/01/06 Depreciation	11,960	(1)
31/12/06 Profit and loss (profit)	73,960	(1)	01/01/06 Bank	660,000	(1)
	671,960			671,960	

Revaluation Reserve Account (10)

	€			€	
01/01/03 Revenue reserve	50,000	(1)	01/01/02 Land and buildings	140,000	(1)
01/01/06 Revenue reserve	268,000	(1)	Provision for depreciation	68,800	(1)
Balance	190,100	(2)	01/01/05 Land and buildings	183,000	(1)
			Provision for depreciation	45,200	(1)
			01/01/06 Land and buildings	55,000	(1)
			Provision for depreciation	16,100	(1)
	508,100			508,100	

Revenue Reserve Account (2)

	€	
01/01/03 Revaluation reserve	50,000	(1)
01/01/06 Revaluation reserve	268,000	(1)
	318,000	

(b) Balance Sheet as on 31/12/06 (5)

	Cost €	Acc. Depr. €	NBV €
Fixed assets			
Land and buildings	860,000 (1)	17,200 (1)	842,800 (1)
Capital and reserves			
Revaluation reserve			190,000 (1)
Revenue reserve			318,000 (1)

3 Control Accounts

Learning objectives

In this chapter you will learn about:

1 The rules to be followed for operating debtors' and creditors' accounts

2 The purpose and advantages of control accounts

3 Preparation of an adjusted debtors' control account and creditor's control account and adjusted list/schedule of debtors/creditors to take into account a number of omissions and corrections

Debtors' Account

A debtor is someone who owes the business money, usually for goods sold on credit. A debtors' account is an asset account. The **main** balance will appear on the debit side. Transactions that **increase the amount owed** increase the amount of the asset and are entered on the **debit side**. Transactions that **decrease the amount owed** decrease the asset and are entered on the **credit side**.

Creditors' Account

A creditor is someone to whom the business owes money, usually for goods purchased on credit. A creditors' account is a liability account. The **main** balance will appear on the credit side. Transactions that **increase the amount due to be paid** increase the amount of the liability and are entered on the **credit side**. Transactions that **decrease the amount due to be paid** decrease the liability and are entered on the **debit side**.

Control Accounts

The control accounts contain the same entries that appear in individual debtors' and creditors' accounts. These entries are recorded in exactly the same way as they appear in the individual accounts.

The control accounts, however, are prepared using **totals** taken from the books of first entry and the ledgers. The debtors' control account is prepared using the totals from the sales book, sales returns book, cash book, general journal and ledger accounts such as discount and interest. The creditors' control account is prepared using totals taken from the purchases book, purchases returns book, cash book, general journal and ledger accounts such as interest and discount.

Purpose of Control Accounts

The main purpose of control accounts is to check that the individual debtors' and creditors' accounts are correct. If all transactions have been entered correctly, the balance in the control account will be the same as the balance of the individual accounts added together.

Advantages of Control Accounts

- They ensure that the debtors' and creditors' figures are accurate and can be relied upon by comparing the balance of the control account with the total as per the schedule of debtor's/creditors' balances.
- They allow for errors to be found quickly as they identify the ledger or ledgers in which an error may have been made.
- They allow for quick calculation of the debtors' and creditors' figures for inclusion in the firm's balance sheet.

The usual entries to be found in the debtors' and creditors' control accounts are:

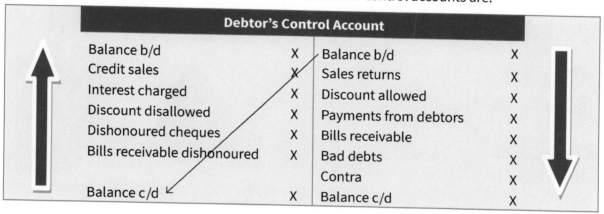

Debtor's Control Account			
Balance b/d	X	Balance b/d	X
Credit sales	X	Sales returns	X
Interest charged	X	Discount allowed	X
Discount disallowed	X	Payments from debtors	X
Dishonoured cheques	X	Bills receivable	X
Bills receivable dishonoured	X	Bad debts	X
		Contra	X
Balance c/d	X	Balance c/d	X

This account shows both a debit and a credit balance; the main balance is on the debit side. Certain circumstances can arise whereby the debtors are owed money by the firm, resulting in a credit balance.

Point to note

Reasons for a credit balance in a debtors' control account:
- Sales returns received after full payment has been received
- Discount allowed after full payment has been received
- Overpayment of a debt by a debtor

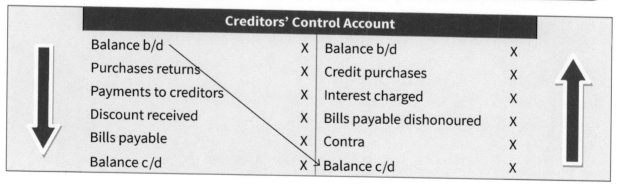

Creditors' Control Account			
Balance b/d	X	Balance b/d	X
Purchases returns	X	Credit purchases	X
Payments to creditors	X	Interest charged	X
Discount received	X	Bills payable dishonoured	X
Bills payable	X	Contra	X
Balance c/d	X	Balance c/d	X

This account also shows both a debit and a credit balance; the main balance is on the credit side. Certain circumstances can arise whereby the creditors owe the firm money, resulting in a debit balance.

Point to note

Reasons for a debit balance in a creditors' control account:
- Purchases returns received after full payment has been received
- Discount received after full payment has been received
- Overpayment of a debt to a creditor

The following points should be noted well:

Cash sales and cash purchases

These are not to be entered in either the control accounts or the individual accounts.

VAT

Figures for sales, purchases, etc. in the control accounts must be shown including VAT as this is how they appear in the individual accounts.

Bills receivable

The amount owed by a debtor is reduced; thus, these are entered on the credit side of a debtors' account. They are **not** entered in a creditors' account.

Bills payable

The amount owed to a creditor is reduced; thus, these are entered on the debit side of a creditors' account. They are **not** entered in a debtors' account.

Contra entry

A contra entry can occur when a firm is **both** a supplier and a customer, making the firm **both** a debtor and a creditor. It involves one amount being offset against another; for example, a firm may owe €300 for sales but also be owed €400 for purchases. This leaves an amount due to be paid of €100. Crediting the debtors' account with €300 and debiting the creditors' account with €300 will give this result.

A contra entry always **reduces** both the debtors' account and the creditors' account.

Study Tips

- The layout of the control accounts is given above. **The balances of the individual accounts when added together are referred to as the list or schedule of debtors/ creditors.**

- In past exam questions a number of errors and omissions have been presented that require correction. Each part of the question needs to be examined closely to determine whether it will be necessary to:

  — Correct the list only

  — Correct the control account only

  — Correct both the control account and the list

- The following may be used as a guide:

Reference to individual or customer's account only	Correct list only
Reference to books of first entry or general accounts such as interest, discount only	Correct control account only
An entry not included in the books An entry included and later altered, the alteration not being included in the books An entry included partially, usually incorrectly	Correct both the list and control account

Including items in both the list and the control account when the item should appear in only one **or** the other shows poor understanding of the topic and will lead to marks being lost. Read the question very carefully; the relevant information will be there to allow you to identify where the correction needs to go.

Procedure

1 Read each part carefully.
2 Decide whether the list or the control account, or both, are affected.
3 Remembering the rules, carry out the correction.
4 Prepare an adjusted debtors'/creditors' control account.
5 Prepare an adjusted schedule of debtors/creditors.

Study Tips

Important points

- Control accounts have regularly arisen as a **60-mark question** in **Section** 1.
- It is necessary to be familiar with both debtors' and creditors' control accounts.
- Pay special attention to the theory included in recent exam questions.
- Practising these questions should improve your ability to deal with correction of errors (suspense) questions as well as the various adjustments relating to debtors and creditors that arise in questions such as those on final accounts.

Sample questions and solutions

Question 1 – Debtors' ledger control account

The debtors' ledger control account of T. McCabe showed the following balances – €39,000 dr and €410 cr on 31/12/2007. These figures did not agree with the schedule (list) of debtors' balances extracted on the same date. An examination of the books revealed the following:

(i) A credit note was sent to a customer for €620. The only entry made in the books was €62 debited to the customer's account.

(ii) Cash sales of €2,500 and credit sales of €540 had both been entered by McCabe in the credit side of the customer's account.

(iii) Discount allowed of €120 had been entered correctly in the books; this discount was subsequently disallowed. The only entry made in relation to discount disallowed was a debit in the discount account of €12.

(iv) Bills payable amounting to €590 have been entered in the credit side of a debtors' account.

(v) Interest amounting to €55, charged to a customer's overdue account, had been entered in the interest account as €155. Following a complaint from the customer, the interest was reduced **by** €30. This reduction was not entered in the books.

(vi) A credit note for €400 was sent to a customer and entered in the books. The accounts clerk forgot to deduct a restocking charge of 10%. When the error was discovered, the clerk sent another credit note for €360 and debited it to the debtors' account. No other entry was made in relation to the restocking charge.

You are required to:

(a) Prepare the adjusted debtors' ledger control account   (24)
(b) Prepare the adjusted schedule of debtors showing the original balance   (30)
(c) Outline the advantages of control accounts to a firm   (6)

(60 marks)

Solution

Note 1 There has been an omission from the control account and an error in the customer's account; both the control account and the list are affected.

Top Tips!

- Enter the sales returns into the control account; remember that entries are recorded in exactly the same way as they appear in the individual accounts; returns reduce the amount owed so enter on the credit side.
- Returns were debited in error to the customer's account. To remedy this, the amount of the error needs to be credited out and the actual returns entered on the credit side.

Entry Required		Error Made		Correction	
Control a/c		Debtors' a/c		Debtors' a/c	
	Returns 620	Returns 62			Returns 682
					Subtract from list 682

Note 2 There has been an error in the customer's account; only the list is affected.

Top Tips!

- The cash sales need to be removed completely from the customer's account.
- The credit sales have been entered on the credit side incorrectly and need to be both removed and entered correctly.

Error Made		Correction	
Debtors' a/c		*Debtors' a/c*	
	Cash sales 2,500	*Cash sales* 2,500	
	Credit sales 540	*Credit sales* 1,080	
			Add to list a total of 3,580

Note 3 There has been an error and omission from the control account and an omission from the customer's account; both the control account and the list are affected.

Top Tips!

- The debit of €12 in the discount account is essentially discount allowed. This means there is now a total of €132 to be entered as discount allowed in the control account.
- Enter discount disallowed in the customer's account.

Correction		Entry Required	
Control a/c		Debtors' a/c	
Discount disallowed 132		Discount disallowed 120	
			Add to list 120

Note 4 There has been an error in the customer's account; only the list is affected.

> **Top Tip!**
>
> Bills payable are **not entered** in the debtors' account as they relate to creditors. Remove the bills payable by debiting them from the customer's account.

Error			Correction		
Debtors' a/c			Debtors' a/c		
	Bills payable	590	Bills payable	590	
					Add to list 590

Note 5 There has been an error and omission in the control account and an omission from the customer's account; both the control account and the list are affected.

> **Top Tips!**
>
> - Interest entered incorrectly in the interest account was later **reduced from €55 by €30 to €25**; the net effect on the interest account should be €25 on the debit side. To achieve this, credit the account with €130.
> - Interest has been reduced by €30; credit the customer's account with €30 to account for the reduction.

Correction		Amendments		
Control a/c		Debtors' a/c		
	Interest 130		Interest	30
				Subtract from list 30

Note 6 There has been an omission from the control account and an error in the customer's account; both the control account and the list are affected.

10% of 400 = 40; restocking charge is 40

> **Top Tips!**
>
> - Reduce the amount of the returns to take into account the restocking charge.
> - An additional credit note was debited to the customer's account, resulting in the account showing €40 on the credit side; credit the account with a further €320 to show the correct amount for the returns: 400 – 40 = 360.

Amendment		Error		Correction		
Control a/c		Debtors' a/c		Debtors' a/c		
Charge 40		Returns 360	Returns 400		Returns	320
			Net effect 40			
						Subtract from list 320

(a) Adjusted Debtors' Ledger Control Account

	€		€
Balance b/d	39,000	Balance b/d	410
Discount disallowed (iii)	132	Credit note (i)	620
Restocking charge (vi)	40	Interest (v)	130
Balance c/d	410	Balance c /d	38,422
	39,582		39,582
Balance b/d	38,422	Balance b/d	410

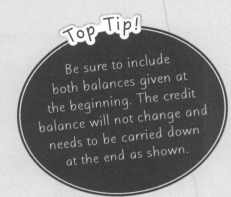

Top Tip!

Be sure to include both balances given at the beginning. The credit balance will not change and needs to be carried down at the end as shown.

(b) Schedule of Debtors' Accounts Balances

	€	€	
Balance as per list of debtors		34,754	**End figure**
Add			
Sales – cash and credit error (ii)	3,580		
Discount disallowed (iii)	120		
Bills payable entered in error (iv)	590	4,290	
		39,044	
Less			
Credit note (i)	682		
Reduction in interest	30		
Credit note – error and restocking charge	320	1,032	
Net balance as per adjusted control account (38,422 – 410)		38,012	

Top Tip!

To complete the schedule of debtors, it is necessary to work back from the answer you have calculated in the adjusted control account and calculate your end figure. **Draft the schedule first and do the calculations at the end.**

(c) Advantages of control accounts – see p.64.

Question 2 – Creditors' ledger control account

The creditors' ledger control account of S. Long showed the following balances – €31,450 cr and €415 dr on 31/12/2008. These figures did not agree with the schedule (list) of creditors' balances extracted on the same date. An examination of the books revealed the following:

(i) Long was charged interest on an overdue account of €158. The only entry made in the books for this interest had been €185 credited to the creditors' account. After a complaint was made by Long, this interest was reduced to €88. No entry was made in the books in respect of this reduction.

(ii) Cash purchases of €1,200 and credit purchases of €820 have both been debited to a supplier's account.

(iii) Discount disallowed by a supplier of €45 has been entered in the discount account as discount received. This was the only entry made in respect of the discount disallowed.

(iv) An invoice received from a supplier showing the purchase of goods for €1,400 less trade discount of 15% has been entered in the purchases book as €1,610. This invoice has not been posted to the creditors' account.

(v) Long returned goods worth €350 to a supplier and this was entered correctly in the books.

When the credit note was received, it showed a restocking charge of 10%. The amount of the credit note was immediately credited to the supplier's account; this was the only entry made in the books in relation to the restocking charge.

(vi) Bills payable of €230 have been credited to a supplier's account.

You are required to:

(a) Prepare the adjusted creditors' ledger control account   (24)

(b) Prepare the adjusted schedule of creditors showing the original balance   (30)

(c) Give reasons why the balance in the creditors' control account may not agree with the balance in the schedule of creditors.

(6)

(60 marks)

Solution

Note 1   There has been an omission from the control account and an error and omission from the customer's account; both the control account and the list are affected.

> No entry has been made in the interest account. Therefore, enter €88 (the new interest) into the control account. The incorrect interest was entered into the correct side of the creditors' account; the interest was later reduced. Enter €97 into the debit side of the creditors' account to ensure that the account now shows the correct charge.

Control a/c		Error Creditors' a/c		Correction Creditors' a/c	
Interest	88	Interest	185	Interest	97
				Subtract from list 97	

Note 2   There has been an error in the customer's account; only the list is affected.

> The cash purchases need to be removed completely from the customer's account. The credit purchases have been entered on the debit side incorrectly and need to be both removed and entered correctly.

Error Creditors' a/c		Correction Creditors' a/c	
Cash purchases	1,200	Cash purchases	1,200
Credit purchases	820	Credit purchases	1,640
		Add to list a total of 2,840	

Note 3   There has been an error in the control account and the customer's account; both the control account and the list are affected.

> Top Tips!
>
> • Discount received disallowed has been entered as discount received; it is necessary to remove the error and enter the discount disallowed. Credit the control account with €90.
>
> • Discount received disallowed has been omitted from the creditors' account. Enter on the correct side, i.e. the credit.

Correction		Entry Required	
Control a/c		Creditors' a/c	
	Discount disallowed 90		Discount disallowed 45
			Add to list 45

Note 4 There has been an error in the control account and an omission from the customer's account; both the control account and the list are affected.

Amount of invoice €1,400 − €210 (15%) = €1,190

Top Tips!

- The correct amount of the invoice must be entered in the creditors' account.
- Purchases have been entered as €1,610 instead of €1,190; purchases are overstated by €420. Debiting the control account with €420 will correct this.

Correction		Entry Required	
Control a/c		Creditors' a/c	
Purchases	420	Purchases	1,190

Note 5 There has been an omission from the control account and an error in the customer's account; both the control account and the list are affected.

10% of €350 = €35; restocking charge is €35

Top Tips!

- Reduce the amount of the returns to take into account the restocking charge.
- An additional credit note was credited to the customer's account, resulting in the account showing €35 on the debit side. Debit the account with a further €280 to show the correct amount for the returns: €350 − €35 = €315.

Entry Required		Error				Correction	
Control a/c		Debtors' a/c				Creditors' a/c	
	Charge 35	Returns	350	Returns	315	Returns 280	
		Net effect	35				
						Subtract from list 280	

Note 6 There has been an error in the customer's account; only the list is affected.

Top Tip!

Bills payable have been entered on the wrong side of the creditors' account. Remove the bills payable from the credit side and enter them on the debit side by debiting the creditors' account with €460.

Error		Correction	
Creditors' a/c		Creditors' a/c	
	Bills payable 230	Bills payable 460	
		Subtract from list 460	

(a) Adjusted Creditors' Ledger Control Account				
	€		**€**	
Balance b/d	415	Balance b/d	31,450	
Invoice overstated (iv)	420	Interest (i)	88	
		Discount disallowed (iii)	90	
		Restocking charge (v)	35	
Balance c/d	31,243	Balance c/d	415	
	32,078		32,078	
Balance b/d	415	Balance b/d	31,243	

Top Tip!

Be sure to include both balances given at the beginning; the debit balance will not change and needs to be carried down at the end as shown.

(b) Schedule of Creditors' Accounts Balances		
	€	**€**
Balance as per list of creditors		27,587 **End figure**
Add		
Purchases – cash and credit error (ii)	2,840	
Discount disallowed (iii)	45	
Purchases omitted (iv)	1,190	4,075
		31,662
Less		
Reduction in interest (i)	97	
Credit note recorded incorrectly (v)	280	
Bills payable recorded incorrectly (vi)	460	837
Net balance as per adjusted control account (31,243 – 415)		30,825

(c) The balance in the creditors' control account may not agree with the balance in the schedule of creditors because:

- An error occurred that affected the control account but not the schedule of creditors or vice versa
- The double entry for a transaction was not completed
- One or more of the subsidiary books were totalled incorrectly and the incorrect figures were then used in the control account

Question 3 – Debtors' ledger control account (2007, HL, Section 1, Q2)

Debtors' control account

The debtors' ledger control account of J. Forrester showed the following balances – €30,000 dr and €530 cr on 31/12/2006. These figures did not agree with the schedule (list) of debtors' balances extracted on the same date. An examination of the books revealed the following:

(i) Discount disallowed to a customer amounting to €46 had been treated as discount allowed in the discount account.

(ii) Interest amounting to €90, charged to a customer's overdue account, had been posted to the interest account as €110. Following a complaint by the customer, this was reduced to €40. This reduction was not entered in the books.

(iii) Cash sales of €1,600 and credit sales of €820 had both been entered by Forrester on the credit of the customer's account.

(iv) A credit note was sent to a customer for €520. The only entry made in the books was €52 debited to the customer's account.

(v) An invoice sent by Forrester to a customer for €1,560 had been entered in the appropriate day book as €1,650. When posting from this book to the ledger, no entry had been made in the customer's account.

(vi) Forrester had accepted sales returns of €300 from a customer and entered this correctly in the books. The accounts clerk sent out a credit note showing a restocking charge of 10% of sales price, but made the necessary adjustment only in the customers' account. Later this charge was reduced to 4% but this reduction was not reflected in the accounts.

You are required to:

(a) Prepare the adjusted debtors' ledger control account (22)

(b) Prepare the adjusted schedule of debtors showing the original balance (30)

(c) Explain: (i) A contra item

(ii) How 'opening balance €530' above could arise (8)

(60 marks)

Solution

(a) Adjusted Debtors' Ledger Control Account (22)

	€		€
Balance b/d	30,000 (1)	Balance b/d	530 (1)
Discount disallowed (i)	92 (3)	Interest (ii)	70 (4) (4)
Restocking charge (vi)	12 (4)	Credit note (iv)	520 (4) (4)
Balance c/d	530 (1)	Sales overstated (v)	90 (4) (4)
		Balance c/d	29,424
	30,634		30,634
Balance b/d	29,424	Balance b/d	530

(b) Schedule of Debtors' Accounts Balances (30)

	€	€
Balance as per list of debtors		24,734 (4)
Add		
Sales – cash and credit error (iii)	3,240 (5)	
Sales (v)	1,560 (5)	4,800
		29,534
Less		
Interest (ii)	50 (5)	
Credit note (iv)	572 (50)	
Reduction in charge (vi)	18 (5)	640
Net balance as per adjusted control account		28,894 (1)

(c) (8)

(i) Contra item (5)

A contra item is an offset of a debtor against a creditor where the debtor and creditor are the same person.

(ii) Opening balance €530 (3)

This could arise because of:

- A full payment of a debt followed by a credit note (returns or reduction)
- Overpayment of a debt
- Full payment followed by discount

Farm Accounts

4

Learning objectives

In this chapter you will learn about:

1 The different types of farm accounts prepared
2 The purpose of preparing farm accounts
3 The different types of farm income
4 The preparation of farm final accounts to include enterprise accounts, profit and loss account and balance sheet

The Accounts of a Farm

These are similar to those already prepared for business.

Statement of capital

The statement of capital is prepared on the first day of the year. All amounts owned and all amounts owed **on that day** must be included.

Total assets – Total liabilities = Capital

Top Tip!

As is the case with both club and service firm accounts, look for hidden assets and liabilities: bank balance, loan and loan interest due and investments.

Receipts and payments account

The receipts and payments account is the farm's analysed cashbook; this shows amounts paid and amounts received and contains the bank balance at the beginning of the period and the end. The analysed headings relate to the different farm enterprises. This analysed cashbook can be summarised into a receipts and payments account at the year end (see Question 1, p.77 for an example).

Enterprise account

For a farm, the normal trading account is replaced by an enterprise account. Farmers may engage in a number of activities, e.g. raising cattle, sheep or deer, growing grain, etc.; each of these activities can be seen as a separate enterprise. An enterprise account can be prepared for each activity; this account shows very clearly all income generated and all expenditure directly related to the activity. The result will be either a profit or a loss on the activity, which is then transferred to the profit and loss account.

Drawings from farm produce

- It is often the case that the farmer will take produce from the farm for his/her own use, e.g. milk or cattle; items taken for personal use are drawings. In this case, drawings are being taken from the sales account: debit drawings **and** credit sales.

- This increases sales; any drawings taken from farm produce must be **added on to the sales figure**. Taking items from produce reduces the amount available for sale. By adding back on the amount that was taken, the true amount produced can be calculated for inclusion in the accounts.

Stock

- To incorporate the stock of the enterprise into the enterprise account, include opening stock with expenditure and closing stock with income.

Profit and loss account

The profit and loss account is completed as with any other type of business:
Income − Expenses = Net Profit/Loss

Income = Income from enterprise accounts, plus any other general income not directly related to one of the enterprises, such as rent receivable, premiums, other government payments and investment income

Expenditure = General expenses not already accounted for, such as depreciation and interest

The net profit/loss is transferred to the balance sheet as a reserve as normal.

As with club and service firm accounts, include **all** income and **all** expenditure for the **current** year only; capital expenditure is not included (e.g. purchase of machinery, repayment of loan).

Balance sheet

This is prepared in exactly the same way as with other businesses; current assets will include stock such as cattle, sheep or grain.

In calculating the drawings figure, be sure to include all expenses attributable to the household **and** any amounts taken from farm produce.

Income

Main source of income:	Sales of produce, e.g. cattle, sheep, grain
Special income/receipts:	**Single payment:** Payment made to farmers based on hectares of land; this was introduced in 2005 and replaced many of the other payments received by farmers
	Rural Environment Protection Scheme: Payment made to farmers to protect the environment within their own farms
	Disadvantaged Areas Compensatory Allowance Scheme (REPS): Payments made to farmers in disadvantaged areas only
	Conacre: This is rent paid by a farmer to another landowner for use of land during the year

Reasons for Preparing Farm Accounts

There are many reasons that accurate farm accounts should be prepared:

- To calculate the value of the farm (net worth)
- To calculate the profit or loss of the farm
- To assist loan or grant applications
- For tax purposes
- To allow comparison between the various farming enterprises and between the current year and previous years
- For planning and budgeting purposes
- To allow an accurate calculation of the farmer's cost of living

Top Tip!

Suggested method for exam questions

1. Calculate the net worth; look for hidden assets/liabilities.
2. Prepare the enterprise accounts: identify the enterprises in which the farmer is engaged; identify income or expenditure that relates specifically to those enterprises; identify any drawings from farm produce and add to the relevant sales; apportion expenses correctly, making sure to adjust for any amount due or prepaid.
3. Prepare the profit and loss account, transferring the profits from the enterprise accounts, including any other income and all relevant expenses.
4. Prepare the balance sheet; be sure to include any new assets purchased and an accurate figure for drawings, including amounts taken from farm produce as well as expenses.

Study Tips

- This question has arisen as a **60-mark question** in **Section 1**.
- It could also be examined as a 100-mark question in Section 2, where you may be asked to prepare a balance sheet.
- Preparing farm accounts is similar to preparing the accounts of a club or service firm. Practising the completion of any of these topics should increase your proficiency in dealing with all three, along with necessary adjustments.

Sample questions and solutions

Question 1

Included among the assets and liabilities of John and Ann Jones, who carry on a mixed farming business, on 1/1/2008 were the following: land and buildings €520,000, value of cattle €32,000, machinery at cost €35,000, value of grain €5,600, milk cheque due €630, stock of fuel €250, creditors for fertilisers amounting to €740 and electricity due €320.

The following is a summary taken from their cheque payments and lodgements for the year ended 31/12/2008.

Lodgements	€	Cheque Payments	€
Balance	5,110	Seeds	5,210
Milk	28,900	Cattle	11,400
Calves	8,200	Machinery	12,500
Grain	17,500	General farm expenses	7,500
Cattle	21,600	Dairy wages	5,450
Forestry premium	2,100	Repairs	4,500
EU subsidy – cattle	3,460	Veterinary fees and medicines	1,980
3 months' interest from		Light, heat and fuel	3,540
4% investment bond	120	Fertiliser	4,700
Rent receivable	1,400	Repayment of €18,000 loan on 31/12/2008 together with 2½ years' interest	19,800
		Balance	11,810
	88,390		88,390

The following information and instructions are to be taken into account:
  (i)   The value of cattle on 31/12/2008 is €36,000.
        The value of grain on 31/12/2008 is €8,200.
 (ii)   Farm produce used by the family during the year: milk worth €650.
(iii)   General farm expenses and fertiliser are to be apportioned 75% to cattle and milk and 25% to grain.
 (iv)   Other expenses are to be apportioned 90% to farm and 10% to household.
  (v)   General farm expenses include a cheque for college fees for a family member for €800.
 (vi)   Machinery owned on 31/12/2008 is to be depreciated at the rate of 10% of cost per annum.
(vii)   The forestry premium is 60% of the premium for the year.
(viii) On 31/12/2008 there was rent receivable prepaid of €220, creditors for fertilisers amounted to €320, a milk cheque was due of €210 and there was stock of fuel of €370.

You are required to:
  (a) Prepare a statement of capital for the farm as on 1/1/2008   (16)
  (b) Prepare an enterprise analysis account for cattle and milk and crops for the year ended 31/12/2008   (30)
  (c) Prepare a general profit and loss account for the year ended 31/12/2008   (24)
  (d) Prepare a balance sheet as on 31/12/2008   (24)
  (e) Give 3 reasons why farmers should keep a full set of accounts   (6)
                                                                                          (100 marks)

Solution

Note 1   Bank

Balance on 1/1/2008 is on debit side; enter as an asset in statement of capital

Balance on 31/12/2008 will be brought down on debit; enter as a current asset in balance sheet

Note 2   Investment

3 months' investment income was paid during the year = €120

1 month = €40

12 months = €480; record as income in profit and loss account

Rate of interest payable for the year was 4%

4% = €480

1% = €120; 100% = €12,000; include in statement of capital as an asset

Investment income due: €480 − €120 = €360; record as a current asset in balance sheet

Note 3 Loan

Loan = €18,000 which was paid off on 31/12/2008; therefore it was still owing on 1/1/2008 and must be included in liabilities at the beginning of the year

Total interest paid is €19,800 − €18,000 = €1,800

€1,800 = 2½ years' interest; the loan was repaid on 31/12/2008, thus 1 year's interest is for 2008, leaving 1½ years' interest for previous years due at the beginning of 2008

2½ years = 30 months

1,800 ÷ 30 = 60; 60 × 12 months = €720   Profit and loss account

60 × 18 months = €1,080   Statement of capital

Note 4 Milk sales

	€
Bank	28,900
Add Drawings	650
Less Due beginning	630
Add Due end	210
	29,130

> **Point to note**
>
> **Apportionment of expenses**
>
> **Before dividing up expenses** between different enterprise accounts, it is very important to **adjust figures** for any amounts that may be **prepaid** or **due** at the beginning or end of the year. Only income and expenditure that relates to the current year should be included.
>
> NOTE: Expenses may also be apportioned between the farm and household. Any expenses attributed to the household are included as drawings.

Note 5 General farm expenses

	€
Bank	7,500
Less Drawings	800
	6,700

Apportionment of expenses	Total
	€
General farm expenses	6,700
Fertiliser	4,280

Note 6 Fertiliser

	€
Bank	4,700
Less Creditors beginning	740
Add Creditors end	320
	4,280

Cattle and milk (75%)	Crops (25%)
€	€
5,025	1,675
3,210	1,070

Note 7 Rent receivable

	€	
Bank	1,400	
Less Prepaid end	220	Current liability
	1,180	Income, profit and loss a/c

Note 8 Forestry premium

		€	
Bank	60%	2,100	
	100%	3,500	Income in profit and loss a/c
Due		1,400	Current asset in balance sheet

Note 9   Light, heat and fuel

	€
Bank	3,540
Less Due beginning	320
Add Stock beginning	250
Less Stock end	370
	3,100

Note 10   Depreciation of machinery

10% of €47,500 (€35,000 + €12,500) = €4,750

Apportionment of expenses	Total	Farm (90%)	Household (10%)
	€	€	€
Light, heat and fuel	3,100	2,790	310
Repairs	4,500	4,050	450
Depreciation of machinery	4,750	4,275	475
Interest	720	648	72

Note 11   Drawings

	€
Milk	650
College fees	800
Light, heat and fuel	310
Repairs	450
Interest	72
Depr. of machinery	475
Total	2,757

(a) Statement of Capital 1/1/2008			
		€	€
Assets			
Land and buildings		520,000	
Machinery		35,000	
Cattle		32,000	
Grain		5,600	
Milk cheque due		630	
Stock of fuel		250	
Bank	N1	5,110	
Investment	N2	12,000	610,590
Liabilities			
Creditors for fertilisers		740	
Electricity due		320	
Loan	N3	18,000	
Loan interest	N3	1,080	20,140
Capital on 1/1/2008			590,450

(b)

Enterprise Analysis Account – Cattle and Milk		€	€
Income			
Sales – milk	N4	29,130	
Cattle and calves (21,600 + 8,200)		29,800	
Closing stock		36,000	
EU subsidy – cattle		3,460	98,390
Expenditure			
Purchases – cattle		11,400	
Opening stock		32,000	
Dairy wages		5,450	
Veterinary fees and medicines		1,980	
General farm expenses	N5	5,025	
Fertiliser	N6	3,210	59,065
Gross profit			39,325

Enterprise Analysis Account – Crops		€	€
Income			
Sales – grain		17,500	
Closing stock		8,200	25,700
Expenditure			
Purchases – seeds		5,210	
Opening stock		5,600	
General farm expenses	N5	1,675	
Fertiliser	N6	1,070	13,555
Gross profit			12,145

(c) General Profit and Loss Account for Year Ended 31/12/2008		€	€
Income			
Gross profit – cattle and milk		39,325	
Gross profit – crops		12,145	
Forestry premium	N8	3,500	
Rent receivable	N7	1,180	
Investment interest		480	56,630
Expenditure			
Light, heat and fuel	N9	2,790	
Repairs		4,050	
Depreciation of machinery	N10	4,275	
Loan interest		648	11,763
Net profit			44,867

(d) Balance Sheet as on 31/12/08

	Cost €	Depr. €	Net €
Fixed assets			
Land and buildings	520,000	0	520,000
Machinery	47,500	4,750	42,750
	567,500	4,750	562,750
Financial assets			
4% investment bond			12,000
			574,750
Current assets			
Bank		11,810	
Stock of cattle		36,000	
Stock of grain		8,200	
Stock of fuel		370	
Milk cheque due		210	
Forestry premium due		1,400	
Investment income due		360	
		58,350	
Less **Current liabilities**			
Rent receivable prepaid	220		
Creditors for fertilisers	320	540	
Working capital			57,810
Total net assets			632,560
Financed by			
Capital and reserves			
Capital 1/1/2008		590,450	
Add Net profit		44,867	
		635,317	
Less Drawings **N11**		2,757	
Capital 31/12/2008			632,560

(e) Reasons for preparing farm accounts (any 3 as listed in the chapter)

1. To calculate the value of the farm (net worth)
2. To calculate the profit or loss of the farm
3. To assist loan or grant applications

Question 2 (2009, HL, Section 1, Q4)

Among the assets and liabilities of Tom and Anne Barry, who carry on a mixed farming business, on 1/1/2008 are: land and buildings at cost €510,000; machinery at cost €90,000; electricity due amounting to €450; cattle of value €80,000; milk cheque due amounting to €2,600; stock of fuel worth €850 and sheep of value €20,000.

The following is a summary taken from their cheque payments and lodgements for the year ended 31/12/2008.

Lodgements	€	Cheque Payments	€
Balance 1/1/2008	33,100	Fertiliser	2,500
Milk	29,000	General farm expenses	13,200
Sheep	24,000	Dairy wages	2,000
Cattle	16,000	Sheep	20,000
Lambs	14,300	Cattle	15,000
Calves	6,100	Light, heat and fuel	3,600
Single payment – sheep	2,500	Machinery	7,000
Single payment – cattle	3,000	Repairs	6,600
Wool	1,400	Veterinary fees and medicines	1,850
Forestry premium	1,900	Bank loan plus 18 months' interest at 4% per annum on 30/4/2008	9,540
Six months' interest from 3% investment bond	900	Balance 31/12/2008	50,910
	€132,200		€132,200

The following information and instructions are to be taken into account.

	Cattle	Sheep
(i) The value of livestock on 31/12/2008 was:	€84,000	€23,000

(ii) Farm produce used by the family during the year: milk worth €900; lamb worth €500.

(iii) General farm expenses, fertiliser, and veterinary fees and medicines are to be apportioned 70% to cattle and milk and 30% to sheep.

(iv) Other expenses are to be apportioned 80% to farm and 20% to household.

(v) Depreciation is to be provided on the following:

Machinery at the rate of 10% of cost per annum

Land and buildings at the rate of 2% per annum (land at cost was €300,000)

(vi) Veterinary fees and medicines include a cheque for family health insurance for €1,100.

(vii) On 31/12/2008 a milk cheque for €1,600 was due, creditors for fertilisers amounted to €500 and stock of fuel was €600.

You are required to:

(a) Prepare a statement of capital for the farm as on 1/1/2008   (20)

(b) Prepare an enterprise analysis account for cattle and milk and sheep for the year ended 31/12/2008   (20)

(c) Prepare a general profit and loss account for the year ended 31/12/2008   (12)

(d) (i) Say which account, other than drawings, is affected by 'farm produce used by the family'? Explain your answer

    (ii) Prepare the Barrys' drawings account   (8)

(60 marks)

Solution

(a) Statement of Capital 1/1/2008

Assets		€		€
Land and buildings		510,000	(2)	
Machinery		90,000	(2)	
Investments		60,000	(3)	
Milk cheque due		2,600	(1)	
Cattle		80,000	(1)	
Sheep		20,000	(1)	
Fuel		850	(1)	
Bank		33,100	(2)	796,550
Liabilities				
Electricity due		450	(1)	
Bank loan		9,000	(2)	
Loan interest due	W1	420	(3)	(9,870)
Capital 1/1/2008				786,680 (1)

(b)

Enterprise Analysis Account – Cattle and Milk

Income		€		€
Sales – milk	W2	28,000	(2)	
– cattle and calves	(16,000 + 6,100)	22,100	(1)	
Drawings by family		900	(1)	
Single payment – cattle		3,000	(1)	
Increase in stock	(84,000 – 80,000)	4,000	(1)	58,000
Expenditure				
Purchases – cattle		15,000	(1)	
Dairy wages		2,000	(1)	
General farm expenses		9,240	(1)	
Fertiliser	W3	2,100	(1)	
Vet fees	W4	525	(1)	28,865
Gross profit				29,135

Enterprise Analysis Account – Sheep

Income		€		€
Sales – sheep and lambs	(24,000 + 14,300)	38,300	(1)	
Drawings by family		500	(1)	
Single payment – sheep		2,500	(1)	
Wool		1,400	(1)	
Increase in stock (23,000 – 20,000)		3,000	(1)	45,700
Expenditure				
Purchases – sheep		20,000	(1)	
General farm expenses		3,960	(1)	
Fertiliser	W3	900	(1)	
Vet fees	W4	225	(1)	25,085
Gross profit				20,615

(c) General Profit and Loss Account for Year Ended 31/12/08

Income		€		€
Gross profit – cattle and milk		29,135		
– sheep		20,615		
Interest	W5	1,800	(1)	
Forestry premium		1,900	(1)	53,450
Expenditure				
Light, heat and fuel (80%)	W6	2,720	(4)	
Repairs (80%)		5,280	(1)	
Depreciation – machinery (80%)		7,760	(1)	
Depreciation – buildings (80%)	W7	3,360	(1)	
Loan interest	W1	96	(1)	(19,216)
Net profit				34,234 (2)

(d) (i) Drawings are debited and sales are credited. Sales are credited instead of purchases because the farm produce is produced rather than purchased. (3)

(ii)

Drawings Account			(5)	
	€		€
Milk	900	Capital a/c	7,304
Lamb	500		
Interest	24		
Light and heat	680		
Health insurance	1,100		
Repairs	1,320		
Depreciation – machinery	1,940		
Depreciation – buildings	840		
	7,304		7,304

Workings

1 Interest
  18 months' interest = 4% x 1.5 = 6%
  106% = 9,540; therefore 6% = 540

Interest for year 2008	120	
Less Drawings	(24)	96
2 Milk sales	29,000	
Add Due 31/12	1,600	
Less Due 1/1	(2,600)	28,000
3 Fertiliser	2,500	
Add Due 31/12	500	3,000
4 Veterinary fees	1,850	
Less Health insurance	(1,100)	750
5 Investment interest	900	
Interest due	900	1,800
6 Light, heat and fuel	3,600	
Add Stock 1/1	850	
Less Due 1/1	(450)	
Less Stock 31/12	(600)	
Less Drawings (20% of 3,400)	(680)	2,720
7 Depreciation – land and buildings: 510,000 – 300,000 = 210,000 x 2% =		4,200

5 Club Accounts

Learning objectives

In this chapter you will learn about:

1 The different types of club accounts prepared

2 The different types of club income and how this income is treated in the accounts

3 The preparation of club final accounts to include trading account for any bar/restaurant, income and expenditure account and balance sheet

The Accounts of a Club

Clubs and voluntary organisations exist for the benefit of their members rather than to make a profit. By their nature they require different types of accounts to be prepared. These accounts are in fact similar to those of any firm; the same rules and considerations apply at all times. Certain phrases are changed to reflect the fact that the main objective of these organisations is not profit.

Statement of accumulated fund

The capital of a club is known as the accumulated fund. It is prepared on the first day of the year. All assets and liabilities of the club **on that day** must be listed.

Total assets − Total liabilities = Accumulated fund

Top Tip!

Look for hidden assets and liabilities: the **bank balance** contained in the receipts and payments account; any **loans** that may have been repaid during the year; any **interest due** on loans at the beginning of the year; **levies due** from the previous year; **investment** (if there is investment interest due then there must be an investment).

Point to note

Subscriptions prepaid = Current liability

Subscriptions due = Current asset

Points to note

- Bar receipts must include only receipts that relate to the current year (see Question 1, Note 4, p.90 for an illustration of this point). *Subtract* debtors at the beginning; these are amounts owed from last year and were included in last year's sales. *Add* debtors at the end; these are amounts owed for this year which need to be included in this year's sales.

- Bar purchases are treated the same way; *subtract* creditors at the beginning of the year and *add* creditors at the end of the year.

Receipts and payments

Receipts and payments are contained in the club's cashbook; this shows amounts paid and amounts received and contains the bank balance at the beginning and end of the period and the end.

Bar/restaurant trading account

This is used to calculate profit/loss on any bar/restaurant. This is then transferred to the income and expenditure account.

Income and expenditure account

This replaces the profit and loss account. The term net profit is replaced by **excess income over expenditure** and net loss is replaced by **excess expenditure over income**.

Balance sheet

The financed by section is altered slightly for a club. It must include life membership, levy reserve fund, accumulated fund and excess of income/expenditure. The other sections remain the same.

Top Tip!

When preparing the income and expenditure account, include **all** income and **all** expenditure for the **current** year only; capital expenditure is **not** included, e.g. purchase of equipment, repayment of loan, transfers of funds to other accounts. Adjust figures for prepaid and due amounts.

Income

Main source of income

The main sources of income for a club are usually subscriptions and/or fundraising activities; these are included as income in the income and expenditure account.

Special income/receipts

Levies: Special (**extra**) payments made to the club **by its members** to fund a project such as an extension. A levy is not a loan. As levies are received, they are debited to the bank account and credited to a levy reserve fund account. This reserve is included in the financed by section of the balance sheet after accumulated fund; levies are **not included** as income.

Life membership: A fee that entitles a member to use of club facilities for the remainder of his/her life. As life memberships are received, they are debited to the bank account and credited to a life membership account, which is included in the financed by section of the balance sheet as a long-term liability. Transfer life membership in instalments to the income and expenditure account as **income** when instructed.

Top Tip!

When **writing off life membership**, be sure to include any life membership received in the current year; divide the total amount by the number of years given. The amount to be written off is entered as **income** and the remainder (Total life membership – Written-off amount) is entered in the **financed by** section.

Entrance fees: Fees sometimes payable by new members in their first year of membership. Include them as income in the income and expenditure account unless told to treat them as a capital receipt. In this case, add to the accumulated fund in the financed by section of the balance sheet.

Sponsorship: If annual sponsorship occurs, then simply include it with income in the income and expenditure account; one-off sponsorship is added to the accumulated fund in the financed by section of the balance sheet.

Grants: If an annual grant is received, then include it with income in the income and expenditure account; a one-off grant is added to the accumulated fund in the financed by section of the balance sheet.

Donations, gifts: If these are small in relation to the club's income, treat them as income in the income and expenditure account; if large, then add to the accumulated fund in the financed by section of the balance sheet.

Top Tips!

Procedure

- Prepare the accumulated fund; make sure to look for hidden assets/liabilities.
- Prepare the bar/restaurant trading account, adjusting the sales and purchases for any debtors and creditors.
- Prepare the income and expenditure account; be sure to adjust the subscriptions figure, calculate profit/loss on activities such as catering and competitions, include depreciation and life membership and adjust any expenses.
- Prepare the balance sheet; include any new assets purchased, the depreciation calculated, new investments, changes to life membership, and changes to the levy reserve fund.

Top Tip!

Levies due at the beginning of the year may not have been paid, but they **are** included in the figure given for the levy reserve fund at the beginning of the year. To get the new figure for the levy reserve fund, add the current year's levy to the original figure and include in the financed by section.

Study Tips

- In past exam questions the theory section has been worth 15 marks out of 100 marks and 10 marks out of 60 marks. The importance of this section must not be overlooked.
- If asked to respond to a proposal to reduce subscriptions by a percentage, then **always calculate what this percentage would be in money terms**, e.g. find 10% of current-year subscriptions. Refer to the bank balance, investments, any excess income over expenditure, sponsorship and entrance fees. Always state that sponsorship and entrance fees are income not guaranteed for future years. **Give factual information based on the accounts and the figures given.**
- Study the sample questions and answers given here.
- A club account question can arise in **Section 2** for **100 marks** or **Section 1** for **60 marks**. In past exam questions there has been no balance sheet to prepare with a 60-mark question.
- Practising these questions will be very useful in dealing with service firm and farm accounts and adjustments in general. Recognising and dealing with the hidden assets and liabilities is good training for reading questions well and for preparing incomplete records.

Question 1

Included among the assets and liabilities of the Wood Brook Golf Club on 1/1/2008 were the following:

clubhouse and courts €480,000; bar stock €2,300; equipment (at cost) €25,600; life membership €48,000; bar debtors €310; bar creditors €1,055; subscriptions prepaid €400; 8% government investments €25,000; investment income due €500; levy reserve fund €40,000; and electricity due €150.

The following is a summary of the club's receipts and payments for the year ended 31/12/2008:

Receipts	€	Payments	€
Bank current account	3,220	Sundry expenses	88,290
Subscriptions	122,450	Bar purchases	41,300
Investment income	1,500	Equipment	14,900
Entrance fees	17,500	Catering costs	5,020
Bar receipts	58,620	Repayment of €40,000 loan on 31/12/2008	
Catering receipts	8,170	together with 1¼ years' interest	44,500
Annual sponsorship	21,000	Transfer to building society	25,000
		Balance	13,450
	232,460		232,460

You are given the following information and instructions:
(i) Bar stock on 31/12/2008 was €2,100.
(ii) Bar debtors and bar creditors on 31/12/2008 were €275 and €1,750 respectively.
(iii) Equipment owned on 31/12/2008 is to be depreciated at the rate of 20% of cost.
(iv) Clubhouse and courts are to be depreciated at a rate of 2%.
(v) Subscriptions include:
    Subscriptions for 2009 amounting to €600
    2 life memberships of €4,000 each
    Levy for 2008 of €200 on 200 members
    Levy of €200 on 6 members for 2007
(vi) Life membership was to be written off over a 10-year period commencing in 2008.

You are required to:
(a) Show the club's accumulated fund (capital) as on 1/1/2008 (30)
(b) Show the income and expenditure account for the year ending 31/12/2008 (35)
(c) Show the club's balance sheet as on 31/12/2008 (20)
(d) Indicate the points you, as the treasurer, might make if the members at the AGM of the club proposed to reduce the annual subscription by 15% (15)

(100 marks)

Solution

Note 1   Bank

The balance in the receipts and payments account at the beginning of the year is on the debit side; it is an asset of the club and is entered as such in the accumulated fund.

The balance in the receipts and payments account at the end is also an asset and will be entered in the balance sheet as a current asset.

If the balance at the beginning or end were to appear on the credit side, it would be treated as a current liability.

Note 2   Loan

Loan = €40,000

This was not paid off until 31/12/2008; therefore it was still owing on 1/1/2008 and must be included in liabilities at the beginning of the year.

Total interest paid is €44,500 − €40,000 = €4,500

€4,500 = 1¼ years' interest; the loan was repaid on 31/12/2008, thus 1 year's interest is for 2008, leaving ¼ of a year's interest for the previous year due at the beginning of 2008

1¼ years = 15 months

€4,500 ÷ 15 = €300:   €300 × 12 months = €3,600 **Income and expenditure account**

€300 × 3 months = €900 **Accumulated fund**

Note 3   Levies

There are levies due for 2007: €200 × 6 = €1,200; these are amounts due to the club and as such are included with assets at the beginning of the year.

Note 4   Bar trading account

Remember to adjust receipts and purchases for debtors and creditors at the beginning and the end.

	€	€
Bar receipts (58,620 − 310 + 275)		58,585
Less Cost of sales		
Opening stock	2,300	
Purchases (41,300 − 1,055 + 1,750)	41,995	
	44,295	
Less closing stock	2,100	42,195
Bar profit		16,390

Top Tips!

• *Subtract* bar debtors at the beginning (amounts owed from last year's sales, not to be included).

• *Add* bar debtors at the end (amounts owed from this year's sales not yet received, which need to be included in the sales figures).

Note 5   Subscriptions

Only subscriptions that relate to the current year can be included in the income and expenditure account. Life membership and the levy reserve fund are dealt with separately from subscriptions and therefore must be subtracted.

	€
Subscriptions received	122,450
Add Subscriptions prepaid beginning	400
Less Subscriptions prepaid end	(600)
Less Life membership (€4,000 × 2)	(8,000)
Less Levies for 2007 (€200 × 6)	(1,200)
Less Levies for 2008 (€200 × 200)	(40,000)
Subscriptions (I + E a/c)	73,050

Point to note

It is only the life memberships paid this year that have been included with subscriptions; therefore it is only these 2 payments of €4,000 each that are deducted and not the total life membership.

Note 6   Investment income

Investment income due of €500 at the beginning of the year is a current asset and is therefore included in the accumulated fund.

The income and expenditure account must show all income that should have been received in the current year **and only** this income.

8% investments of €25,000; €25,000 × 8% = €2,000 is the investment income receivable in this year; include this in the income and expenditure account.

The amount actually received in 2009 is €1,500 (receipts and payments account). However, part of this money includes a payment of the amount that was due at the beginning of the year:

	€	
	1,500	paid
Less	500	due beginning
	1,000	paid in relation to this year
	2,000	income and expenditure a/c
Less	1,000	received in relation to this year
	1,000	due end; show in the balance sheet as a current asset

Note 7   Life membership

New life membership: €48,000 + €8,000 = €56,000

This amount is to be written off over 10 years: 56,000 ÷ 10 = €5,600

Life membership €5,600 is included in the income and expenditure account as **income**

Life membership €56,000 − €5,600 = €50,400 is included in the financed by section of the balance sheet as a **long-term liability**

Note 8   Depreciation

Remember to include any new fixed assets that have been purchased during the year; these will be found on the credit side of the receipts and payments account.

Equipment: originally €25,600 + €14,900 purchased = €40,500

20% of €40,500 = €8,100 recorded as expenditure in the income and expenditure account and in the balance sheet under fixed assets

Clubhouse and courts: 2% of €480,000 = €9,600 recorded as expenditure in the income and expenditure account and in the balance sheet under fixed assets

Note 9   Catering/competitions

Always deduct expenses from receipts to show whether the club made a profit or a loss on these activities and show the profit/loss only in the income and expenditure account.

	€
Catering receipts	8,170
Less Catering costs	5,020
Profit from catering	3,150

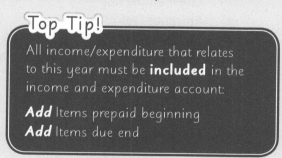

Top Tip!

All income/expenditure that relates to this year must be **included** in the income and expenditure account:

Add Items prepaid beginning
Add Items due end

Note 10   Items prepaid and due

	€
Sundry expenses	88,290
Less electricity due beginning	150
Expenses (I + E a/c)	88,140

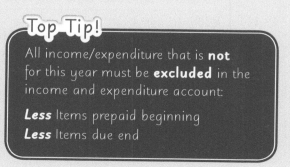

Top Tip!

All income/expenditure that is **not** for this year must be **excluded** in the income and expenditure account:

Less Items prepaid beginning
Less Items due end

Note 11 Levy reserve fund

Original fund + levies **for this year only**

€40,000 + €40,000 = €80,000

The levy reserve fund is shown in the financed by section of the balance sheet as a long-term liability.

(a) Accumulated Fund as on 1/1/2008		€	€
Assets			
Clubhouse and courts		480,000	
Equipment		25,600	
Bar stock		2,300	
Bar debtors		310	
Bank current account	N1	3,220	
8% government investments		25,000	
Investment income due		500	
Levy due	N3	1,200	538,130
Liabilities			
Life membership		48,000	
Levy reserve fund		40,000	
Subscriptions prepaid		400	
Bar creditors		1,055	
Electricity due		150	
Loan	N2	40,000	
Loan interest	N2	900	(130,505)
Accumulated fund 1/1/2008			407,625

(b) Income and Expenditure Account for Year Ended 31/12/08		€	€
Income			
Bar profit	N4	16,390	
Subscriptions	N5	73,050	
Investment income	N6	2,000	
Life membership	N7	5,600	
Entrance fees		17,500	
Annual sponsorship		21,000	
Profit from catering (8,170 − 5,020)	N9	3,150	138,690
Less **Expenditure**			
Sundry expenses (88,290 − 150)	N10	88,140	
Loan interest		3,600	
Depreciation – clubhouse and courts	N8	9,600	
– equipment	N8	8,100	(109,440)
Excess income over expenditure for year			29,250

(c) Balance Sheet as on 31/12/08					
			Cost €	Depr. €	NBV €
Fixed assets					
Clubhouse and courts			480,000	9,600	470,400
Equipment			40,500	8,100	32,400
			520,500	17,700	502,800
Investments					
8% government investments				25,000	
Building society				25,000	50,000
					552,800
Current assets					
Bar debtors				275	
Bar stock				2,100	
Investment interest due				1,000	
Bank				13,450	
				16,825	
Less **Creditors: amounts falling due within 1 year**					
Bar creditors			1,750		
Subscriptions prepaid			600	2,350	
Working capital					14,475
Total net assets					567,275
Financed by:					
Life membership					50,400
Levy reserve fund	**N11**				80,000
Accumulated fund					
Balance at 1/1/2008				407,625	
Add Excess income over expenditure				29,250	436,875
					567,275

(d) Points you would make as treasurer if the members proposed to reduce the annual subscription by 15%:

1   Calculate the effect of the reduction on the income of the club in the current year:
Subscriptions €73,050 × 15% = €10,958
Always calculate this figure.
A reduction in subscriptions of 15% for 2008 would involve a reduction in club income of €10,958.

Point to note

This is an essential part of the question and worth 15 marks. Students **must** include a number of points to achieve full marks.

2   Evaluate the financial situation of the club at present: amount in the bank, investments, savings and loans.
Although the club is **financially sound**, it has **€13,450 in the bank, €25,000 in investments** and **€25,000 in the building society** and has **paid off a loan of €40,000**. These funds are set aside for future **capital expenditure**.

3   State whether there is an excess of income over expenditure or excess expenditure over income and ascertain where the income is coming from. In particular, highlight sources that are not guaranteed in the future, e.g. sponsorship, entrance fees. The club has an **excess of income over expenditure of €29,250**. However, almost all of this surplus is provided by **entrance fees of €17,500** and **sponsorship of €21,000** and this income **cannot be guaranteed** in future years.

4 State any other relevant point and give advice on whether or not to decrease the subscriptions. It can be argued that a **reduction** in subscriptions could **attract more members** and thus **bring in entrance fees** as well as **increased bar profit**. However, it **would not be prudent to reduce subscriptions** at present and instead it would be advisable to retain the present level of fees and **use these fees to improve facilities for the members and thus attract more members**.

Question 2

Included among the assets and liabilities of the Millbank Tennis Club on 1/1/2009 were the following:

clubhouse and courts €350,000; bar stock €1,750; equipment (at cost) €16,000; bar debtors €115; bar creditors €660; wages due €770; life membership €12,000; subscriptions prepaid €440; 12% government investments €15,000; investment income due €450; levy reserve fund €5,000.

The following is a summary of the club's receipts and payments for the year ended 31/12/2009.

Receipts	€	Payments	€
Bank current account	2,120	Bar purchases	10,320
Investment income	900	Competition prizes	1,130
Bar receipts	11,530	Equipment	14,000
Subscriptions	46,710	Caretaker's wages	12,200
Annual sponsorship	5,000	Repayment of €30,000 loan on 31/12/2009	
Entrance fees	3,000	together with 2½ years' interest	33,000
Competition receipts	1,490	Sundry expenses	26,745
Balance	26,645		
	97,395		97,395

You are given the following information and instructions:
   (i) Bar stock on 31/12/2008 is €1,860.
  (ii) Bar debtors and bar creditors on 31/12/2008 were €90 and €750 respectively.
 (iii) Equipment owned on 31/12/2009 is to be depreciated at the rate of 20% of cost.
  (iv) Rates have been prepaid in the amount of €235.
   (v) Clubhouse and courts are to be depreciated at a rate of 2%.
  (vi) Subscriptions include:
        Subscriptions for 2010 amounting to €120
        2 life memberships of €2,000 each
        Levy for 2009 of €50 on 100 members
        Levy of €50 on 5 members for 2008
 (vii) Life membership was to be written off over an 8-year period commencing in 2009.

You are required to:
   (a) Show the club's accumulated fund (capital) on 1/1/2009   (30)
   (b) Show the income and expenditure account for the year ending 31/12/2009   (35)
   (c) Show the club's balance sheet on 31/12/2009   (20)
   (d) Indicate the points you, as the treasurer, might make if the members at the AGM of
        the club proposed to reduce the annual subscription by 10%   (15)

(100 marks)

Solution

Note 1 Loan

Loan = €30,000 paid off on 31/12/2009

Interest = €3,000 = 2½ years = 30 months

Loan repaid on 31/12/2009; thus 1 year's interest is for 2009, leaving 1½ years' interest due at the beginning of 2009

3,000 ÷ 30 = 100   100 × 12 months = €1,200 Income and expenditure account

                 100 × 18 months = €1,800 Accumulated fund

Note 2 Levies

There are levies due for 2008: €50 × 5 = €250; include in current assets at the beginning of the year.

Note 3 Bar trading account

	€	€
Bar receipts (11,530 − 115 + 90)		11,505
Less Cost of sales		
Opening stock	1,750	
Purchases (10,320 − 660 + 750)	10,410	
	12,160	
Less Closing stock	1,860	10,300
Bar profit		1,205

Note 4 Subscriptions

	€
Subscriptions received	46,710
Add Subscriptions prepaid beginning	440
Less Subscriptions prepaid end	(120)
Less Life membership (€2,000 × 2)	(4,000)
Less Levies for 2008 (€50 × 5)	(250)
Less Levies for 2009 (€50 × 100)	(5,000)
Subscriptions (I + E a/c)	37,780

Note 5 Investment income

12% investments of €15,000; 15,000 × 12% = €1,800 Income and expenditure account

Amount received in 2009 is €900 Receipts and payments account

	€	
	900	paid
Less	450	due beginning from the accumulated fund
	450	paid in relation to this year
	1,800	income and expenditure a/c
Less	450	received in relation to this year
	1,350	due end; show in the balance sheet as a current asset

Note 6 Life membership

€12,000 + €4,000 = €16,000

€16,000 ÷ 8 = €2,000

€2,000 Income and expenditure account as income

€16,000 − €2,000 = €14,000 Balance sheet as a long-term liability

Note 7 Depreciation

Equipment: €16,000 + €14,000 = €30,000; 20% of €30,000 = €6,000

Clubhouse and courts: 2% of €350,000 = €7,000

Note 8 Profit from competition

	€
Competition receipts	1,490
Less Competition costs	1,130
Profit from competition	360

Note 9 Levy reserve fund

€5,000 + €5,000 = €10,000 Balance sheet as a long-term liability

(a) Accumulated Fund as on 1/1/09			
		€	€
Assets			
Clubhouse and courts		350,000	
Bar stock		1,750	
Equipment		16,000	
Bar debtors		115	
8% government investments		15,000	
Investment income due		450	
Levies due	N2	250	
Bank		2,120	385,685
Liabilities			
Bar creditors		660	
Life membership		12,000	
Subscriptions prepaid		440	
Levy reserve fund		5,000	
Wages due		770	
Loan	N1	30,000	
Loan interest	N1	1,800	(50,670)
Accumulated fund 1/1/2009			335,015

(b) Income and Expenditure Account for Year Ended 31/12/09			
		€	€
Income			
Bar profit	N3	1,205	
Subscriptions	N4	37,780	
Profit from competition (1,490 – 1,130)	N8	360	
Investment income	N5	1,800	
Entrance fees		3,000	
Sponsorship		5,000	
Life membership	N6	2,000	51,145
Less **Expenditure**			
Depreciation			
Clubhouse and courts	N7	7,000	
Equipment	N7	6,000	
Sundry expenses (26,745 – 235)		26,510	
Caretaker's wages (12,200 – 770)		11,430	
Loan interest		1,200	(52,140)
Excess expenditure over income for year			(995)

		Cost €	Depr. €	NBV €
Fixed assets				
Clubhouse and courts		350,000	7,000	343,000
Equipment		30,000	6,000	24,000
		380,000	13,000	367,000
12% government investments				15,000
				382,000
Current assets				
Bar debtors			90	
Bar stock			1,860	
Investment interest due			1,350	
Rates prepaid			235	
			3,535	
Current liabilities				
Bank		26,645		
Bar creditors		750		
Subscriptions prepaid		120	27,515	(23,980)
Total net assets				358,020
Financed by				
Life membership				14,000
Levy reserve fund	N9			10,000
Accumulated fund				
Balance at 1/1/2009			335,015	
Less Excess expenditure over income			(995)	334,020
Capital employed				380,020

(d) Points you would make as treasurer if the members proposed to reduce the annual subscription by 10%:

Subscriptions 37,780 × 10% = 3,778

A reduction in subscriptions of 10% for 2009 would involve a reduction in club income of €3,778.

The club is **not financially sound** at present. It has a **bank overdraft of €26,645**, a **negative figure for working capital of €23,980**. It has **paid off a loan of €30,000** and has **investments of €15,000**. These investments do not cover the amount of the bank overdraft.

The club has an **excess of expenditure over income of €995**. The club is in a position of not being able to cover its day-to-day expenses. **Entrance fees of €3,000** and **sponsorship of €5,000** make up part of the income and these **cannot be guaranteed** in future years.

It **would not be prudent to reduce subscriptions** at present, as this would bring about a reduction in services to members unless further funds could be raised through:

- Greater and regular sponsorship
- Increased life membership
- Introduction of another levy (unlikely members would agree)
- Other fundraising activities

Instead it would be advisable to retain the present level of fees and **use these fees to improve the financial situation before any further capital expenditure is undertaken**.

Question 3 (2008, HL, Section 1)

Included among the assets and liabilities of the Bard's Valley Golf Club on 1/1/2007 were the following:

clubhouse and court €750,000, bar stock €7,000, equipment (at cost) €26,000, life membership €40,000, bar debtors €535, bar creditors €6,000, levy reserve fund €50,000, investment interest receivable due €400, wages due €2,500, subscriptions received in advance €1,600.

The club treasurer has supplied the following account of the club's activities during the year ended 31/12/2007.

Receipts	€	Payments	€
Bank current account	14,000	Bar purchases	78,500
Interest from 5% government investments	1,600	Catering costs	8,000
		Sundry expenses	186,400
Entrance fees	15,000	Equipment	45,000
Catering receipts	14,000	Golf lessons for club teams	4,600
Annual sponsorship	25,000	Repayment of €30,000 loan on 31/5/2007	
Subscriptions	250,000	together with 1½ years' interest	33,600
Bar receipts	110,460	Transfer to building society on 31/12/2007	60,000
		Balance	13,960
	430,060		430,060

You are given the following additional information and instructions:
- (i) Bar stock on 31/12/2007 was €8,500.
- (ii) Equipment owned on 31/12/2007 is to be depreciated at the rate of 20% of cost.
- (iii) Clubhouse and courts are to be depreciated by 2%.
- (iv) Bar debtors and creditors on 31/12/2007 were €275 and €3,220 respectively.
- (v) Subscriptions include:
  - 1 life membership, bringing total life memberships to 21
  - Subscriptions for 2008 amounting to €2,600
  - Levy for 2007 of €250 on 200 members
  - Levy of €250 on 10 members for 2006
- (vi) Life membership was to be written off over a 10-year period commencing in 2007.

You are required to:
- (a) Show the club's accumulated fund (capital) on 1/1/2007   (25)
- (b) Show the income and expenditure account for the year ending 31/12/2007   (25)
- (c) (i) Explain, with the use of an example, what is meant by a special-purpose profit and loss account
  - (ii) If it were proposed to introduce a further 4-year levy to fund a €250,000 extension, indicate what points you as an ordinary member would now make   (10)

  (60 marks)

Solution

(a) Accumulated Fund as on 1/1/07 (25)

Assets		€	
Clubhouse		750,000 (1)	
Bar stock		7,000 (1)	
Equipment		26,000 (1)	
Bar debtors		535 (1)	
Investments	W1	24,000 (2)	
Investment interest due		400 (2)	
Bank current account		14,000 (2)	
Levy due (250 × 10)		2,500 (2)	824,435
Liabilities			
Life membership		40,000 (2)	
Bar creditors		6,000 (1)	
Levy reserve fund		50,000 (2)	
Wages due		2,500 (1)	
Loan		30,000 (1)	
Loan interest due	W2	2,600 (2)	
Subscriptions prepaid		1,600 (2)	132,700
Accumulated fund 1/1/2007			691,735 (2)

(b) Income and Expenditure Account for Year Ended 31/12/07 (25)

Income		€	€
Bar profit		35,980 (4)	
Investment interest	W3	1,200 (2)	
Entrance fees		15,000 (1)	
Catering profit (14,000 – 8,000)		6,000 (1)	
Annual sponsorship		25,000 (1)	
Subscriptions	W4	194,500 (5)	
Life membership		4,200 (2)	281,880
Less **Expenditure**			
Sundry expenses (186,400 – 2,500)		183,900 (2)	
Golf lessons		4,600 (1)	
Loan interest		1,000 (2)	
Depreciation – equipment		14,200 (1)	
Depreciation – clubhouse		15,000 (1)	(218,700)
Excess income over expenditure for year			63,180 (2)

Bar Trading Account	€	€
Sales (110,490 + 275 − 535)		110,200
Less Cost of goods sold		
Stock 1/1/2007	7,000	
Add Purchases (78,500 + 3,220 − 6,000)	75,720	
	82,720	
Less Closing stock	(8,500)	(74,220)
Bar profit		35,980

Workings

1 Investments: 5% = 1,200, 100%   24,000
2 Loan interest due 1/1/2007: 3,600 − 1,000   2,600
3 Investment interest: 1,600 − 400   1,200
4 Subscriptions: 1,600 + 250,000 − 2,000 − 50,000 − 2,500 − 2,600   194,500

(c)   **(10)**

(i) Sometimes non-profit-making organisations such as a club prepare a profit and loss **(3)** account for activities that are carried out to make a profit, e.g. running a club lottery, dances, bar, restaurants etc. All expenses and revenues relating to that particular activity are entered in a special profit and loss account and the profit/loss is then transferred to the income and expenditure account.

(ii) The proposed levy would raise €200,000 over 4 years (250 × 200 × 4). **(7)** As a member I would make the case that the club is capable of generating enough income from within, as it has a **surplus of income of €63,180**. The club is financially sound, as it has cash of €13,960, building society investment of €60,000 and 5% government investments of €24,000, totalling €97,960 even after it has paid off a loan and interest of €33,600 and purchased equipment for €45,000.

However, a sizeable proportion of the surplus is provided by **entrance fees** of €15,000 and **sponsorship of €25,000**. This income **cannot be guaranteed** in future years.

Service Firms

6

Learning objectives

In this chapter you will learn about:

1 Types of accounts prepared by a service firm
2 Purpose of preparing service firm accounts
3 Preparation of service firm accounts to include statement of capital and reserves, profit and loss account and balance sheet

The Accounts for a Service Firm

The main line of business for these firms is in providing a service to their customers. Included in this category are doctors, dentists, hairdressers, plumbers, etc. As well as providing their service, they may also sell some products to their customers to earn additional profit as a sideline to the main business. These firms exist to make a profit.

The accounts prepared for a service firm are: statement of capital and reserves, profit and loss account and balance sheet.

It may be necessary to prepare a separate profit and loss account for a sideline business. Any profit or loss from this enterprise is then transferred to the main profit and loss account.

Reasons for Preparing Service Firm Accounts

- To calculate the profit or loss on the services provided for the year
- To ensure good credit control by calculating the amounts owed by the firm and to the firm
- As private limited companies, returns must be made to the revenue commissioners and the registrar of companies
- For planning and budgeting purposes

Statement of Capital and Reserves

This statement is prepared on the first day of the year. All assets and liabilities of the firm on that day must be listed. Include the issued share capital as a liability and note any loans repaid during the year, the bank balance, etc.

Total assets – Total liabilities = Reserves

Top Tip!

It is usually necessary to calculate accumulated depreciation for previous years on the fixed assets. This depreciation **reduces the value of the assets**; assets are shown in the statement of capital at book value. The accumulated depreciation must also be taken into account if revaluations or disposals occur during the year. Read through the question carefully as **the information may only be given at the end of the question.**

Profit and Loss Account for Sideline Area of the Business

Include all the necessary information to calculate whether a profit or loss has been made on this section of the business. Once the profit or loss has been calculated, **it and only it is entered** in the main profit and loss account.

Profit and Loss Account

It usually necessary to adjust the main source of income to take account of fees in arrears (due) and fees paid in advance (prepaid). Expenses will also need adjusting for due and prepaid amounts. The profit and loss account must show **all** the income and expenditure for the current year only. Capital expenditure is not included (purchase of fixed assets, repayment of loan, transfer of funds, etc.). Include depreciation charges for the year.

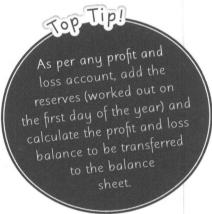

Balance Sheet

Prepare this as per any balance sheet; for fixed assets be sure to take into account any additions, disposals or revaluations.

Income in arrears, e.g. client fees due	Current asset
Income in advance, e.g. deposits received	Current liability
Expenses due, e.g. creditors for supplies	Current liability
Expenses prepaid, e.g. stock of oil	Current asset

Exam Procedure

1 If necessary, prepare the statement of capital and reserves. Make sure to calculate accumulated depreciation for previous years and look for hidden assets/liabilities.
2 Prepare the profit and loss account for the sideline business, if any.
3 Prepare the profit and loss account. Be sure to adjust the income and expenses figure for amounts due and prepaid at the beginning and end of the year and include depreciation.
4 Prepare the balance sheet. Include any new fixed assets purchased, the depreciation calculated, all current assets and liabilities, the revaluation reserve and the profit and loss balance.

Study Tips

- A service firm question can arise in **Section 2** for **100 marks** or **Section 1** for **60 marks**.
- **The service firm may be that of a sole trader or company. Students need to be familiar with the very slight differences in these accounts to ensure that an accurate answer can be prepared in good time under exam conditions. In this book, Question 1 is for a company and Question 2 is for a sole trader.**
- In past exam questions there has been no calculation of reserves at the beginning of the year in 60-mark questions.
- Practising these questions will be very useful in dealing with club accounts and farm accounts and with adjustments in general.

Sample questions and solutions

Question 1

The following were included in the assets and liabilities of Verve Health Centre Ltd on 1/1/2009:

buildings at cost €540,000; equipment at cost €80,000; furniture at cost €15,000; stock of health food for sale €700; heating oil €590; creditors for supplies to health centre €2,120; 6% investments €50,000; contract cleaning prepaid €410; clients' fees paid in advance €6,700; authorised capital €500,000; and issued capital €400,000.

All fixed assets have 3 years' accumulated depreciation on 1/1/2009.

The following is the receipts and payments account for the year ended 31/12/2009:

Receipts and Payments Account of Verve Health Centre for Year Ended 31/12/09			
	€		**€**
Balance at bank 1/1/2009	8,420	Wages and salaries	81,680
Clients' fees	312,800	Repayment of €60,000 loan on	
Investment income	2,250	1/3/2009 with 2 years' interest	66,000
Shop receipts	73,000	Furniture	23,000
		New extension	90,000
		Cleaning	4,100
		Light and heat	2,900
		Insurance	7,900
		Telephone	1,790
		Purchases – shop	59,800
		Purchases – supplies	46,500
		Balance at bank 31/12/2009	12,800
	396,470		396,470

The following information and instructions are to be taken into account:

(i) Closing stock at 31/12/2009 was as follows: shop €1,100; heating oil €430.

(ii) Cleaning is done under contract payable monthly in advance and includes a payment of €540 for January 2010.

(iii) Clients' fees include fees for 2010 of €2,510. Clients' fees in arrears at 31/12/2009 total €370.

(iv) Wages and salaries include €20,000 per annum paid to the receptionist, who also runs the shop. It is estimated that 40% of this salary, 30% of the telephone, 25% of insurance and €330 of the light and heat are attributable to the shop.

(v) On 1/1/2009 Verve Health Centre Ltd had the buildings revalued at €720,000.

(vi) During the year equipment which had cost €3,000 on 1/1/2007 was disposed of for €2,200. The amount received was incorrectly included with client fees. This was the only entry made in respect of this transaction. It is the company's policy to apply a full year's depreciation in the year of purchase and no depreciation in the year of disposal.

(vii) Electricity due on 31/12/2009 totalled €150.

(viii) Creditors for supplies to Verve Health Centre Ltd at 31/12/2009 are owed €3,000.

(ix) Depreciation is to be provided as follows:
    Buildings: 2% of cost for the full year
    Equipment: 15% of cost per annum
    Furniture: 20% of cost per annum

You are required to:

(a)	Calculate the company's reserves on 1/1/2009	(20)
(b)	Calculate the profit/loss from the shop for the year ended 31/12/2009	(12)
(c)	Prepare a profit and loss account for the year ended 31/12/2009	(36)
(d)	Prepare a balance sheet as on 31/12/2009	(32)

(100 marks)

Solution

Note 1   Accumulated depreciation

3 years' depreciation has accumulated on the fixed assets. These amounts have not been given, thus need to be calculated and included in the statement of capital and reserves.

Buildings €540,000 × 2% = €10,800 × 3 years = €32,400

Equipment €80,000 × 15% = €12,000 × 3 years = €36,000

Furniture €15,000 × 20% = €3,000 × 3 years = €9,000

Note 2   Loan

Loan = €60,000 paid off on 1/3/2009 but still owing on 1/1/2009, so include with liabilities

Total interest paid is €6,000 = 2 years; €6,000 ÷ 24 = €250 per month

2 months' interest for 2009 = €500; €5,500 interest due, so include with liabilities

Note 3   Clients' fees

	€
Clients' fees	312,800
Add Amounts paid in advance beginning	6,700
Less Amounts paid in advance end	2,510
Add Arrears end	370
Less Receipt from equipment	2,200
	315,160

Note 4   Light and heat

	€
Paid	2,900
Add Stock of fuel beginning	590
Less Stock of fuel end	430
Add Electricity due	150
Less Shop	330
P+L a/c	2,880

Note 5   Expenses relating to shop

Wages and salaries	40% of 20,000 = €8,000
Insurance	25% of 7,900 = €1,975
Telephone	30% of 1,790 = €537
Light and heat	€330

Top Tip!

Clearly identify the purchases that relate to the health shop **and** those that apply to the main business and **adjust the correct figure** for any amounts owing, i.e. creditors.

Note 6   Purchases of supplies

The creditors in this question relate to purchases made for supplies for the main business.

	€
Purchases	46,500
Less Creditors beginning	2,120
Add Creditors end	3,000
	47,380

Note 7   Revaluation of buildings at the beginning of the year

Buildings cost €540,000 with accumulated depreciation of €32,400
Revalue land and buildings to €720,000
Revaluation reserve €180,000 + €32,400 = €212,400
Buildings €540,000 + €120,000 (increase in value) + €90,000 (extension) = €810,000
Depreciation for the year €810,000 × 2% = €16,200

Note 8   Disposal of equipment

Old equipment cost €3,000, bought on 1/1/2007
Accumulated depreciation €3,000 × 15% = €450 × 2 years = €900
Depreciation charge on equipment for the year €77,000 × 15% = €11,550

Equipment Account				Depr. of Equipment Account				Disposal Account			
Balance	80,000	Disposal	3,000	Disposal	900	Balance	36,000	Equip.	3,000	Depr.	900
		Balance	77,000	Balance	46,650	Profit and		Profit	100	Bank	2,200
						loss	11,550				
	80,000		80,000		47,550		47,550		3,100		3,100

Note 9   Depreciation of furniture

Furniture €15,000 + €23,000 (new) = €38,000 × 20% = €7,600
Accumulated depreciation €9,000 + €7,600 = €16,600

Note 10 Investment income

	€
6% of 50,000	3,000
Received	2,250
Due	750

Note 11 Cleaning

	€
Paid	4,100
Add Prepaid beginning	410
Less Prepaid end	540
	3,970

(a) Statement of Capital and Reserves on 1/1/09

Assets		€	€
Buildings (540,000 − 32,400)	N1	507,600	
Equipment (80,000 − 36,000)	N1	44,000	
Furniture (15,000 − 9,000)	N1	6,000	
Stock of health food		700	
Stock of heating oil		590	
Contract cleaning prepaid		410	
Bank		8,420	
Investment		50,000	617,720
Liabilities			
Creditors for supplies		2,120	
Clients' fees paid in advance		6,700	
Loan		60,000	
Loan interest	N2	5,500	
Issued capital		400,000	474,320
Reserves 1/1/2009			143,400

(b) Profit and Loss Account for the Health Shop

		€	€
Receipts			73,000
Less Cost of sales (700 + 59,800 − 1,100)			59,400
Gross profit			13,600
Less Expenses			
Wages and salaries	N5	8,000	
Insurance	N5	1,975	
Telephone	N5	537	
Light and heat	N4	330	10,842
Profit from shop			2,758

(c) Profit and Loss Account for Year Ended 31/12/09

Income		€	€
Clients' fees	N3	315,160	
Profit from health shop		2,758	
Profit from sale of equipment	N8	100	
Investment income	N10	3,000	321,018
Expenditure			
Purchases − supplies	N6	47,380	
Wages and salaries (81,680 − 8,000)		73,680	
Loan interest	N2	500	
Cleaning	N11	3,970	
Light and heat		2,880	
Insurance (7,900 − 1,975)		5,925	
Telephone (1,790 − 537)		1,253	
Depreciation − buildings	N7	16,200	

contd →

Profit and Loss Account for Year Ended 31/12/09 (continued)			
Expenditure			
Depreciation – equipment	N8	11,550	
Depreciation – furniture	N9	7,600	170,938
Net profit for the year			150,080
Add Reserves 1/1/2009			143,400
Profit and loss balance 31/12/2009			293,480

(d) Balance Sheet as on 31/12/09		Cost	Depr.	Net
		€	€	€
Fixed assets				
Buildings	N7	810,000	16,200	793,800
Equipment	N8	77,000	46,650	30,350
Furniture	N9	38,000	16,600	21,400
		925,000	79,450	845,550
Investment				50,000
				895,550
Current assets				
Bank			12,800	
Stock from shop			1,100	
Stock of heating oil			430	
Clients' fees due			370	
Investment income due	N10		750	
Cleaning prepaid			540	
			15,990	
Less **Creditors: amounts falling due within 1 year**				
Creditors for supplies		3,000		
Electricity due		150		
Clients' fees paid in advance		2,510	5,660	
Working capital				10,330
Total net assets				905,880
Financed by				
Share capital and reserves		Authorised	Issued	
Ordinary shares		500,000	400,000	
Revaluation reserve			212,400	
Profit and loss			293,480	
Capital employed				905,880

Question 2

Included among the assets and liabilities of B. Farley, a medical consultant, on 1/1/2010 were:

surgery €320,000; equipment €55,000; motor car €45,000; stock of medical supplies €3,310; heating oil €410; creditors for medical supplies €1,470; money owed from private patients €1,700; money owed from medical insurance scheme €5,200; 4% fixed mortgage €150,000; capital €295,950.

The following is the receipts and payments account for the year ended 31/12/2010.

Receipts and Payments Account of B. Farley for Year Ended 31/12/10			
	€		€
Balance at bank 1/1/2010	4,100	Wages and salaries	43,100
Receipts from private patients	76,300	Sponsorship of local charity	500
Medical insurance scheme	67,000	Mortgage interest	4,000
Sale of equipment (cost €16,000)	8,000	Light and heat	2,700
6 months' interest from 8%		Insurance	4,560
Investment	2,400	Repairs	510
		Furniture	6,000
		Telephone	2,950
		Medical supplies	6,870
		Drawing	46,890
		Balance at bank 31/12/2009	39,720
	157,800		157,800

The following information and instructions are to be taken into account:

(i) Stock of medical supplies on 31/12/2010 was €2,600. Stock of heating oil was €530.

(ii) The closing figure for the bank does not take into account a dishonoured cheque worth €250 from a private patient that was lodged late in December.

(iii) A private patient was declared bankrupt in December and it has been decided that the amount owed of €450 is to be written off as a bad debt.

(iv) 25% of the furniture and 30% of the telephone are attributable to the private section of the business.

(v) The closing figure for cash drawings includes wages of €6,270 for 3 weeks paid to a substitute doctor. B. Farley is also required to provide a further 2 weeks' wages.

(vi) Creditors for medical supplies on 31/12/2009 amount to €3,000.

(vii) Depreciate fixed assets on 31/12/2010 as follows:

Surgery   2% of cost
Equipment and furniture   15% of cost
Motor car   20% of cost

NOTE: Fixed assets are given at cost and depreciation on them has been accumulated for 2 years by 31/12/2009. There is nil depreciation on disposed equipment in year of disposal.

(viii) Fees due from private patients and the medical insurance scheme are €2,350 and €4,800 respectively. Advance deposits from private patients for 2011 amount to €590.

You are required to prepare:

(a) An income and expenditure account for year ended 31/12/2010 (35)

(b) A balance sheet as at 31/12/2010 (25)

(60 marks)

Solution

Note 1   Accumulated depreciation

2 years' depreciation has accumulated on the fixed assets:

Surgery   €320,000 × 2% = 6,400 × 2 years = €12,800
Equipment   €55,000 × 15% = 8,250 × 2 years = €16,500
Motor car   €45,000 × 20% = 9,000 × 2 years = €18,000

Note 2   Receipts from private patients

	€
Receipts	76,300
Less Due beginning	1,700
Add Due end	2,350
Less Prepaid end	590
	76,360

Note 3   Amounts due from private patients

	€
Due 31/12/2010	2,350
Add Dishonoured cheque	250
Less Bad debt	450
	2,150

Note 4   Receipts from medical insurance scheme

	€
Receipts	67,000
Less Due beginning	5,200
Add Due end	4,800
	66,600

Note 5   Medical supplies

	€
Opening stock	3,310
Add Purchases (6,870 − 1,470 + 3,000)	8,400
Less Closing stock	2,600
	9,110

Note 6   Investment income

6 months = €2,400; 1 year = €4,800; due €2,400
      8% = €4,800
      1% = €600
   100% = €60,000 investment

Note 7   Drawings

	€
Cash (46,890 − 6,270)	40,620
Furniture (25% of 6,000)	1,500
Telephone (30% of 2,950)	885
	43,005

Note 8   Wages

€6,270 ÷ 3 = €2,090 × 2 = €4,180 due
€43,100 + €6,270 + €4,180 = €53,550

Note 9   Disposal of equipment

2 years' depreciation: €16,000 × 15% = €2,400 × 2 = €4,800
€55,000 − €16,000 = €39,000 × 15% = €5,850 P+L
Accumulated depreciation: €16,500 − €4,800 + €5,850 = €17,550

Equipment Account				Depr. of Equipment Account				Disposal Account			
	€		€		€		€		€		€
Balance	55,000	Disposal	16,000	Disposal	4,800	Balance	16,500	Equip.	16,000	Depreciation	4,800
		Balance	39,000	Balance	17,550	P+L	5,850			Bank	8,000
										Loss	3,200
	39,000		39,000		22,350		22,350		16,000		16,000

Note 10 Mortgage interest

	€
4% of 150,000	6,000
Paid	4,000
Due	2,000

Profit and Loss Account for Year Ended 31/12/10			
		€	€
Income			
Receipts from private patients	N2	76,360	
Medical insurance scheme	N4	66,600	
Investment income	N6	4,800	147,760
Expenditure			
Medical supplies	N5	9,110	
Wages and salaries	N8	53,550	
Bad debts		450	
Loss on equipment	N9	3,200	
Light and heat (410 + 2,700 − 530)		2,580	
Mortgage interest	N10	6,000	
Telephone (2,950 − 885)		2,065	
Sponsorship		500	
Insurance		4,560	
Repairs		510	
Depreciation − surgery		6,400	
Depreciation − equipment		5,850	
Depreciation − motor car		9,000	
Depreciation − furniture (4,500 × 15%)		675	104,450
Net profit for year			43,310

Balance Sheet as on 31/12/10				
		Cost €	Depr. €	Net €
Fixed assets				
Surgery	N1	320,000	19,200	300,800
Equipment	N9	39,000	17,550	21,450
Motor car	N1	45,000	27,000	18,000
Furniture		4,500	675	3,825
		408,500	64,425	344,075
Investment	N6			60,000
				404,075
Current assets				
Bank (39,720 − 250)				39,470
Stock of medical supplies				2,600
Stock of heating oil				530
Amounts due from private patients	N3			2,150
Investment income due				2,400
Medical insurance scheme				4,800
				51,950

contd →

Balance Sheet as on 31/12/10 (continued)				
Less **Creditors: amounts falling due within 1 year**				
Creditors for supplies		3,000		
Mortgage interest due		2,000		
Wages due	**N8**	4,180		
Advance deposits from private patients		590	9,770	
Working capital				42,180
Total Net assets				446,255
Financed by				
Mortgage				150,000
Capital			295,950	
Add Net profit			43,310	
			339,260	
Less Drawings	**N7**		43,005	296,255
Capital employed				446,255

Question 3 (2012, HL, Section 2, Q6)

The following were included in the assets and liabilities of the New Era Gym and Health Centre Ltd on 01/01/2011:

buildings and grounds €520,000; equipment €75,000; vehicles at cost €60,000; stock in shop €3,600; stock of heating oil €1,800; creditors for supplies to gym and health centre €1,500; 5% investments €40,000; contract cleaning prepaid €300; clients' deposits paid in advance €5,000. The authorised capital of the company was €400,000 and the issued capital was €350,000. **All fixed assets have 3 years' accumulated depreciation on 01/01/2011.**

The following is a receipts and payments account for the year ended 31/12/2011.

Receipts and Payments Account of New Era Gym and Health Centre Ltd for Year Ended 31/12/11			
	€		€
Balance at bank 01/01/2011	6,500	Laundry	3,000
Clients' fees	320,000	Telephone	1,400
Investment income	1,100	Wages and salaries	84,300
Shop receipts	42,000	Repayment of €30,000 loan on 01/04/2011	
Balance 31/12/2011	108,600	with 15 months' interest	36,000
		Equipment	20,000
		New extension	220,000
		New vehicle	40,000
		Contract cleaning	3,400
		Light and heat	3,300
		Insurance	6,200
		Purchases – shop	26,000
		Purchases – supplies	34,600
	478,200		478,200

The following information and instructions are to be taken into account.

  (i) Closing stock at 31/12/2011 was as follows: shop €1,600, heating oil €400.

 (ii) Cleaning is done under contract payable monthly in advance and includes a payment of €700 for January 2012.

(iii) Clients' fees include deposits for 2012 of €5,500. Clients fees in arrears at 31/12/2011 amount to €600.

(iv) Wages and salaries include €20,000 per annum paid to the secretary, who also runs the shop. It is estimated that 40% of this salary, €300 of light and heat, €900 of insurance and €400 of telephone are attributable to the shop.

 (v) Creditors for supplies to the gym and health centre at 31/12/2011 are owed €2,000.

(vi) Electricity due on 31/12/2011 is €340.

(vii) Depreciation is to be provided as follows:

Buildings: 2% of cost for the full year

Equipment: 10% of cost for the full year

Vehicles: 20% of cost per annum from date of purchase to date of sale

NOTE: The vehicle held on 01/01/2011 was purchased on 01/01/2008 and was traded in on 01/07/2011 against a new vehicle. The trade-in allowance was €8,000 against a new vehicle valued at €48,000.

(viii) On 31/12/2011 the New Era Gym and Health Centre Ltd decided to revalue buildings at €850,000.

You are required to:

(a) Calculate the company's reserves (profit and loss balance) on 01/01/2011   (18)

(b) Calculate the profit/loss from the shop for the year ended 31/12/2011   (10)

(c) Prepare a profit and loss account for New Era Gym and Health Centre Ltd for the year ended 31/12/2011   (36)

(d) Prepare a balance sheet as on 31/12/2011   (30)

(e) Advise the company on how to fund the purchase of equipment for the new extension; the equipment is expected to cost €150,000   (6)

(100 marks)

Solution

(a) Statement of Capital and Reserves on 1/1/2011			
Assets	€		€
Buildings and grounds (520,000 – 31,200)	488,800	(2)	
Equipment (75,000 – 22,500)	52,500	(2)	
Vehicles (60,000 – 36,000)	24,000	(2)	
Stock in shop	3,600	(1)	
Stock of oil	1,800	(1)	
5% investments	40,000	(1)	
Contract cleaning prepaid	300	(1)	
Cash at bank	6,500	(1)	617,500
Liabilities			
Creditors for supplies	1,500	(1)	
Clients' deposits paid in advance	5,000	(1)	
Loan	30,000	(1)	
Interest on loan (12 months @ 400 per month)	4,800	(2)	
Issued capital	350,000	(1)	(391,300)
Reserves			226,200 (1)

(b) Shop Profit and Loss Account for Year Ended 31/12/11

		€		€	
Shop receipts				42,000	(1)
Less Expenses					
Cost of goods sold	W1	28,000	(5)		
Light and heat		300	(1)		
Insurance		900	(1)		
Telephone		400	(1)		
Wages and salaries (40% × 20,000)		8,000	(1)	(37,600)	
Profit from shop				4,400	

(c) Profit and Loss Account for Year Ended 31/12/11

		€		€
Income				
Investment income		2,000	(1)	
Profit from shop		4,400	(1)	
Clients' fees	W2	320,100	(5)	326,500
Expenditure				
Wages and salaries (84,300 – 8,000)		76,300	(2)	
Insurance (6,200 – 900)		5,300	(2)	
Light and heat	W3	4,740	(5)	
Purchases – supplies	W4	35,100	(3)	
Loan interest		1,200	(1)	
Laundry		3,000	(1)	
Postage and telephone (1,400 – 400)		1,000	(2)	
Depreciation – Buildings		14,800	(1)	
– Equipment		9,500	(1)	
– Vehicles		10,800	(1)	
Loss on sale of vehicle		10,000	(2)	
Contract cleaning	W5	3,000	(3)	(174,740)
Net profit for year				151,760 (4)
Add Reserves 01/01/2011				226,200 (1)
Profit and loss balance 31/12/2011				377,960

(d) Balance Sheet as at 31/12/2011	Cost €		Depreciation €		NBV €	
Fixed assets						
Buildings and grounds	850,000	(1)			850,000	
Equipment (75,000 + 20,000)	95,000	(2)	32,000	(2)	63,000	
Vehicles	48,000	(1)	4,800	(2)	43,200	
	993,000		36,800		956,200	
5% investments					40,000	(2)
					996,200	
Current assets						
Investment income due	900	(3)				
Closing stock – shop	1,600	(1)				
– oil	400	(1)				
Cleaning prepaid	700	(1)				
Clients' fees due	600	(2)	4,200			
Less **Creditors: amounts falling due within 1 year**						
Electricity due	340	(1)				
Clients' advance deposits	5,500	(2)				
Bank	108,600	(2)				
Creditors for supplies	2,000	(2)	(116,440)		(112,240)	
					883,960	
Financed by						
Share capital and reserves	Authorised		Issued			
Ordinary shares	400,000	(1)	350,000	(1)		
Revaluation reserve			156,000	(3)		
Profit and loss balance			377,960		883,960	
					883,960	

(e) Funding options for new equipment

My advice to the company would be:

	€
Sell investments	40,000
Sell remaining shares	50,000
Borrow	60,000
	150,000

The company would be able to pay back the loan quickly, as the accounts show that it had a surplus €151,760 in 2011 and is generating enough cash. Although it owes the bank €108,600, it has paid out amounts up to €310,000 on non-recurring and non-trading items.

Workings

1 Cost of goods sold

Stock 1/1/2011	3,600	
Add Purchases	26,000	
Less Stock 31/12/2011	(1,600)	28,000

2 Clients' fees

Amount received	320,000	
Advance deposits	5,000	
Fees due	600	
Less Fees prepaid	(5,500)	320,100

3 Light and heat

Amount paid	3,300	
Stock of oil 1/1/2011	1,800	
Electricity due	340	
Stock of oil 31/12/2011	(400)	
Charge to shop	(300)	4,740

4 Purchases	34,600 + 2,000 – 1,500	35,100
5 Contract cleaning	3,400 + 300 – 700	3,000

Incomplete Records

7

Learning objectives

In this chapter you will learn about:

1 The preparation of final accounts from limited information using:
- **Control account and cashbook method**
- **Balance sheet mark-up/margin method**

2 Advice for those who do not keep proper accounts

When a business has not kept proper ledger accounts, the information available is very limited. It is necessary to piece together this information and, with your knowledge of double entry, prepare a trading, profit and loss account and balance sheet containing as much detail as possible for the business. The method used will depend on the type of information supplied in the question. As you are attempting to put the information together rather like a jigsaw, it is a good idea to have a procedure to follow.

Control Account and Cashbook Method

The question will provide information on cash payments, bank receipts and payments and a list of some assets and liabilities, both at the beginning and the end of the year, as well as other information such as loans and drawings.

Steps

1 Prepare a statement of capital by listing the assets and liabilities at the beginning of the year. This will allow you to calculate the opening capital; if the capital has been given, an intangible asset such as goodwill may need to be found (see sample Question 1, p.117).

2 Prepare a bank account to find the closing bank figure to include in the balance sheet. Do not balance the account until the end.

3 Prepare a cash account to find cash sales. Make sure to include any drawings taken from cash.

4 Prepare a debtors' control account to find credit sales.
Total the cash and credit sales to get the total sales figure.

5 Prepare a creditors' control account to find credit purchases.
Total the cash and credit purchases to get the total purchases figure.
Adjust purchases for any drawings taken from stock.

6 Calculate the expenses and gains figures for the profit and loss account, taking into account amounts due and prepaid at the beginning and end of the year and any amounts attributable to the private section of the business (drawings). Note if there has been any depreciation on the fixed assets over the year.

7 Calculate the figure for drawings; note that drawings can include a number of items, such as cash, stock, a proportion of certain expenses, fixed assets, etc.

8 Prepare the trading, profit and loss account and balance sheet.

Balance Sheet Mark-up/Margin Method

In this method there is no cashbook and thus the information available is very limited. Assets and liabilities at the beginning and end of the year and information regarding payments and lodgements made and amounts taken by the owner are usually provided. This method works on the principle that, after accounting for amounts taken from the business by the owners (drawings) and amounts lodged into the business by the owners (capital introduced), any change in capital **must be** as result of a net profit or loss. Therefore, if all the available information is used to complete the balance sheet, the missing figure for net profit can be found. This net profit figure is used to work back and find all remaining missing figures.

Steps

1 Find the opening capital; list assets and subtract any liabilities at the beginning of the year.

2 Calculate the expenses and gains to be charged to the profit and loss account; be sure to adjust figures for amounts due and prepaid and for any drawings.

3 Note any capital introduced and calculate the drawings figure.

4 Prepare the balance sheet as normal using the information provided and any amounts calculated such as goodwill, investments, expenses prepaid/due and gains prepaid/due. The financed by section will contain the missing figure of net profit. A suggested layout is given below:

> **Top Tip!**
> If the owner lodges money in the bank account and then purchases a business, the amount invested is the opening capital; find out if there is any goodwill by adding up the assets purchased and subtracting the liabilities.

Financed by		
Creditors: amounts falling due after more than 1 year		
Loan		X
Capital and reserves		
Capital – opening balance	X	
Add Capital introduced	X	
Less Drawings	(X)	X
		X
Add Net profit (missing figure)		
Capital employed (same as total net assets)		X

> **Top Tips!**
> - Net profit can be found when all other known figures are entered.
> - Subtract Long-term liabilities + Capital + Capital introduced − Drawings from the capital employed figure (the total net assets figure). If capital employed is greater, then there is a net profit; if it is less, then there is a net loss.

5 Prepare a skeleton trading, profit and loss account by filling in all known figures. It will now be necessary to work back to find the missing figures of gross profit, sales and purchases.

> **Points to note**
> - **When working back the following applies:** Net profit + Expenses − Income = Gross profit
> - Gross profit is usually a percentage of sales (margin); if you have gross profit you can find sales. (Gross profit may also be given as a percentage of cost (mark-up); if you have gross profit you can find cost of sales.)
>   Sales − Gross profit = Cost of sales   Cost of sales + Closing stock − Opening stock = Purchases

Study Tips

- Incomplete records is a popular **100-mark question**, and both the control account method and balance sheet method need to be practised.

- Great care needs to be taken to include all information that has been provided.

- Note, for example, there are a small number of expenses; because of this, each figure is worth high marks and therefore **must** be accurate.

- Read the question carefully and ensure that you have used **all information** given at some stage.

- **Pay great attention to the theory part of the question to ensure full marks;** note the advice to give to a trader who keeps incomplete records and additional information that would be provided by the double-entry system **(see sample questions)**.

- Margin is gross profit as a percentage of sales.

- Mark-up is gross profit as a percentage of cost (i.e. cost of sales in this instance).

- This method of using the profit or percentage profit to work back to find another figure is also used in product costing in management accounting.

Sample questions and solutions

Question 1 – Cashbook and control account method

On 1/1/2009, G. Kelly purchased a business for €255,000 consisting of the following tangible assets and liabilities: buildings €178,000; stock €21,600; debtors €16,000; 4 months' rates prepaid €660; cash €600; trade creditors €19,200; and wages due €2,460.

During 2009 Kelly did not keep a full set of accounts but was able to supply the following information on 31/12/2009:

Cash payments:	Lodgements €64,000; general expenses €21,500; purchases €63,000
Bank payments:	Furniture €30,000; creditors €41,900; light and heat €5,800; interest €11,200; annual rates €2,220; covenant for charitable organisation €2,700; vehicle €16,000; rent for 1 year €10,800
Bank lodgements:	Debtors €57,000; cash €64,000; dividends €2,400

Each week Kelly took goods from stock to the value of €120 and cash to the value of €110 for household expenses.

Kelly borrowed €160,000 on 1/5/2009, part of which was used to build an extension costing €120,000. It was agreed that the sum borrowed would be repaid in 8 equal instalments on 1 December each year. Interest was to be charged at the rate of 12% per annum on the initial sum, to be paid monthly at the end of each month.

The figure for rent was in respect of an adjoining building rented by Kelly on 1/8/2009. It was payable in advance and Kelly estimated that ¼ of the building was used as a private residence and that 20% of the light and heat **used** and 30% of the furniture should also be attributed to the private section of the premises.

Included in the assets and liabilities of the firm on 31/12/2009 were: stock €19,800 (including stock of heating fuel €400); debtors €18,600; trade creditors €16,500; cash €820; electricity due €550.

You are required to show:

(a) The trading, profit and loss account for the year ended 31/12/2009   (52)

(b) The balance sheet as at 31/12/2009   (40)

(c) What additional information would be available if Kelly's accounts were prepared using the double-entry system   (8)

(100 marks)

Solution

Note 1   Statement of capital at the beginning of the year

Point to note

A business has been purchased and the tangible assets and liabilities are listed; the amount paid for the business is the capital, as this is the amount invested by the owner; the missing figure will be the intangible asset goodwill.

Statement of Capital 1/1/2009			
Assets	**€**	**Liabilities**	**€**
Buildings	178,000	Creditors	19,200
Stock	21,600	Wages due	2,460
Debtors	16,000	Capital	255,000
Rates	660		
Cash	600		
	216,860		
Goodwill	59,800		
	276,660		276,660

Note 2   Cash account

Cash Account			
	€		**€**
Balance b/d	600	Lodgements	64,000
Cash sales	**154,440**	General expenses	21,500
		Purchases	63,000
		Drawings (110 × 52)	5,720
		Balance c/d	820
	155,040		155,040

Top Tips!

- Prepare a cash account to find the cash sales; **remember to include any drawings from cash and any opening and closing cash balance**.

- Use a T account format for this adjustment to avoid errors.

Note 3   Debtors' control account

Debtors' Control Account			
	€		**€**
Balance b/d	16,000	Bank	57,000
Credit sales	**59,600**	Balance c/d	18,600
	75,600		75,600
Balance b/d	18,600		

		€	
Total sales	Cash	154,440	
	Credit	59,600	
	Total	214,040 T	

Top Tips!

- Prepare a debtors' control account to get the credit sales figure. The balance for debtors at the end of the year will be b/d on the debit; therefore it is c/d on the credit.

- Use a T account format for this adjustment.

Note 4 **Creditors' control account**

Creditors' Control Account				
	€			**€**
Bank	41,900	Balance b/d		19,200
Balance c/d	16,500	**Credit purchases**		39,200
	58,400			58,400
		Balance b/d		16,500

			€	
Total purchases	**Cash**		**63,000**	
	Credit		**39,200**	
			102,200	
	Less **Drawings**		**6,240**	**(120 × 52)**
			95,960	**T**

Top Tips!
- Prepare a creditors' control account to get the credit purchases figure. The balance for creditors at the end of the year will be b/d on the credit; therefore it is c/d on the debit.
- Use a T account format for this adjustment.
- **Remember to adjust the purchases figure for any drawings taken from stock** (goods taken for personal use cannot be sold and therefore cannot be included in the trading account).

Note 5 **Rates**

	€	
4 months prepaid beginning	660	
Annual rates 2,220 ÷ 12 × 8	1,480	
P+L a/c (12 months)	2,140	
Rates prepaid 2,220 ÷ 12 × 4	740	Current asset BS

Note 6 **General expenses**

	€
Cash	21,500
Less Wages due beginning	2,460
P+L a/c	19,040

Note 7 **Loan**

Interest Loan was received on 1/5/2009; 8 months' interest payable for 2009:

$160,000 \times 12\% = 19,200 \div 12 \times 8 = 12,800$ P+L a/c

                              11,200 Paid

                                1,600 Current liabilities BS

Repayment of loan $160,000 \div 8 = 20,000$; an instalment was due on 1/12/2009, but this has not yet been paid:

Loan instalment due   20,000 Current liability BS

Loan   140,000 Long-term liability BS

Note 8 **Rent** (paid on 1/8/2009 for 1 year)

¼ of rent is drawings: $10,800 \div 4 = 2,700$

                     $10,800 - 2,700 = 8,100$

                     $8,100 \div 12 \times 5 = 3,375$ P+L a/c

                     $8,100 \div 12 \times 7 = 4,725$ Current asset, rent prepaid

Note 9   Light and heat

	€
Bank	5,800
Add Electricity due	550
Less Stock of oil end	(400)
	5,950
Less Drawings (20%)	1,190
P+L a/c	4,760

Top Tip!

Drawings are a percentage of the amount **used**. First, calculate the actual amount of light and heat used in this year, i.e. adjust the amount paid for all amounts prepaid/due. Then, calculate the given percentage on this figure.

Note 10   Drawings

	€
Cash	5,720
Stock	6,240
Light and heat	1,190
Furniture	9,000 (30% of 30,000)
Rent	2,700
Total	24,850 BS

Note 11   Bank

Bank Account			
	€		€
Cash	64,000	Furniture	30,000
Loan	60,000	Creditors	41,900
Dividends	2,400	Light and heat	5,800
Debtors	57,000	Interest	11,200
		Rates	2,220
		Covenant	2,700
		Vehicle	16,000
		Rent	10,800
		Extension	120,000
		Balance c/d	42,780
	283,400		283,400

Top Tip!

Many of the figures in the bank account affect the other adjustments. Preparing a bank account at the beginning of the question will bring these figures to your attention; however, it would not be advisable to balance the bank account until the end to ensure that all items are included.

Top Tip!

Note carefully that **every** piece of information given in this question has been used. In particular, the **lodgements of dividends by the owner into the bank account are capital introduced** and need to be added to the capital in the financed by section of the balance sheet, and the **payment of money to charity is treated as a business expense**.

(a) Trading, Profit and Loss Account for Year Ended 31/12/09

		€	€
Sales	N2,3		214,040
Less Cost of sales			
Opening stock		21,600	
Purchases	N4	95,960	
		117,560	
Less Closing stock (19,800 − 400)		19,400	
Cost of sales			98,160
Gross profit			115,880
Less Expenses			
Rates	N5	2,140	
General expenses	N6	19,040	
Loan interest	N7	12,800	
Rent	N8	3,375	
Light and heat	N9	4,760	
Covenant for charity		2,700	44,815
Net profit			71,065

(b) Balance Sheet as on 31/12/09

		€	€	€
Intangible fixed assets				
Goodwill	N1			59,800
Tangible fixed assets				
Buildings (178,000 + 120,000)			298,000	
Furniture			21,000	
Vehicle			16,000	335,000
				394,800
Current assets				
Stock			19,400	
Stock of heating oil			400	
Debtors			18,600	
Cash			820	
Bank	N11		42,780	
Rent prepaid			4,725	
Rates prepaid			740	
			87,465	
Creditors: amounts falling due within 1 year				
Creditors		16,500		
Electricity due		550		
Loan interest due	N7	1,600		
Loan instalment due	N7	20,000	38,650	
Working capital				48,815
Total net assets				443,615
Financed by				
Creditors: amounts falling due after more than 1 year				
Loan				140,000
Capital			255,000	
Add Capital introduced			2,400	
Add Net profit			71,065	
			328,465	
Less Drawings	N10		24,850	303,615
Capital employed				443,615

(c) Preparation of accounts using the double-entry system

A double-entry system would produce general ledger accounts and a trial balance. This would lead to lots more information being available such as: total sales figure and total purchases figure; bank balance; capital and drawings; bad debts; expenses/gains due and prepaid; and discounts allowed and received.

Question 2 – Balance sheet mark-up/margin method

C. McCauley lodged €410,000 to a business bank account on 1/1/2009 and on the same day purchased a business for €370,000, including the following assets and liabilities: buildings €340,000; stock €18,200; 3 months' building insurance prepaid €2,100; debtors €25,700; advertising due €3,500; and trade creditors €62,500.

McCauley did not keep a full set of books during 2009, but estimates that the gross profit was 40% of sales, and she was able to supply the following additional information on 31/12/2009:

(i) Each week McCauley took from stock goods to the value of €100. Each month cash of €400 was taken for household expenses.

(ii) On 1/8/2009 McCauley borrowed €260,000, part of which was used to purchase an adjoining premises costing €210,000. It was agreed that McCauley would pay interest on the last day of the month at the rate of 6% per annum. The capital sum was to be repaid in one lump sum in the year 2019 and, to provide for this, the bank was instructed to transfer €2,100 on the last day of every month from McCauley's business account into an investment fund. On 1/9/2009 part of the new premises was rented out for an **annual** rent of €14,400, which was lodged to the business bank account.

(iii) During the year, McCauley had a lottery win of €6,500 and lodged this to the business bank account. The following payments were made during the year: light and heat €8,400; salaries and general expenses €102,285; college fees €7,000; **annual** insurance premium €9,600; interest €3,900; and furniture €12,000.

(iv) McCauley estimated that 25% of the following should be attributed to the private section of the premises: furniture; light and heat used; and interest payable. McCauley also estimated that 20% of college fees should be attributed to a family member and the remainder to an employee.

(v) Included in the assets and liabilities of the firm on 31/12/2009 were: stock €26,000; debtors €32,400; trade creditors €27,580; cash at bank €78,075; electricity due €520; and €525 interest earned by the investment fund to date.

You are required to prepare, with workings:

(a) A statement/balance sheet showing McCauley's profit or loss for the year ended 31/12/2009 (50)
(b) A trading, profit and loss account, in as much detail as possible, for the year ended 31/12/2009 (40)
(c) A summary of the advice you would give to McCauley in relation to the information given above (10)
(100 marks)

> **Points to note**
>
> - The amount lodged into the business bank account is the opening capital, €410,000.
> - The difference between the amount paid for the business and the assets less liabilities is the intangible asset goodwill.

Solution

Note 1   Goodwill

	€
Assets: 340,000 + 18,200 + 2,100 + 25,700 =	386,000
Liabilities: 62,500 + 3,500 =	66,000
Tangible total net assets	320,000
Amount paid for the business	370,000
The difference is goodwill	50,000 BS

Note 2   Drawings

	€
Stock	5,200
Cash	4,800
Interest (25%)	1,625
Light and heat	2,230
College fees (20%)	1,400
Furniture (25%)	3,000
	18,255

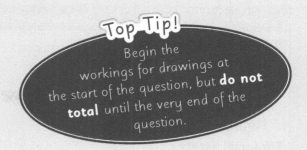

Top Tip!
Begin the workings for drawings at the start of the question, but **do not total** until the very end of the question.

Note 3   Loan interest
Received 1/8/2009 5 months
6% of 260,000 = 15,600 ÷ 12 × 5 = €6,500
6,500 − 1,625 (drawings = 25%) = €4,875
6,500 − 3,900 (paid) = €2,600 due

Top Tips!
- Note when the loan was received, then calculate how much interest is due. Drawings are on the **amount payable**. This means the amount of interest that should have been paid for this year, in this case 5 months.
- Note the **purpose of the loan**: in this case buildings increase.

Note 4   Investment

	€	
2,100 × 5 months	10,500	
Interest earned	525	P+L a/c
Total in the account	11,025	

Note 5   Rent receivable
14,400 ÷ 12 × 4 = €4,800 P+L a/c
€9,600 Prepaid, current asset

Note 6   Light and heat
Note that drawings are a percentage of the amount used.

	€
Bank	8,400
Add Due	520
	8,920
Drawings	2,230
P+L a/c	6,690

Note 7   Insurance (note the prepaid at the beginning)
9,600 ÷ 12 × 9 = 7,200 + 2,100 = €9,300 P+L a/c
9,600 ÷ 12 × 3 = €2,400 Prepaid

Note 8   Salaries and general expenses

	€
Bank	102,285
Less Due beginning	(3,500)
Add College fees (80%)	5,600
	104,385

Point to note
Money lodged to the business by the owner during the year is **capital introduced**. Note the lottery win of €6,500.

Points to note

The calculation of the missing figures is shown below for illustration purpose only; these figures are best calculated by working back in the accounts.

Net profit
410,000 + 6,500 − 18,255 + 260,000 = 658,275
718,600 − 658,275 = 60,325

Gross profit
60,325 + 125,250 − 5,325 = 180,250 = 40%
1% = 4,506.25
100% = 450,625 sales

Cost of sales
450,625 − 180,250 = 270,375

Purchases
270,375 + 26,000 − 18,200 = 278,175
278,175 + 5,200 = 283,375

(a) Balance Sheet as on 31/12/09

		€	€	€
Intangible fixed assets				
Goodwill	N1			50,000
Tangible fixed assets				
Buildings (340,000 + 210,000)			550,000	
Furniture			9,000	559,000
Financial assets				
Investment	N4			11,025
				620,025
Current assets				
Stock			26,000	
Debtors			32,400	
Bank			78,075	
Insurance prepaid			2,400	
			138,875	
Creditors: amounts falling due within 1 year				
Creditors		27,580		
Electricity due		520		
Loan interest due	N3	2,600		
Rent receivable prepaid	N5	9,600	40,300	
Working capital				98,575
Total net assets				718,600
Financed by				
Creditors: amounts falling due after more than 1 year				
Loan				260,000
Capital			410,000	
Add Capital introduced			6,500	
Less Drawings	N2		(18,255)	398,245
				658,245
Net profit **(missing figure)**				**60,355**
Capital employed				718,600

(b) Trading, Profit and Loss Account for Year Ended 31/12/09

		€	€
Sales **(100%)**			**450,700**
Less Cost of sales			
Opening stock		18,200	
Purchases (**283,420** − 5,200)		**278,220**	
		296,420	
Less Closing stock		26,000	
Cost of sales			**270,420**
Gross profit **(40%)**			**180,280**
Add Income			
Investment income	N4	525	
Rent receivable	N5	4,800	5,325
			185,605 *contd* →

(b) Trading, Profit and Loss Account for Year Ended 31/12/09 (continued)			
Less Expenses			
Insurance	N7	9,300	
Salaries and general expenses	N8	104,385	
Loan interest	N4	4,875	
Light and heat	N6	6,690	125,250
Net profit			**60,355**

(c) A business that does not keep proper accounts needs the following advice

Businesses should keep a detailed cashbook and general ledger, supported by the sales, sales returns, purchases, purchases returns day books and general journal.

This would enable the preparation of an accurate trading, profit and loss account and would avoid reliance on estimates.

Question 3 (2005, HL, Section 2, Q7)

On 1/1/2004, J. Connolly purchased a business for €195,000, consisting of the following tangible assets and liabilities: premises €162,000; stock €15,200; debtors €17,000; 3 months' premises insurance prepaid €860; trade creditors €18,700; and wages due €1,700.

During 2004 Connolly did not keep a full set of accounts but was able to supply the following information on 31/12/2004:

Cash payments:	Lodgements €96,000; general expenses €23,700; purchases €53,000
Bank payments:	Equipment €22,000; creditors €33,100; light and heat €5,800; interest €2,325; annual premises insurance premium €6,000; standing order for charitable organisation €3,200, vehicle €26,000; rent for 1 year €2,400
Bank lodgements:	Debtors €34,000; cash €96,000; dividends €3,800

Connolly took goods from stock to the value of €100 and cash €80 per week for household expenses during the year.

Connolly borrowed €84,000 on 1/7/2004, part of which was used to purchase an adjoining warehouse costing €70,000. It was agreed that the sum borrowed would be repaid in 12 equal instalments on the 1 June each year. Interest was to be charged at the rate of 10% per annum on the initial sum, to be paid monthly at the end of each month.

The figure for rent was in respect of an adjoining building rented by Connolly on 1/10/2004. It was payable in advance and Connolly estimated that $1/3$ of the building was used as a private residence and that 20% of the light and heat used should also be attributed to the private section of the premises.

Included in the assets and liabilities of the firm on 31/12/2004 were: stock €17,300 (including stock of heating fuel €300); debtors €18,100; trade creditors €15,500; cash €650; electricity due €720.

You are required to show:

(a) The trading, profit and loss accounts for the year ended 31/12/2004 (52)

(b) The balance sheet as at 31/12/2004 (40)

(c) What additional information would be available if Connolly's accounts were prepared using the double-entry system (8)

(100 marks)

Solution

(a) Trading, Profit and Loss Account for Year Ended 31/12/04 (52)

		€		€	
Sales	**W1**			212,610	(9)
Less Cost of sales					
Opening stock		15,200	(2)		
Purchases	**W2**	77,700	(7)		
		92,900			
Closing stock		(17,000)	(2)	75,900	
Gross profit				136,710	
Less Expenses					
General expenses	**W3**	22,000	(5)		
Donation to charity		3,200	(2)		
Light and heat	**W4**	4,976	(7)		
Interest	**W5**	4,200	(4)		
Insurance	**W6**	5,360	(6)		
Rent	**W7**	400	(5)		
				40,136	
Net profit				96,574	(3)

Workings

1 Sales

Credit sales 34,000 + 18,100 − 17,000	35,100	
Cash sales 96,000 + 23,700 + 53,000 +		
4,160 + 650	177,510	
Total sales	**212,610**	

2 Purchases

Credit purchases		
33,100 + 15,500 −18,700	29,900	
Cash purchases	53,000	
Total purchases	82,900	
Less Drawings of stock	(5,200)	
Total purchases	**77,700**	

3 General expenses 23,700 − 1,700   22,000

4 Light and heat 5,800 + 720 −

      300 − 1,244   4,976

5 Loan interest 2,325 + 1,875   4,200

6 Insurance 6,000 + 860 − 1,500   5,360

7 Rent 2,400 − 1,200 − 800   400

8 Drawings

      5,200 + 4,160 + 800 + 1,244   11,404

(b) Balance Sheet as on 31/12/04 (40)

	€		€	€	
Intangible fixed assets					
Goodwill				20,340	(3)
Tangible fixed assets					
Buildings	232,000	(2)			
Vehicles	26,000	(1)			
Equipment	22,000	(1)		280,000	
				300,340	

contd →

(b) Balance Sheet as on 31/12/04 (continued)				
Current assets				
Stock	17,300	(1)		
Debtors	18,100	(1)		
Bank	46,975	(5)		
Cash	650	(1)		
Insurance prepaid	1,500	(3)		
Rent prepaid	1,200	(3)		
	85,725			
Creditors: amounts falling due within 1 year				
Creditors	15,500	(1)		
Electricity due	720	(1)		
Interest due	1,875	(3)		
Loan repayment due	7,000	(2)	25,095	60,630
				360,970
Financed by				
Creditors: amounts falling due after more than 1 year				
Loan				77,000 (2)
Capital			195,000 (2)	
Capital introduced			3,800 (3)	
Net profit			96,574	
			295,374	
Less Drawings	**W8**		11,404 (5)	
				283,970
				360,970

(c) Additional information available if accounts prepared using double-entry system (8)

Total sales figure; total purchases figure; trial balance; bank balance; capital; goodwill; bad debts; expenses due and prepaid; discounts

Question 4 (2007, HL, Section 2, Q7)

On 1/1/2006, P. Lynch purchased a business for €590,000, which included the following tangible assets and liabilities: premises €560,000; stock €19,000; debtors €12,000; 3 months' premises insurance prepaid €1,600; trade creditors €18,200; wages due €2,600 and cash €200.

During 2006 Lynch did not keep a full set of accounts but was able to supply the following information on 31/12/2006:

Cash payments:	Lodgements €116,000, general expenses €73,800, purchases €105,200
Bank payments:	Furniture €14,000, creditors €38,800, light and heat €5,400, interest €2,250, annual premises insurance premium €6,800, delivery van €28,400
Bank lodgements:	Debtors €61,000, cash €116,000, dividends €3,000

Each week Lynch took goods from stock to the value of €150 and cash to the value of €200 for household expenses.

Lynch borrowed €180,000 on 1/9/2006, part of which was used to purchase an adjoining premises and residence costing €155,000. It was agreed that Lynch would pay interest on the last day of each month at a rate of 5% per annum. The capital sum was to be repaid in a lump sum in the year 2015 and to provide for this the bank was to transfer €1,200 on the last day of each month from Lynch's business bank account into an investment fund commencing on 30/9/2006.

Lynch estimated that 25% of the furniture, 20% of interest **payable** for the year and 25% of light and heat **used** should be attributed to the private section of the premises.

Included in the assets and liabilities of the firm on 31/12/2006 were: stock €16,400, debtors €20,200, trade creditors €30,400, cash €400, electricity due €480 and €25 interest earned by the fund to date.

You are required to:

(a) Prepare, with workings, the trading, profit and loss accounts for the year ended 31/12/2006   (52)

(b) Show the balance sheet with workings as at 31/12/2006   (40)

(c) (i) Explain the term 'accounting concept'

    (ii) Name **two** fundamental accounting concepts

    (iii) Illustrate an accounting concept applying to the accounts of P. Lynch   (8)

(100 marks)

Solution

(a) Trading, Profit and Loss Account for Year Ended 31/12/06		(52)	
	€	€	
Sales		374,800	(11)
Less Cost of sales			
Opening stock	19,000 (2)		
Purchases (156,200 – 7,800)	148,400 (7)		
	167,400		
Closing stock	(16,400) (2)	(151,000)	
Gross profit		223,800	
Less Expenses			
General expenses	71,200 (5)		
Insurance	6,700 (6)		
Interest	2,400 (4)		
Light and heat	4,410 (6)	84,710	
		139,090	
Add Income from investment fund		25	(3)
Net profit		139,115	(6)

(b) Balance Sheet as on 31/12/06			(40)
Intangible fixed assets	€	€	€
Goodwill			18,000 (3)
Tangible fixed assets			
Buildings	715,000 (2)		
Delivery vans	28,400 (1)		
Furniture	10,500 (2)		753,900
Financial assets			
Investment fund			4,825 (2)
			776,725
Current assets			
Stock	16,400 (1)		
Debtors	20,200 (1)		
Bank	104,550 (5)		
Cash	400 (2)		
Prepayments (insurance)	1,700 (3)	143,250	

contd →

(b) Balance Sheet as on 31/12/06 (continued)

Creditors: amounts falling due within 1 year				
Creditors	30,400	(1)		
Interest due	750	(3)		
Electricity due	480	(1)	(31,630)	111,620
				888,345
Financed by				
Creditors: amounts falling due after more than 1 year				
Loan				180,000 (2)
Capital	590,000	(2)		
Capital introduced			3,000 (3)	
Net profit			139,115	
			732,115	
Less Drawings			(23,770) (6)	708,345
				888,345

(c) (8)

(i) **Accounting concepts**
Accounting concepts are the accounting practices or rules that are applied in the preparation of financial statements.

(ii) **Fundamental accounting concepts**
Accruals, going concern, consistency and prudence.

(iii) **The accruals concept**
All expenses incurred in a particular period must be included in the accounts of that period, regardless of whether they are paid or not. Similarly, all revenue income must be included in the accounts of that period whether received or not, e.g. electricity due for the current year must be included in the accounts, although the bill may not be paid until the following year, as the expense refers to the current year. Insurance prepaid should not be included in the current year's accounts as the payment refers to the following year.

Workings

1 Sales – credit (61,000 + 20,200 – 12,000)	69,200	
– cash (116,000 + 73,800 + 105,200 + 10,400 + 400 – 200)	305,600	
Total sales =	374,800	
2 Purchases		
Credit purchases (–18,200 + 30,400 + 38,800)	51,000	
Cash purchases	105,200	
Total purchases	156,200	
Less Drawings of stock	(7,800)	
Total purchases = €148,400		
3 General expenses (73,800 – 2,600) =	71,200	
4 Insurance (1,600 + 6,800 – 1,700) =	6,700	
5 Interest (3,000 – 600) =	2,400	
6 Light and heat (5,400 + 480 – 1,470) =	4,410	
7 Drawings (7,800 + 10,400 + 1,470 + 600 + 3,500) =	23,770	

NOTE: For a further example of a balance sheet mark-up/margin method question, see the 2003 exam paper, Question 7.

8 Correction of Errors – Suspense Accounts

Learning objectives

In this chapter you will learn about:

1 The procedure for dealing with errors in the accounts and omissions from the accounts
   - Journal entries for errors and omissions
   - Preparation of suspense account
   - Correction of net profit
   - Correction of balance sheet
2 The outline of errors that do not affect the trial balance

Accounts are prepared using the double-entry principle that for every debit there must be a corresponding credit. A trial balance is a list of balances taken from the ledger accounts. If the double-entry rule has been followed, the debit and credit balances should add up to the same figure.

However, mistakes can occur and the debit and the credit sides may not be the same; essentially the trial balance will not balance. When this happens the difference is placed in a temporary account called a suspense account until the errors can be found. Once the errors have been discovered, the accounts are corrected by entries in the general journal and the figure in the suspense account will be cancelled out. If the final accounts have already been prepared, it will be necessary to correct the net profit and the balance sheet to take into account the changes made by the corrections.

Past Leaving Certificate questions involve correcting errors and omissions with journal entries, preparing the suspense account, correcting the net profit and correcting the balance sheet. This topic tests students' knowledge of basic double entry and the effects that certain entries have on the trading, profit and loss account and balance sheet and should be approached with the attitude that it is a revision of knowledge you already have.

Top Tip!

Always check the **nature** of the business, e.g. if the business is that of a garage owner then motor vehicles bought or sold are purchases or sales, whereas in a grocery business motor vehicles are fixed assets.

Read and reread each part of the question very carefully to ensure that you interpret the information correctly and follow this procedure:

1 Use T accounts to deal with the corrections: your first set of T accounts should show **the error**, i.e. the incorrect entry or entries. The next set of T accounts will be what **should have happened**, i.e. the correct entries. **Compare** what did happen with what should have happened and it will be easy to see what accounts need to be debited and credited to **correct the mistake**. Any difference between the debit and the credit sides of the accounts in question is entered into the suspense account so that the debit and credit sides will be equal.

2 **Omissions will not affect the suspense account**: these are items left out of the books that need to be included; follow the double-entry rules to enter these transactions.

3　Prepare the suspense account from the general journal. Items stay on the same side: debit in the journal means debit in the suspense account; credit in the journal means credit in the suspense account. By balancing the account you will find the original difference.

4　Correct the net profit using the entries in the general journal. Any adjustments to purchases, purchases returns, sales, sales returns and expenses/gains will affect the net profit.

Top Tips!

When preparing the corrected net profit, remember to check which side the item is on in the general journal:

Debit side　　Reduces the net profit (*Subtract*)
Credit side　　Increases net profit (*Add*)

Draw on your existing knowledge:

- **Sales and gains** increase net profit and appear on the **credit** side of ledger accounts; thus entries on the credit side of the journal will increase net profit and must be **added**.

- **Purchases and expenses** reduce net profit; these appear on the **debit** side of the ledger accounts; thus entries on the debit side of the journal will reduce net profit and need to be **subtracted**.

5　Prepare the corrected balance sheet using the entries in the general journal. Changes to any assets, liabilities, drawings and capital will need to be taken into account.

Top Tip!

When preparing the corrected balance sheet, the effect will depend on which side the item is on in the general journal:

For assets　　Debit side increases (*Add*)
　　　　　　Credit side decreases (*Subtract*)

For liabilities　Debit side decreases (*Subtract*)
　　　　　　Credit side increases (*Add*)

Errors Revealed by the Trial Balance

Some errors can be found by examining the trial balance – for example:

- Completing the double entry incorrectly – i.e., entering one amount on the debit side of a ledger account and a different amount on the credit side of another ledger account
- Completing only one side of the double entry – i.e., entering the debit side of a transaction but not the credit side
- Mathematical errors, such as addition or subtraction errors or transcription errors with figures – e.g. entering €5,300 instead of €3,500

Errors Not Revealed by the Trial Balance

Some errors do not affect the trial balance; this means that these errors can be present in the books and the trial balance will still balance. Students must be aware of the 6 types of errors that can occur and a relevant example of each.

1 Error of original entry

- A mistake made in the books of first entry, such as sales or purchases books, and then carried through into the ledger: an **incorrect amount** entered correctly
- Credit sales of €500 entered in the sales book as €300; then debtors would be debited with €300 and the sales account credited with €300 instead of €500

2 Error of omission

- A transaction **left out of the books** completely
- Electricity payment of €250 by cheque not recorded; thus neither the debit nor the credit side is affected as the transaction has not been recorded

3 Error of commission

- A transaction that involves a **correct amount** being posted on the **correct side** of the **correct type** of account, but the **wrong account**
- Goods purchased on credit from Brown Ltd for €1,000; purchases debited with €1,000 but Black Ltd instead of Brown Ltd credited with €1,000

4 Error of principle

- A transaction that involves a **correct amount** being posted on the **correct side** but to the **wrong type** of account
- A garage purchases a motor vehicle for €10,000 and pays by cheque; bank credited correctly but equipment instead of purchases debited with €10,000

5 Compensating error

- This type of error occurs when **two errors have the effect of cancelling each other out**
- Payment of telephone bill €200 by cheque recorded as debit expenses €100 and credit bank €200; there is €100 too little on the debit side. If another error were to occur, such as sales on credit to a debtor of €2,500 credited to the sales account correctly but debited to the debtors' account as €2,600, this would compensate for the incorrect expenses figure and the debit and credit sides would be the same, yet there would be two errors in the accounts

6 Complete reversal of errors

- The **correct figures** are posted to the **correct accounts** but on the **incorrect sides**
- The purchase of goods on credit for €12,000 from Red Ltd recorded as credit purchases and creditors debited instead of vice versa

- Correction of errors has appeared in previous exam questions as both a **100-mark** and a **60-mark** question, most commonly as a 100-mark question.
- For 100 marks it is necessary to present the corrections in general journal format, prepare a suspense account to show the original difference, and correct the net profit and the balance sheet.
- For 60 marks students have been asked to journalise the corrections and correct the net profit. **Any part of the question** could arise for 60 marks, so it is advisable to practise all parts.
- Read the question carefully as the wording in the question will allow you to work out what needs to be done. In the case of an **error** occurring, use T accounts to work out what happened, what should have happened and what needs to be done to correct it. If there has been an **omission**, enter the relevant transaction in the books. Lay your work out clearly. Your corrections must be **presented in the general journal format** and there must be an appropriate **narration**.
- Make sure to give enough time to complete all parts of the question. **Follow your corrections** through in the suspense account, the corrected net profit and the balance sheet, in order to obtain the maximum number of marks.
- Be able to list, explain and give examples of errors not revealed by the trial balance.

Sample questions and solutions

Question 1

The trial balance of K. Leonard, a garage owner, failed to agree on 31/12/2009. The difference was entered in a suspense account and the following balance sheet was prepared.

Balance Sheet as on 31/12/09			
Fixed assets	€	€	€
Premises		550,000	
Equipment		40,000	590,000
Current assets			
Stock (including suspense)		62,000	
Debtors		24,500	
Cash		600	
		87,100	
Current liabilities			
Creditors	31,700		
Bank	19,000	50,700	36,400
			626,400
Financed by			
Capital		600,000	
Add Net profit		48,400	
		648,400	
Less Drawings		22,000	626,400

On checking the books, the following errors and omissions were discovered:

(i) A motor car purchased on credit from F. Brown for €21,000 has been entered as €12,200 on the incorrect side of Brown's account and credited as €2,100 to the equipment account.

(ii) Leonard won a private holiday prize for two worth €10,000 in total. One ticket had been given to a sales person as part payment of sales commission for the year and the other to a creditor as full payment for a debt of €5,300. No entry had been made in the books.

(iii) During the year repairs carried out to Leonard's private houses of €350 were paid from the business bank account but debited in error to the general expenses account as €530.

(iv) A debtor who owed Leonard €2,000 sent a cheque for €1,800 in full settlement. This was recorded correctly in the books. However, no entry has been made in the books of the subsequent dishonouring of this cheque and the writing-off of the remainder of the debt following the receipt of a cash payment of 20 cent in the euro.

(v) Leonard returned motor vehicles previously purchased on credit from a supplier for €11,500 and entered the transaction in the relevant accounts as €15,500. However, when the credit note was received it showed a transport charge of €300 to cover the cost of returning the vehicles. The only entry made in respect of this credit note was a credit of €11,800 to the creditors' account.

You are required to:

(a) Journalise the necessary corrections (55)

(b) Show the suspense account (10)

(c) Prepare a statement showing the correct net profit (15)

(d) Prepare a corrected balance sheet (20)

(100 marks)

Solution

Part (i)

Did happen

Creditors (F. Brown)		Equipment	
12,200			2,100

Should have happened

Creditors (F. Brown)		Purchases	
	21,000	21,000	

Correction

Creditors (F. Brown)		Purchases		Equipment		Suspense	
	33,200	21,000		2,100		10,100	

> **Point to note**
>
> Note that **the business is a garage**; motor vehicles are purchases, meaning the correct entry is debit purchases, credit creditors.

Part (ii)

> **Point to note**
>
> A difference between an amount owed and an amount paid is treated as discount; a debit entry in the discount account is discount allowed, a credit entry in the discount account is discount received.

There was an omission that now needs to be entered in the books.

The owner has given a personal prize to pay business expenses; this is recorded as capital introduced.

Capital		Commission		Creditors		Discount	
	10,000	5,000		5,300			300

Part (iii)

Did happen

Bank		General Expenses	
	350	530	

Top Tip!

The owner paid private expenses from the business and this was treated incorrectly as payment of a business expense. Remove this error from the business expenses account and enter the correct figure into the drawings account. Due to the fact that an incorrect figure was posted, there will also be an entry in the suspense account.

Should have happened

Bank		Drawings	
	350	350	

Correction

General Expenses		Drawings		Suspense	
	530	350		180	

Top Tip!

Look out for new items that appear as a result of omissions; these may be new entries in the corrected net profit or balance sheet.

Part (iv)

This entry involves the reversal of a correct entry due to the dishonouring of a cheque and the inclusion of omission.

Reversal

Debtors		Bank		Discount	
2,000			1,800		200

Writing-off of the bad debt;
€2,000 × 20 cent = €400

Cash		Debtors		Bad Debts	
400			400	1,600	
			1,600		

Point to note

The dishonoured cheque **and** the writing-off of the bad debt must both be entered in the accounts.

Part (v)

Did happen

Creditors		Purchases Returns	
15,500	11,800		15,500
3,700			

↗

Net effect

Point to note

There were two wrong entries in the creditors' account. When this occurs it is useful to determine what the overall net effect is so that you can see what needs to be done to put it right. Goods returned by the business are debited in the creditors' account and credited in the purchases returns. Any charges imposed by the seller will reduce the value of the returns.

Should have happened

Creditors		Purchases Returns	
11,200			11,200

Correction

Creditors		Purchases Returns		Suspense	
7,500		4,300			11,800

(a) Journal Entries		
	Dr **€**	**Cr** **€**
Purchases	21,000	
Equipment	2,100	
Suspense	10,100	
Creditors		33,200
Being correction of incorrect recording of credit purchases		
Commission	5,000	
Creditors	5,300	
Discount		300
Capital		10,000
Being private funds used to pay sales commission and a business debt		
Drawings	350	
Suspense	180	
General expenses		530
Being correction of payment of private repairs recorded incorrectly as business repairs		
Debtors	2,000	
Bank		1,800
Discount disallowed		200
Cash	400	
Bad debts	1,600	
Debtors		2,000
Being recording of a dishonoured cheque and a bad debt		
Creditors	7,500	
Purchases returns	4,300	
Suspense		11,800
Being recording of a credit note received incorporating a transport charge		

Point to note

No entry in the books = No suspense figure. **No error** has been made; the suspense is not affected.

Top Tip!

The debit and credit sides of the journal entries must be equal. Remember that for every debit there must be a credit; if both sides are not equal you have made a mistake and must go back and re-read the question.

(b) Suspense Account

		€			€
Creditors	(i)	10,100	Creditors	(v)	11,800
General expenses	(ii)	180			
Original difference		1,520			
		11,800			11,800

Top Tip!

The suspense figure was in stock; the balancing figure of €1,520 (original difference) was entered on the debit side of stock. This means that, in order to get the trial balance to equal, €1,520 was put on the debit side of stock. Now that the errors have been corrected, this figure must be removed. To remove, credit stock with €1,520: a credit in an asset account reduces the asset. The correct figure for stock is €62,000 − €1,520 = €60,480.

(c) Statement of Correct Net Profit

		€
Original net profit as per books		48,400
Less Purchases	(i)	(21,000)
Less Sales commission	(ii)	(5,000)
Add Discount	(ii)	300
Add General expenses	(iii)	530
Add Discount	(iv)	200
Less Bad debts	(iv)	(1,600)
Less Purchases returns	(v)	(4,300)
Correct net profit		17,530

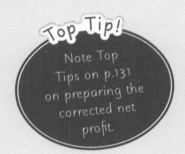

Top Tip!

Note Top Tips on p.131 on preparing the corrected net profit.

(d) Balance Sheet as on 31/12/09

	€	€	€
Fixed assets			
Premises		550,000	
Equipment (40,000 + 2,100)		42,100	592,100
Current assets			
Stock (62,000 − 1,520)		60,480	
Debtors (24,500 + 2,000 − 2,000)		24,500	
Cash (600 + 400)		1,000	
		85,980	
Current liabilities			
Creditors (31,700 + 33,200 − 5,300 − 7,500)	52,100		
Bank (19,000 + 1,800)	20,800	72,900	13,080
			605,180
Financed by			
Capital (600,000 + 10,000)		610,000	
Add Net profit		17,530	
		627,530	
Less Drawings (22,000 + 350)		22,350	605,180

Question 2

The trial balance of M. McGrath, a grocer, failed to agree on 31/12/2010. The difference was entered in a suspense account and the final accounts were prepared, which showed a net profit of €34,000.

On checking the books, the following errors and omissions were discovered:
  (i) Goods for resale bought on credit for €13,200 have been credited to the equipment account as €3,200 and debited to a creditors' account as €10,100.
 (ii) A private debt of €520 owed by McGrath had been offset in full against a business debt of €700 owed to the firm for groceries. No entry has been made in the books in respect of this offset.
(iii) Goods previously sold on credit for €970 have been returned to McGrath. These goods have been incorrectly entered as €70 on the credit side of the general expenses account and €790 on the debit side of the sales account.
 (iv) A cheque for €3,600 paid by McGrath out of a private bank account for 18 months' rent of a storeroom up to 30/6/2011 has not been entered in the books.
  (v) McGrath returned goods previously purchased on credit amounting to €6,400. This transaction was entered in the relevant accounts incorrectly as €4,600. However, a credit note was received from the supplier showing a restocking charge of €120 to cover the cost of the return. The only entry made in respect of this credit note was a credit of €6,280 in the creditors' account.

You are required to:
  (a) Journalise the necessary corrections   (40)
  (b) Prepare a statement showing the correct net profit   (20)
                                                                        (60 marks)

Solution

Part (i)

Did happen

Creditors		Equipment	
10,100			3,200

Point to note

Goods purchased on credit should be entered as debit purchases and credit creditors.

Should have happened

Purchases		Creditors	
13,200			13,200

Correction

Equipment		Purchases		Creditors		Suspense	
3,200		13,200			23,300	6,900	

Part (ii)

There was an omission that now needs to be entered in the books.

The owner has paid a private debt with business funds; this is recorded as drawings. The amount offset was more than the private debt, so the difference is accounted for as discount allowed by the owner.

Drawings		Debtors		Discount	
520			700	180	

Part (iii)

Did happen

Sales		General Expenses	
790			70

Point to note

Goods returned to the business are accounted for as debit sales returns and credit debtors.

Should have happened

Sales Returns		Debtors	
970			970

Correction

General Expenses		Sales		Sales Returns		Debtors		Suspense	
70			790	970			970	720	

Part (iv)

There was an omission that now needs to be entered in the books. The owner has used private funds to pay a business expense; this is capital introduced. We need to take into account the fact that part of the payment is for the current year and part relates to next year.

Rent			Capital	
P+L	2,400			3,600
Prepaid	1,200			

Point to note

18 months' rent was paid:

12 months for this year and 6 months for the following year; only this year's rent can be charged to the profit and loss account

3,600 ÷ 18 = 200	
200 × 12 = 2,400	Profit and loss account
200 × 6 = 1,200	Rent prepaid

Part (v)

Did happen

Creditors		Purchases Returns	
4,600	6,280		4,600
	1,680		

Net effect

Should have happened

Creditors		Purchases Returns	
6,280			6,280

Correction

Creditors		Purchases Returns		Suspense	
7,960			1,680		6,280

(a) Journal Entries

	Dr €	Cr €
Equipment	3,200	
Purchases	13,200	
Suspense	6,900	
Creditors		23,300
Being correction of incorrect recording of credit purchases		
Drawings	520	
Discount	180	
Debtors		700
Being recording of owner's private debt offset against a business debt for goods sold		
General expenses	70	
Sales returns	970	
Suspense	720	
Sales		790
Debtors		970
Being correction of incorrect figures and incorrect treatment of sales returns		
Rent/Profit and loss	2,400	
Rent/Balance sheet	1,200	
Capital		3,600
Being private funds used to pay 12 months' rent for the current year and 6 months' rent for the following year		
Creditors	7,960	
Purchases returns		1,680
Suspense		6,280
Being recording of a credit note received incorporating a restocking charge		

(b) Statement of Correct Net Profit

		€
Original net profit as per books		34,000
Less Purchases	(i)	(13,200)
Less Discount	(ii)	(180)
Less General expenses	(iii)	(70)
Less Sales returns	(iii)	(970)
Add Sales	(iii)	790
Less Rent	(iv)	(2,400)
Add Purchases returns	(v)	1,680
Correct net profit		19,650

Question 3 (2002, HL, Section 1, Q3)

The trial balance of J. Townsend, a garage owner, failed to agree on 31/12/2001. The difference was entered in a suspense account and the final accounts were prepared, which showed a net profit of €29,000.

On checking the books, the following errors **and omissions** were discovered:

(i) A motor car, purchased on credit from M. Browne, for €12,000, had been entered on the incorrect side of Browne's account and credited as €21,000 in the equipment account.

(ii) Car parts, previously sold on credit for €850, had been returned to Townsend. These **returns** had been incorrectly entered as €50 on the credit of the equipment account and as €580 on the debit of the purchases account.

(iii) A cheque for €3,000, paid by Townsend out of a private bank account for 15 months' rent of a garage up to 31/3/2002, had not been entered in the books.

(iv) Townsend had returned a motor car, previously purchased on credit from a supplier for €10,500, and had entered this transaction in the relevant ledger accounts incorrectly as €15,100. However, a credit note subsequently arrived from the supplier, showing a restocking charge of €400 to cover the cost of the return. The only entry made in respect of this credit note was a credit entry of €10,100 in the creditors' account.

(v) €1,400 received from the sale of an old display cabinet (book value €1,200), which was used by Townsend to store private materials, had not been entered in the books.

You are required to:

(a) Journalise the necessary corrections (40)

(b) Prepare a statement showing the correct net profit (20)

(60 marks)

Solution

(a) Journal Entries	Dr €		Cr €	
(i) Equipment account	21,000	(2)		
Purchases account	12,000	(3)		
M. Browne account			24,000	(3)
Suspense account			9,000	(3)
Being purchase of equipment entered on incorrect side of creditors' account and entered as incorrect amount on incorrect side of equipment account				
(ii) Sales returns account	850	(2)		
Debtors' account			850	(2)
Suspense	530	(2)		
Equipment	50	(2)		
Purchases			580	(2)
Being correction of incorrect figures and incorrect treatment of returns inwards of car parts				
(iii) Rent account	2,400	(2)		
Landlord/debtors for rent account	600	(2)		
Capital account			3,000	(2)
Being private funds used to pay 9 months' rent for the current year and 3 months' rent for the following year				

contd →

(a) Journal Entries (continued)		
(iv) Purchases returns accounts	5,000 (2)	
Creditors' account	5,100 (2)	
Suspense account		10,100 (2)
Being recording in books of credit note and correction of incorrect entry relating to the return of the motor car		
(v) Bank	1,400 (3)	
Furniture		1,200 (2)
Profit and loss account		200 (2)
Being recording of sale of old display cabinet (book value €1,200) for €1,400 and use of proceeds for private expenses		

(b) Statement of Correct Net Profit		(20)
		€
Original new profit		29,000 (3)
Add Purchases		580 (2)
Profit on sale		200 (2)
Less Purchases	(12,000) (2)	
Sales	(850) (2)	
Rent	(2,400) (3)	
Purchases returns	(5,000) (3)	20,250 (3)
Correct net profit		9,530 (3)

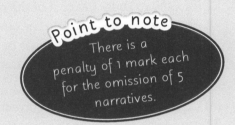

Point to note

There is a penalty of 1 mark each for the omission of 5 narratives.

Question 4 (2006, HL, Section 2, Q7)

The trial balance of M. O'Meara, a garage owner, failed to agree on 31/12/2005. The difference was entered in a suspense account and the following balance sheet was prepared.

Balance Sheet as on 31/12/05			
	€	€	€
Fixed assets			
Premises		700,000	
Equipment		60,000	
Furniture		20,000	780,000
Current assets			
Stock (including suspense)		91,400	
Debtors		35,200	
Cash		500	
		127,100	
Less **Current liabilities**			
Creditors	54,000		
Bank	28,000	82,000	45,100
			825,100
Financed by			
Capital		790,000	
Add Net profit		64,100	
		854,100	
Drawings		29,000	825,100
			825,100

On checking the books, the following errors were discovered:

  (i) A motor car, purchased on credit from D. Foran for €13,000, had been entered on the incorrect side of Foran's account as €1,300 and credited as €3,100 in the equipment account.

 (ii) O'Meara had returned a motor car, previously purchased on credit for €14,600 from a supplier. O'Meara entered this transaction as €16,400 on the correct sides of the correct accounts in the ledger. A credit note subsequently arrived from the supplier, showing a restocking charge of €500 to cover the cost of the return. The only entry made in respect of this credit note was a credit of €14,100 in the creditors' account.

(iii) A debtor who owed O'Meara €1,000 sent a cheque for €800 and €150 in cash in full settlement. This was correctly recorded in the books. However, no entry has been made in the books of the subsequent dishonouring of this cheque or of the writing-off of the remaining debt in full because of bankruptcy.

(iv) A private debt for €770, owed by O'Meara, had been offset in full against a business debt of €820 owed to the firm for car repairs previously carried out. No entry had been made in the books in respect of this offset.

 (v) A cheque for €2,250 paid by O'Meara out of a private bank account for 15 months' hire of diagnostic equipment up to 31/3/2006 had not been entered in the books.

You are required to:

(a) Journalise the necessary corrections   (50)
(b) Show the suspense account   (6)
(c) Prepare a statement showing the correct net profit   (14)
(d) Prepare a corrected balance sheet   (20)
(e) Explain, with examples, the difference between 'error of commission' and 'error of principle'   (10)

     (100 marks)

Solution

(a) Journal Entries		**(50)**
	Dr **€**	**Cr** **€**
(i) Purchases account	13,000 (3)	
Equipment account	3,100 (3)	
Suspense account		1,800 (2)
Creditors' account		14,300 (2)
Being correction of incorrect recording of the purchase of a motor car on credit		
(ii) Purchases returns account	2,300 (3)	
Creditors' account	11,800 (3)	
Suspense account		14,100 (3)
Being recording of return of motor car and credit note incorporating a restocking charge		
(iii) Debtors' account	850 (3)	
Bank account		800 (3)
Discount account		50 (3)

contd →

(a) Journal Entries (continued)

Bad debts account	850 (3)	
Debtors' account		850 (3)
Being recording of a dishonoured cheque and a bad debt		
(iv) Drawings account	770 (3)	
Discount account	50 (3)	
Debtors' account		820 (3)
Being recording of owner's private debt offset against a business debt for repairs owed to firm		
(v) Rent /profit and loss account	1,800 (2)	
Rent /balance sheet	450 (2)	
Capital account		2,250 (3)
Being private funds used to pay 12 months' rent for the current year and 3 months' rent for the following year		

(b) Suspense Account (6)

	€		€
Original difference	15,900	Equipment (i)	1,800 (3)
		Creditors (ii)	14,100 (3)
	15,900		15,900

(c) Statement of Correct Net Profit (14)

		€	€
Original net profit as per books			64,100 (1)
Add Discount allowed disallowed	(iii)	50 (2)	
		64,150	
Less Purchases	(i)	13,000 (2)	
Purchases returns	(ii)	2,300 (2)	
Bad debts	(iii)	850 (1)	
Discount	(iv)	50 (1)	
Rent	(v)	1,800 (2)	(18,000)
Correct net profit			46,150 (3)

(d) Balance Sheet as on 31/12/05 (20)

	€	€	€
Fixed assets			
Premises			700,000 (½)
Equipment (60,000 + 3,100)			63,100 (2)
Furniture			20,000 (½)
			783,100
Current assets			
Stock (91,400 − 15,900)	75,500 (2)		
Debtors (35,200 + 850 − 850 − 820)	34,380 (4)		
Cash	500 (½)		
Rent prepaid	450 (½)	110,830	
Less **Creditors: amounts falling due within 1 year**			
Creditors (54,000 + 14,300 − 11,800)	56,500 (3)		
Bank (28,000 + 800)	28,800 (2)	(85,300)	25,530
			808,630
Financed by			
Capital (790,000 + 2,250)		792,250 (2)	
Add Net profit		46,150	
		838,400	
Less Drawings (29,000 + 770)		(29,770) (2)	808,630
			808,630 (1)

(e) (10)

An **error of commission** occurs when the correct amount is posted to the correct side of the incorrect account, e.g. goods sold on credit to Pat O'Brien debited in error to John O'Brien's account.

An **error of principle** arises when an item is posted to the incorrect class of account, e.g. an electrical shop owner purchased a vehicle and entered it in the purchases account instead of the vehicles account.

9 Interpretation of Accounts (Ratio Analysis)

Learning objectives

In this chapter you will learn about:

1. The list of frequently used ratios
2. Comments for shareholders
3. Comments for debenture holders
4. The causes of fall in gross profit percentage
5. Action to take for company with poor liquidity/falling profitability
6. The limitations of ratios

Ratios are used to help make sense of the information provided in the final accounts of a business. You must be able to:

1. Calculate the ratios
2. Understand what each ratio is telling you
3. Assess what it means for any of the following interested parties:

   - Current shareholders
   - Someone interested in purchasing shares
   - Current debenture holders
   - A bank manager deciding whether or not to grant a loan

Top Tip!

Learn the ratios.

Calculating Ratios

The first part of the question deals with calculating ratios.

Profitability

Return on capital employed (ROCE)	$\dfrac{\text{Net profit before interest and tax}}{\text{Capital employed}} \times \dfrac{100}{1}$
Return on shareholders' funds (ROSF)	$\dfrac{\text{Net profit} - \text{Preference dividend}}{\text{Ordinary share capital} + \text{P+L balance}} \times \dfrac{100}{1}$
Percentage mark-up on cost	$\dfrac{\text{Gross profit}}{\text{Cost of sales}} \times \dfrac{100}{1}$
Gross profit margin (%)	$\dfrac{\text{Gross profit}}{\text{Sales}} \times \dfrac{100}{1}$
Net profit margin (%)	$\dfrac{\text{Net profit}}{\text{Sales}} \times \dfrac{100}{1}$

A fall/deterioration in profitability is not good for any company.

Top Tips!

- The **ROCE** and the **ROSF** should always be **higher than the return to be gained from risk-free investment** because there is **a risk involved** in investing in a business; investors could potentially lose their money if the business were to fail. The **return from risk-free investment is around 2–4%**.
- The ROCE must be compared to the **interest rate being charged on any existing or proposed loans**. It is **essential** that the firm is able to generate a higher return than the rate which they are paying on borrowings. A ROCE greater than the loan rate shows **efficient use of funds by management**.

Causes of falls in gross profit and net profit percentage should be known, as well as the appropriate action to take to improve them (see Question 1).

Liquidity

Current (working capital) ratio Recommended 1.5 to 2 : 1	Current assets : Current liabilities
Acid test ratio (quick ratio) Recommended 1 : 1	Current assets – Closing stock : Current liabilities

Liquidity is the ability of the firm to **pay short-term debts as they fall due**. Poor liquidity (overtrading) means that the business does not have enough cash to carry out its day-to-day activities. This is a serious problem that can lead to bankruptcy. If it is identified and action is taken, this can be avoided (see Question 2).

Gearing

Fixed-interest capital to Total capital Over 50% = highly geared Below 50% = lowly geared	$\dfrac{\text{Debentures} + \text{Preference shares}}{\text{Capital employed}} \times \dfrac{100}{1}$
Interest cover	$\dfrac{\text{Profit before interest and tax}}{\text{Interest}}$

Gearing analyses how the company is financed. Finance can come either from **fixed-interest sources (debentures, preference shares)** or from **equity/shareholders' capital (issued ordinary shares, retained profits/reserves)**.

High gearing means that more finance comes from fixed-interest capital; interest **has to be paid** regardless of profits. Inability to pay interest puts the company at risk, and there is less money available to pay dividends. Highly geared firms may find it difficult to raise future finance.

Low gearing means that more finance comes from equity capital sources; the firm will have more profits available to pay dividends and to retain in reserves. There will be little threat to the firm from outside investors and it may be easier to raise future finance.

The **interest cover** measures the firm's ability to meet interest payments from the profits generated; firms that have high interest cover are seen as low risk, as profits are able to cover interest adequately.

Investment

Top Tip!

When considering the following ratios, remember shareholders like **good dividends** to be paid. However, they also know that **retaining profits** will help the firm grow, which can lead to even larger profits in the future; there should always be a balance.

Earnings per share (EPS) (answer in cent)	$\dfrac{\text{Net profit} - \text{Preference dividend}}{\text{No. of ordinary shares issued}}$
Divide the profit available to shareholders by the number of ordinary shares issued to find out how much **each** share has earned.	
Dividend per share (DPS) (answer in cent)	$\dfrac{\text{Total ordinary dividend}}{\text{No. of ordinary shares issued}}$
Divide the ordinary dividend by the number of ordinary shares issued to find out how much dividend **each** share has received.	
Dividend yield	$\dfrac{\text{Dividend per share}}{\text{Market price per share}} \times \dfrac{100}{1}$
Dividend yield shows the return received by shareholders (DPS) as a percentage of their investment (the share price). **It is compared to the return from risk-free investment.** Note that the **DPS** is the **amount paid out** to shareholders rather than the **amount earned** by the shares.	
Dividend cover	$\dfrac{\text{Net profit} - \text{Preference dividend}}{\text{Total ordinary dividend}}$
Dividend cover shows how much profit is being retained by the firm.	
Price earnings ratio (P/E ratio) This is the number of years it would take a share to recoup its share price at the current rate of earnings.	$\dfrac{\text{Market price per share}}{\text{EPS}}$
Price earnings ratio shows how long in years it will take a share to recover its present value at the current rate of earnings. A low P/E ratio will mean that the shareholder will be able to recoup their investment relatively quickly. A high P/E will result from a high share price; this shows confidence in the future of the firm and it is likely that EPS will in fact increase.	
Price dividend ratio This is the number of years it would take a share to recoup its share price at the present payout rate.	$\dfrac{\text{Market price per share}}{\text{DPS}}$

Activity

Debtors' average period of credit	$\dfrac{\text{Total debtors}}{\text{Credit sales}} \times \dfrac{12}{1}$
Creditors' average period of credit	$\dfrac{\text{Total creditors}}{\text{Credit purchases}} \times \dfrac{12}{1}$
Stock turnover	$\dfrac{\text{Cost of sales}}{\text{Average stock}}$
Average stock	$\dfrac{\text{Opening stock} + \text{Closing stock}}{2}$

Analysing Ratios

The second part of the question deals with assessing how the business is doing from a particular point of view. The shareholders and debenture holders have different priorities and these need to be taken into account when making comments.

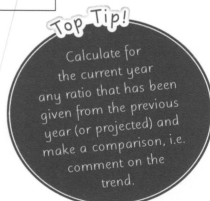

Top Tip!

Calculate for the current year any ratio that has been given from the previous year (or projected) and make a comparison, i.e. comment on the trend.

(ii) Return on capital employed in 2009

$$\frac{\text{Net profit before interest and tax}}{\text{Capital employed}} \times \frac{100}{1}$$

$$\frac{80{,}000}{675{,}000} \times \frac{100}{1} = 11.85\%$$

(iii) The earnings per ordinary share in 2009
(the answer will always be in cent)

$$\frac{\text{Net profit} - \text{Preference dividend}}{\text{No. of ordinary shares issued}}$$

$$\frac{55{,}000}{300{,}000} = 18.33 \text{ cent}$$

(iv) How long would it take 1 ordinary share to recover its 2009 market price (assume current performance is maintained)?

Price earnings ratio

$$\frac{\text{Market price per share}}{\text{EPS}}$$

$$\frac{190}{18.33} = 10.37 \text{ years}$$

(v) The ordinary dividend cover in 2009

$$\frac{\text{Net profit} - \text{Preference dividend}}{\text{Total ordinary dividend}}$$

$$\frac{55{,}000}{24{,}000} = 02.29 \text{ times}$$

Part (b)

> **Top Tip!**
>
> The question will include ratios from **either** the **previous year's accounts** or **projected figures for next year**. These are two different types of information and this will need to be taken into consideration when writing comments.

Additional ratios required

Return on shareholders' funds

$$\frac{\text{Net profit} - \text{Preference dividend}}{\text{Ordinary share capital} + \text{P+L balance}} \times \frac{100}{1}$$

$$\frac{55{,}000}{365{,}000} \times \frac{100}{1} = 15.07\%$$

Dividend per share (DPS)

$$\frac{\text{Total ordinary dividend}}{\text{No. of ordinary shares issued}}$$

$$\frac{24{,}000}{300{,}000} = 8 \text{ cent}$$

Dividend yield

$$\frac{\text{Dividend per share}}{\text{Market price per share}} \times \frac{100}{1}$$

$$\frac{8}{190} \times \frac{100}{1} = 4.21\%$$

Quick ratio

Current assets − Closing stock : Current liabilities

223,000 − 65,000 : 128,000

158,000 : 128,000

1.23 : 1

Current ratio	Current assets : Current liabilities
	223,000 : 128,000
	1.74 : 1

Gearing (Fixed-interest capital/total capital)	$\dfrac{\text{Debentures} + \text{Preference shares}}{\text{Capital employed}} \times \dfrac{100}{1}$
	$\dfrac{160,000 + 150,000}{675,000} \times \dfrac{100}{1} = 45.93\%$

Interest cover	$\dfrac{\text{Profit before interest and tax}}{\text{Interest}}$
	$\dfrac{80,000}{16,000} = 5 \text{ times}$

Gross profit %	$\dfrac{\text{Gross profit}}{\text{Sales}} \times \dfrac{100}{1}$
	Sales − Cost of sales = Gross profit
	820,000 − 650,000 = 170,000
	$\dfrac{170,000}{820,000} \times \dfrac{100}{1} = 20.73\%$

Top Tip!

This question asks for the opinion of shareholders under the headings of performance, state of affairs and prospects. As these headings are given in the question, they should be used in the answer. A suggested layout is as follows:

Performance: Profitability, dividend policy

State of affairs: Liquidity, gearing, investment policy

Prospects: Market value of shares, sector, profitability, liquidity, gearing (in terms of the future)

Performance

Profitability

Lifeline Ltd is a **profitable business**. The **ROCE** is 11.85% in 2009; this is an **improvement** on the 2008 figure of 10%. The **return on equity funds** has also **improved** from 9.5% in 2008 to 15.07% in 2009.

Both these returns are **well above the return to be gained from risk-free investment** of around **4% and above the rate of interest paid on the loan of 10%**. This shows **efficient use of funds available by management** and the **shareholders would be pleased**.

Dividend policy

The **DPS** has **improved** from 6 cent in 2008 to 8 cent in 2009.

The company's **dividend cover** is 2.29 times. The dividend policy shows that the shareholders can expect a decent amount of profit to be paid out each year. Money is also being retained by the firm for further growth, so the long-term prospects are good.

The **dividend yield** is 4.21%; the figure is near **to the return from risk-free investment** and should continue to increase if current trends are maintained, which would please shareholders. The real return to shareholders, based on available profits, would be 9.64% (4.21% × 2.29); this figure is above the return to be gained from risk-free investment of around 5%.

State of affairs

Liquidity

The company **does not have a liquidity problem**; it is **well able to pay short-term debts as they fall due**. The quick ratio shows that the company has €1.23 liquid assets to pay each €1 of short-term debt (this is above the recommended ratio of 1 : 1). This is an **improvement** from 2008 when there was €1 available for each €1 owed. Shareholders would be pleased. The company will be able to pay dividends.

The current ratio also shows an **improvement**. There is now €1.74 in assets available to pay each €1 owed in the short-term; there was only €1.50 available in 2008.

Gearing

The company is **lowly geared at 45.93%**; the shareholders would be pleased. The company is **not dependent on outside borrowings** and is therefore **not at risk from outside investors**. This also means that interest payments are manageable, leaving more profits available for paying dividends. The **interest cover** is 5 times; the company **can pay its interest**.

Investment policy

The investments made by the company cost €110,000. The **market value of investments has improved** by rising to €125,000, which shows **good management of resources**; shareholders would be pleased.

Prospects

Market value

The **share price has improved** from €1.80 last year to €1.90 in 2009, an increase of 5%. This would please shareholders as it indicates **confidence in the company** by the market.

Sector

Lifeline Ltd manufactures health foods at present; this is a **good sector** to be in as people are becoming more **health conscious**. In the future, more money will continue to be spent on these types of products and new products will be developed. This is a growing sector with good prospects.

Profitability/ROCE

The ROCE has improved from 10% to 11.85%; this is a positive trend and bodes well for the future.

Gearing

The company is lowly geared at 45.93%; there is little risk from outside investors, which is a positive sign for the future.

Liquidity

The company does not have a liquidity problem; it has €1.23 in liquid assets to pay each €1 of short-term debt. This is a positive sign for the future.

Overall, the shareholders would be pleased with the performance, state of affairs and prospects of this firm.

Part (c)

The gross profit percentage has fallen in 2009 to 20.73% from 23% in 2008. This decrease could have occurred for the following reasons:

- A decrease in the selling price without a corresponding drop in cost of sales
- An increase in the cost of purchases not passed on to customers: the cost of purchases increases but the selling price remains the same
- Stock losses: theft of stock or purchase of stock that cannot be sold at a profit or stock obsolescence
- A change in the sales mix: customers buying goods with a lower mark-up
- Incorrect stock valuation: an undervaluation of closing stock or overvaluation of opening stock, causing higher cost of goods and thus smaller gross profit
- Mark-downs during sales to get rid of slow-moving stock
- Cash losses that occur when cash sales are not recorded in the books

Question 2

The following figures have been extracted from the final accounts of Flynn Ltd, a building contractor in the construction industry, for the year ended 31/12/2010.

Ratios and information for year ended 31/12/2009	
Earnings per ordinary share	16c
Interest cover	7 times
Gearing	40%
Quick ratio	1.2 : 1
Return on capital employed	14%
Dividend per ordinary share	11c
Market value of 1 ordinary share	€3.10

Trading, Profit and Loss Account for Year Ended 31/12/10

	€	€
Sales		1,150,000
Costs of goods sold		
Stock 1/1/2010	54,000	
Purchases	(980,000)	
Stock 31/12/2010	(64,000)	(970,000)
Operating expenses for year		(130,000)
Interest for year		(18,000)
Net profit for year		32,000
Proposed dividends		(30,000)
Retained profit for year		2,000
Profit and loss balance 1/1/2010		28,000 Cr
Profit and loss balance 31/12/2010		30,000

Balance Sheet as on 31/12/10

	€	€
Intangible assets		143,000
Tangible assets		300,000
Investments (market value €80,000)		95,000
		538,000
Current assets (incl. debtors €35,000)	104,000	
Trade creditors	(52,000)	
Proposed dividends	(30,000)	22,000
		560,000
10% debentures (2016/2017)		180,000
Issued capital		
Ordinary shares @ €1 each	200,000	
8% preference shares @ €1 each	150,000	
Profit and loss balance	30,000	380,000
		560,000

Market value of 1 ordinary share: €2.80

You are required to answer the following:
(a) (i) What are the cash sales if the average period of credit given to debtors is 2 months?
   (ii) What is the dividend yield on ordinary shares for **2009**?
   (iii) How long would it take 1 ordinary share to recoup (recover) its 2010 market price based on the present dividend pay-out rate?
   (iv) What is the interest cover?
   (v) What are the earnings per share? (45)

(b) Would the debenture holders be satisfied with the policies and state of affairs of the company? Use available relevant information to support your answer. (40)

(c) What actions would you advise the company to take? (15)

(100 marks)

Solution

To begin:

Preference dividend	8% of 150,000 = 12,000
Ordinary dividend	30,000 − 12,000 = 18,000
Profit before interest	32,000 + 18,000 = 50,000
Profit after preference dividend	32,000 − 12,000 = 20,000

Part (a)

(i) Find cash sales given the period of credit given to debtors figure.

$$\text{Period of credit given to debtors} \quad \frac{\text{Trade debtors}}{\text{Credit sales}} \times \frac{12}{1} = 2 \text{ months}$$

$\dfrac{35,000}{x} \times \dfrac{12}{1} =$	2
$\dfrac{420,000}{x} =$	2
2x =	420,000
x (credit sales) =	210,000
Cash sales = 1,150,000 − 210,000 =	940,000

(ii) Dividend yield for 2009

$$\frac{\text{DPS}}{\text{Market price}} \times \frac{100}{1}$$

$$\frac{11}{310} \times \frac{100}{1} = 3.55\%$$

Top Tip!
Use previous year's figures in this ratio.

(iii) How long would it take 1 ordinary share to recover its 2010 market price based on the present dividend pay-out rate?

Dividend per share (DPS)

$$\frac{\text{Ordinary dividend}}{\text{Issued ordinary shares}}$$

$$\frac{18,000}{200,000} = 9 \text{ cent}$$

Price dividend ratio

$$\frac{\text{Market price per share}}{\text{DPS}}$$

$$\frac{280}{9} = 31.11 \text{ years}$$

(iv)	Interest cover	$\dfrac{\text{Profit before interest and tax}}{\text{Interest}}$
		$\dfrac{50{,}000}{18{,}000} = 2.78$ times

(v)	Earnings per ordinary share	$\dfrac{\text{Net profit – Preference dividend}}{\text{No. of ordinary shares issued}}$
		$\dfrac{20{,}000}{200{,}000} = 10$ cent

Additional ratios required

Return on capital employed	$\dfrac{\text{Net profit before interest and tax}}{\text{Capital employed}} \times \dfrac{100}{1}$
	$\dfrac{50{,}000}{560{,}000} \times \dfrac{100}{1} = 8.93\%$

Gearing (Fixed-interest capital/total capital)	$\dfrac{\text{Debentures + Preference shares}}{\text{Capital employed}} \times \dfrac{x}{1} = x$
	$\dfrac{180{,}000 + 150{,}000}{560{,}000} \times \dfrac{100}{1} = 58.92\%$

Quick ratio	Current assets – Closing stock : Current liabilities
	104,000 – 64,000 : 82,000
	40,000 : 82,000

Current ratio	Current assets : Current liabilities
	104,000 : 82,000
	1.27 : 1

Dividend cover	$\dfrac{\text{Net profit – Preference dividend}}{\text{Total ordinary dividend}}$
	$\dfrac{20{,}000}{18{,}000} = 1.11$ times

Part (b)

Profitability

The ROCE is 8.93%, which shows a **deterioration** from the previous year of 14% – a fall of over 5%. The return is **higher than what can be gained from risk-free investment of around 4%**. Debenture holders would be concerned by the downward trend and that **the return is lower than the rate being paid on the loan of 10%**. This shows inefficient use of funds by management. The firm is profitable but not as profitable as last year.

Liquidity

The company **has a liquidity problem** and it **may have difficulty paying short-term debts as they fall due**. The acid test ratio shows that the company has €0.49 in liquid assets available to pay each €1 of short-term debt (this is below the recommended ratio of 1 : 1). There has been deterioration from last year when there was €1.20 in liquid assets available for each €1 owed in the short term. **Debenture holders would be concerned** about **the ability to pay interest on the loan**. The current ratio is 1.27 : 1, which is also below the recommended ratio of 2 : 1.

Gearing

The company is **highly geared at 58.93%**, which would concern debenture holders. High gearing means that more finance comes from fixed-interest debt than from equity debt; the **higher the gearing, the more pressure will be on the company to pay interest**. The gearing has **declined from a position of 40%** last year to the new figure of 58.93%. The **interest cover** has also declined from 7 times last year to only 2.79 times for the current year; this is **poor cover** and the debenture holders would be **concerned about the future ability of the company to pay interest**.

Security

The fixed assets provide security for the loan. The fixed assets are valued at €443,000; of this €143,000 are intangible assets, leaving €300,000 of tangible assets. The debenture holders would be satisfied that this is **adequate security for the loan of €180,000**. It would, however, be advisable to ascertain the real value of fixed assets, as no write-offs (depreciation) have been given. There are also investments with a market value of €80,000; the value has fallen so it would be prudent to monitor the situation.

Dividend policy

The **DPS** is 9 cent, while the **EPS** is 10 cent.

The company's **dividend cover** is 1.11 times – this is **very low cover**, suggesting that **too much of the profits are being paid to the shareholders**. Dividends are excessive; only €2,000 was retained by the company in 2010. The debenture holders would not be happy; they would like to see more profits being retained by the company and the creation of a debenture redemption reserve for the future repayment of the loan.

Sector

The **downturn in the construction sector** would affect this company; as demand decreases, so will sales. Currently, it is still difficult for consumers to secure finance from lending institutions. There is also increasing competition in the market from foreign contractors. The prospects for this sector are not good.

Market value

There has been a **fall in the share price** from €3.10 to €2.80. This would indicate a **lack of market confidence** in the company and may discourage investment.

Overall the debenture holders would not be satisfied with the performance, state of affairs and prospects of this firm.

Part (c)

This company needs to raise cash, improve liquidity and increase profitability. The action recommended is:

- Pay out lower dividends; retain more profits in the business to finance future expansion/repay the loan
- Sell investments to raise cash
- Issue any remaining shares to raise cash
- Collect debts from debtors more quickly
- Improve the stock control system and introduce minimum levels to avoid cash being tied up
- Improve the profitability of the company
- Diversify into other areas
- Consider the sale and leaseback of assets

Point to note

To improve profitability:

- Increase the volume of sales (this may require the firm to diversify into other areas)
- Increase the selling price to take into account any increase in the cost of sales
- Have strict security to prevent theft
- Tighten controls on expenses to eliminate unnecessary costs

NOTE: If gross profit percentage was to remain constant/increase and net profit percentage decreased, then expenses would need tighter control; it is the job of management to control expenses.

The following are the actual figures for the year ended 31/12/2006 and the projected figures for the year ended 31/12/2007 of Mila PLC, a manufacturer in the pharmaceutical industry. Mila PLC has an authorised capital of €900,000 made up of 650,000 ordinary shares at €1 each and 250,000 6% preference shares at €1 each. The firm has already issued 325,000 ordinary shares and all the preference shares.

Projected ratios and figures for year ended 31/12/2007	
Earnings per ordinary share	8c
Dividend per ordinary share	6.1c
Interest cover	4 times
Quick ratio	1.1 : 1
Price earnings ratio	14 : 1
Return on capital employed	8.5%
Gearing	58%

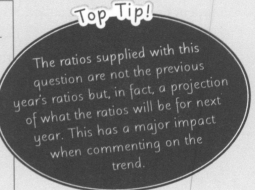

Top Tip!

The ratios supplied with this question are not the previous year's ratios but, in fact, a projection of what the ratios will be for next year. This has a major impact when commenting on the trend.

Trading, Profit and Loss Account for Year Ended 31/12/06	€	€
Sales		820,000
Opening stock	50,000	
Closing stock	55,000	
Costs of goods sold		615,000
Gross profit		205,000
Operating expenses for year		145,000
		60,000
Interest		27,000
Dividends		31,000
Retained profit		2,000
Profit and loss balance 1/1/2006		45,000
Profit and loss balance 31/12/2006		47,000

Balance Sheet as on 31/12/06	€	€
Fixed assets		680,000
Investments (market value 31/12/2006 €210,000)		188,000
		868,000
Current assets	187,000	
Current liabilities		
Trade creditors	(102,000)	
Proposed dividends	(31,000)	54,000
		922,000
Financed by		
9% debentures (2014 secured)		300,000
Capital and reserves		
Ordinary shares @ €1 each	325,000	
6% preference shares @ €1 each	250,000	
Profit and loss balance	47,000	622,000
		922,000

Market value of 1 ordinary share: €1.20

You are required to:

  (a) Calculate the following for 2006:
-     (i) The cash purchases if the period of credit received from trade creditors is 2.4 months
-     (ii) The interest cover
-     (iii) The dividend yield
-     (iv) How long it would take 1 ordinary share to recover its value at the present pay-out rate
-     (v) The projected market value of 1 ordinary share in 2007   (45)

  (b) Indicate if the ordinary shareholders would be satisfied with the performance, state of affairs and prospects of the company. Use relevant ratios and other information to support your answer.   (35)

  (c) Advise the bank manager as to whether a loan of €150,000, on which an interest rate of 10% would be charged, should be granted to Mila PLC for future expansion. Use relevant ratios and other information to support your answer.   (20)

        (100 marks)

Solution

Part (a)   (45)

(i) Cash purchases

Credit purchases $= \dfrac{102,000 \times 12}{2.4}$ $= €510,000$

Cash purchases $= 620,000 - 510,000$ $= €110,000$ (9)

(ii) Interest cover

$\dfrac{\text{Net profit before interest}}{\text{Interest}} \times \dfrac{60,000}{27,000}$ $= 2.22$ times (8)

(iii) Dividend yield

$\dfrac{\text{DPS} \times 100}{\text{Market price}} = \dfrac{4.92\text{c} \times 100}{120\text{c}}$ $= 4.1\%$ (12)

(iv) Period to recoup price

$\dfrac{\text{Market price}}{\text{Dividend per share}} = \dfrac{120}{4.92}$ $= 24.39$ years (8)

(v) Projected market value of ordinary share

Price earnings ratio $\times$ earnings per share $= 14 \times 8\text{c}$ $= €1.12$ (8)

Part (b)   (35)

Performance   (15)

The ROCE and ROSF of 6.5% and 4.8% respectively are both disappointing.   (8)

The ROCE of 6.5% is only marginally better than the return from risk-free investments of around 5%. This indicates an inefficient use of funds and shareholders would be unhappy.

The return on equity funds of 4.8% is less than the return from risk-free investments.

The dividend per share is 4.92c and the dividend yield is 4.1%. This yield is less than the return   (7) from risk-free investments of about 5%.

Dividend cover is 1.125 times, indicating that a very small percentage of the profits is being retained. The dividend cover is low to maintain the yield at 4.1%.

State of affairs (10)

Liquidity The acid test ratio of 0.99 to 1 shows that the company is liquid. (5)
For every €1 of short-term debt, the company has 99c available in liquid assets.

Gearing: The company is highly geared at 59.6%. This indicates that the company is (5)
dependent on outside borrowings and therefore at risk from outside
investors. The interest cover is 2.2 times.

Prospects (10)

Market value (4)

The market value of ordinary shares was €1.20 and is projected to fall to
€1.12 – a **fall** of 6.6% in value. The shareholders would be unhappy with
this as it indicates a lack of market confidence in the company.

ROCE (2)

The ROCE of 6.5% is expected to rise to 8.5%. This represents an improving
prospect.

Liquidity (2)

The acid test figure of 0.99 : 1 is expected to rise to 1.1 : 1, a slight improvement.

Gearing (2)

The company is highly geared at 59.6%, indicating that it is dependent on outside borrowing
and therefore at risk. The gearing will improve in 2007 the projected figure being 58%. This is
still high but the trend is good.

Sector (2)

The company is in the pharmaceutical sector. With an ageing and increasingly health-conscious
population, prospects are good.

Part (c) (20)
Bank loan application – yes/no (2)

Gearing (5)

The company is highly geared.
The gearing will get worse with a further loan of €150,000.
The gearing with the loan will be 65%.
The interest cover will get worse.

Return on capital employed (5)

The ROCE will be 8.5% next year, which is less than the 10% interest to be charged on the loan.

Dividend cover/policy (4)

The dividend cover is 1.1 times and is projected to increase to 1.31 times.
The dividend cover is low.
Not enough of earnings are retained for repayment of the loan.

Purpose for which loan is required (4)

The loan is required for future expansion and should generate extra income to service the loan.

Security (4)

The fixed assets are valued at €680,000, but one should question depreciation policy to ascertain
the real value of the assets.
The investments alone have a market value of €210,000, which would provide security for the loan
of €150,000.
The security is adequate.

Liquidity (4)

The liquidity ratio of 0.99 : 1 is expected to improve to 1.1 : 1 in 2007. However, the extra interest
payment will cause this to be less favourable.

Top Tip!
In this
part of the
question, the first
point is required and
worth 4 marks. Three of
the others are required.
They are worth 2
marks each.

Published Accounts and Regulatory Framework of Accounting 10

Learning objectives

In this chapter you will learn about:

1 The preparation of a published profit and loss account, a published balance sheet and the required explanatory notes
2 The theory required for the Regulatory Framework of Accounting

All limited companies must prepare the following documents to present to their shareholders at the AGM:

- **Published** profit and loss account and balance sheet
- Directors' report
- Auditors' report

The published layout for the profit and loss account and balance sheet must be used when the accounts are being presented to the shareholders **or** to the registrar of companies. As with the cash-flow forecast, the **layout must be followed exactly**; the **order and wording** of entries must be correct.

Layout for a Published Profit and Loss Account

Profit and Loss Account of Brown PLC for Year Ended 31/12/-8		
Turnover		X
Cost of sales		(X)
Gross profit		X
Distribution costs		(X)
Administrative expenses		(X)
		X
Other operating income		X
Operating profit		X
Investment income		X
Profit on sale of fixed assets		X
		X
Interest payable		(X)
Profit on ordinary activities before tax		X
Taxation		(X)
Profit on ordinary activities after tax		X
Dividends paid	X	
Dividends proposed	X	(X)
Profit retained for the year		X
Profit brought forward at 1/1/-8		X
Profit carried forward at 31/12/-8		X

Examples of items to be included under the given headings:

Cost of Sales	Distribution Costs	Administrative	Other Operating Income
Opening stock	Advertising	Directors' fees	Rent receivable
Purchases	Carriage out	Auditors' fees	Discount received
Closing stock	Depr. of motor vehicles	Depr. of buildings	
Carriage in	Selling expenses	General expenses	
Import duty	Commission	Rent and rates	
Manufacturing wages		Bad debts	
		Discount allowed	

Points to note

- **Profit/loss on sale of fixed assets** is referred to as an **exceptional item** and is shown separately in the profit and loss account.
- Unusually **large bad debts** are also referred to as exceptional items and are treated the same way.

Top Tip!

Be sure to show the investment income and interest payable separately.

Layout of a Published Balance Sheet

Balance Sheet of Brown PLC as on 31/12/-8			
Fixed assets			
Intangible assets			X
Tangible assets			X
Financial assets			X
			X
Current assets			
Stock	X		
Debtors	X		
Bank	X	X	
Creditors: amounts falling due within 1 year			
Trade creditors	X		
Dividends due	X		
Taxation due	X		
Other creditors	X	(X)	
Net current assets			X
Total assets *less* Current liabilities			X
Creditors: amounts falling due after more than 1 year			
Debentures			X
Provisions for liabilities and charges			
Liability certain to be incurred			X
Capital and reserves			
Issued shares		X	
Revaluation reserve		X	
Profit carried forward		X	
			X
			X

Note the variations from the layout of the internal accounts.

Profit and loss account

- Sales = turnover
- Cost of sales, distribution cost, administrative expenses = one figure for each
- Taxation = corporation tax only in the profit and loss account
- Profit on sale of fixed asset/unusually large bad debt = exceptional item; show separately
- Dividends = total paid and total due not split into ordinary and preference

Balance sheet

- Intangible, tangible and financial assets = one figure for each
- Debtors = include not only trade debtors but other amounts owed to the business, such as investment interest due
- Creditors = trade creditors
- Other creditors = all other amounts due, such as auditors' fees, debenture interest due
- Tax due = corporation tax due + VAT due
- New heading of provisions for liabilities and charges for a contingent liability that the company strongly believes it will be liable for

A number of explanatory notes are also required to accompany the published profit and loss account and balance sheet. **The exact wording of these notes must be memorised and used.**

1 Accounting policy – fixed assets and stock note
2 Operating profit
3 Interest payable
4 Dividends
5 Tangible fixed assets
6 Exceptional items, e.g. profit on sale of fixed asset
7 Financial assets
8 Debentures
9 Capital expenditure commitments
10 Called-up share capital
11 Contingent liability/gain

Examples of the **most common** notes can be found in the questions in this chapter.

Exceptional item

This is a material item of significant size. It must be shown separately in the profit and loss account because of its size. Examples include: profit or loss on the sale of a fixed asset; a large bad debt.

Contingent liability or gain

This is a liability or gain that the company could possibly or probably be liable to pay. Treatment of contingent liabilities or gains in the accounts depends on whether the company is:

Likely to be liable (include in accounts and notes)
- Include the estimate amount in the profit and loss account under administrative expenses
- Include the estimate amount in the balance sheet under the heading 'Provisions for liabilities and charges'
- Include a note showing the nature of the liability, the expected outcome and the estimate of the amount

Not likely to be liable (include in notes only)
- Include in the notes to the accounts, giving **only** the same information as stated above
(Question 1 provides an example.)

Study Tips

- Published accounts appear as a frequently asked question and can arise in **Section 2** for **100 marks** or **Section 1** for **60 marks**. In previous exam questions there has been no balance sheet to prepare with a 60-mark question.
- **The theory section has been assigned a significant proportion of the marks.** The theory is part of the course and it is possible that it could arise in other sections.
- Be very familiar with the commonly asked notes: accounting policy for fixed assets and stock, operating profit, interest payable, dividends, tangible fixed assets, profit on sales of fixed assets (exceptional item) and contingent liability.

Sample questions and solutions

Question 1

Kilcoyne Ltd has an authorised capital of €600,000 divided into 400,000 ordinary shares at €1 each and 200,000 6% preference shares at €1 each. The following trial balance was extracted from its books at 31/12/2008.

	€	€
Vehicles at cost	240,000	
Vehicles – accumulated depr. on 1/1/2008		42,000
Investment income		8,000
Buildings at cost	650,000	
Buildings – accumulated depr. on 1/1/2008		55,000
Debtors and creditors	288,000	162,000
12% investments	180,000	
Stock at 1/1/2008	68,000	
Goodwill at 1/1/2008	40,000	
Administration expenses	202,000	
Purchases and sales	1,150,000	1,950,000
Rental income		50,000
8% debentures 2014/2015		250,000
Distribution costs	238,000	
Profit on sale of land		70,000
Bank	61,000	
VAT		40,000
Interim dividends	24,000	
Profit and loss at 1/1/2008		51,000
Issued capital		
Ordinary shares		350,000
Preference shares		100,000
Provision for bad debts		23,000
Debenture interest paid	10,000	
Discount		
	3,151,000	3,151,000

The following information is relevant:

(i) Stock on 31/12/2008 is €77,000.

(ii) The goodwill is being written off over 4 years. This writing-off commenced in 2006 and should be included in cost of sales.

(iii) On 1/7/2008, the ordinary shareholders received an interim dividend of €21,000 and the preference shareholders received €3,000. The directors propose the payment of the preference dividend due and a final dividend on ordinary shares to bring that total dividend up to 8c per share.

(iv) During the year, land adjacent to the company's premises that had cost €50,000 was sold for €120,000. At the end of the year the company revalued its buildings at €800,000. The company wishes to incorporate this value in this year's accounts.

(v) Depreciation is to be provided for on buildings at a rate of 2% using the straight line method. There was no purchase or sale of buildings during the year. Vehicles are to be depreciated at the rate of 20% of cost.

(vi) Provide for debenture interest due, investment interest due, auditors' fees €11,500, directors' fees €60,000 and corporation tax €56,000.

(vii) On 1/12/2008 the company received a letter from a former employee who was dismissed on 1/11/2008. The employee is claiming compensation for unfair dismissal. The company's legal advisers believe that the company is likely to be liable under the terms of the employment contract and they estimate the maximum amount of the liability at €25,000.

You are required to:

(a) Prepare the published profit and loss account for the year ended 31/12/2008 and a balance sheet as at that date, in accordance with the Companies Acts and appropriate accounting standards, showing the following notes:

    1 Accounting policy note for tangible fixed assets and stock
    2 Operating profit
    3 Interest payable
    4 Dividends
    5 Tangible fixed assets
    6 Contingent liabilities (85)

(b) Explain the role of the auditor. What conditions are necessary for the auditor to believe that the accounts give a true and fair view? (15)

(100 marks)

Solution

(a)

Workings

1 Cost of Sales	€
Opening stock	68,000
Purchases	1,150,000
Goodwill w/o	10,000
Closing stock	(77,000)
	1,151,000

2 Distribution Costs	€
Distribution costs	238,000
Depr. of vehicles	48,000
	286,000

3 Administrative Expenses	€
Administrative expenses	202,000
Auditors' fees	11,500
Directors' fees	60,000
Depr. of buildings	13,000
Compensation	25,000
	311,500

4 Other Operating Income	€
Rent	50,000

5 Debtors	€
Debtors	288,000
Less BDP	(23,000)
Invest. income due	13,600
	278,600

6 Other Creditors	€
Debenture interest due	10,000
Auditors' fees	11,500
Directors' fees	60,000
	81,500

7 Taxation Due	€
Corporation tax	56,000
VAT	40,000
	96,000

Profit and Loss Account of Kilcoyne PLC for Year Ended 31/12/08

	€	€
Turnover		1,950,000
Cost of sales		(1,151,000)
Gross profit		799,000
Distribution costs		(286,000)
Administrative expenses		(311,500)
		201,500
Other operating income		50,000
Operating profit		251,500
Investment income		21,600
Profit on sale of land		70,000
		343,100
Interest payable		(20,000)
Profit on ordinary activities before tax		323,100
Taxation		(56,000)
Profit on ordinary activities after tax		267,100
Dividends paid	24,000	
Dividends proposed	10,000	(34,000)
Profit retained for the year		233,100
Profit brought forward at 1/1/08		51,000
Profit carried forward at 31/12/08		284,100

Top Tip!

The word **turnover** must be used. Show **one figure only** for:

- Cost of sales
- Distribution costs
- Administrative expenses
- Other operating income

No workings of any kind should be shown on the face of the profit and loss account.

Top Tips!

- Investment income is shown **separately** and **must be after operating profit**.
- Interest payable is shown **separately** and **must be the last item before taxation**.

Balance Sheet of Kilcoyne PLC as on 31/12/08

	€	€	€
Fixed assets			
Intangible assets			30,000
Tangible assets			950,000
Financial assets			180,000
			1,160,000
Current assets			
Stock	77,000		
Debtors	278,600		
Bank	61,000	416,600	

contd →

Balance Sheet of Kilcoyne PLC as on 31/12/08 (continued)			
Creditors: amounts falling due within 1 year			
Trade creditors	162,000		
Dividends due	10,000		
Taxation due	96,000		
Other creditors	81,500	(349,500)	
Net current assets			67,100
Total assets *less* **Current liabilities**			1,227,100
Creditors: amounts falling due after more than 1 year			
Debentures			250,000
Provisions for liabilities and charges			
Claim for compensation			25,000
Capital and reserves			
Issued shares		450,000	
Revaluation reserve		218,000	
Profit carried forward		284,100	
			952,100
			1,227,100

Notes to the accounts

Accounting policy notes

1 Tangible fixed assets

Buildings were revalued at the end of 2008 and have been included in the accounts at their revalued amount. Vehicles are shown at cost. Depreciation is calculated in order to write off the value of the tangible assets over their estimated useful economic life, as follows:

Buildings   2% per annum – straight-line basis

Delivery vans 20% of cost

Stocks   Stocks are valued on a first-in-first-out basis at the lower of cost and net realisable value

Top Tip!

The key word here is **policy**; this note states clearly the policy of the company in relation to its tangible fixed assets and stock. Do not mix this up with the tangible fixed assets note.

2 Operating profit

Operating profit is arrived at after charging:

	€
Depreciation on tangible assets	58,000
Patent amortised	10,000
Directors' remuneration	60,000
Auditors' fees	11,500

3 Interest payable

Interest payable on debentures (repayable by 2014/2015): €20,000

4 Dividends

Ordinary dividends			
Interim/paid	6c per share	21,000	
Final proposed	2c per share	7,000	28,000
Preference dividends			
Interim/paid	3c per share	3,000	
Final proposed	3c per share	3,000	6,000

5 Tangible fixed assets

	Land and buildings	Vehicles	Total
Cost at 1/1/08	700,000	240,000	940,000
Disposal	(50,000)		(50,000)
Revaluation surplus 31/12/08	150,000		150,000
Value at 31/12/08	800,000	240,000	1,040,000
Depreciation 1/1/08	55,000	42,000	97,000
Depreciation charge for the year	13,000	48,000	61,000
	68,000	90,000	158,000
Transfer on revaluation	(68,000)		(68,000)
Depreciation 31/12/08	Nil	90,000	90,000
Net book value 1/1/08	645,000	198,000	793,000
Net book value 31/12/08	800,000	150,000	950,000

6 Contingent liability

The company has provided for an amount of €25,000 for a claim for compensation for unfair dismissal. The company's legal advisers have advised that the company will probably be liable. They have estimated the maximum amount of the liability at €25,000.

> **Top Tip!**
> **Likely to be liable for a contingent liability**: include in the accounts and the notes as above. Include the estimated amount in the profit and loss account under '**Administrative expenses**' and in the balance sheet under the heading '**Provisions for liabilities and charges**'. The note should show the nature of the liability (claim for compensation), the expected outcome (company will probably be liable) and the estimate of the amount (€25,000).

(b)

Refer to the theory section on p.174.

Question 2 (2006, HL, Section 1, Q4)

Ross PLC has an authorised capital of €800,000 divided into 600,000 ordinary shares at €1 each and 200,000 10% preference shares at €1 each. The following trial balance was extracted from its books on 31/12/2005.

	€	€
9% investments 1/1/2005	200,000	
Patent	64,000	
Land and buildings (revalued on 1/7/2005)	860,000	
Delivery vans at cost	140,000	
Delivery vans – accumulated depreciation on 1/1/2005		64,000
Revaluation reserve		265,000
Debtors and creditors	200,000	95,000
Purchases and sales	700,000	1,221,000
Stock 1/1/2005	70,000	
Directors' fees	89,000	
Salaries and general expenses	175,000	
Discount		6,260
Advertising	23,000	
Investment income		9,000
Profit on sale of land		80,000
Rent	30,000	
Interim dividends	29,000	
Profit and loss balance 1/1/2005		78,000
6% debentures including €100,000 issued on 1/8/2005		280,000
Bank		18,440
VAT		3,300
Issued capital		
300,000 ordinary shares at €1 each		300,000
160,000 10% preference shares		160,000
	2,580,000	2,580,000

The following information is also relevant:

(i) Stock on 31/12/2005 was valued on a first-in-first-out basis at €72,000.

(ii) The patent was acquired on 1/1/2003 for €80,000. It is being amortised over 10 years in equal instalments. The amortisation is to be included in cost of sales.

(iii) On 1/7/2005 the ordinary shareholders received an interim dividend of €21,000 and the preference shareholders received €8,000. The directors propose the payment of the preference dividend due and a final dividend on ordinary shares to bring the total ordinary dividend to 15c per share.

(iv) On 1/7/2005 land which cost €100,000 was sold for €180,000. On this date the remaining land and buildings were revalued at €860,000. Included in this revaluation is land now valued at €160,000 but which originally cost €50,000. The revalued buildings had cost €530,000.

(v) Depreciation is to be provided as follows:

Delivery vans at the rate of 20% of cost

Buildings at the rate of 2% of cost per annum until date of revaluation and thereafter at 2% per annum of revalued figure

(vi) Provide for debenture interest due, investment income due, auditors' fees €8,400 and taxation €40,000.

You are required to:

(a) Prepare the published **profit and loss account** for the year ended 31/12/2005, in accordance with the Companies Acts and appropriate reporting standards, showing the following notes:

    1   Tangible fixed assets

    2   Stock

    3   Dividends

    4   Operating profit

    5   Profit on sale of property   (48)

(b) Define an audit. Describe an auditor's report that is 'qualified'.   (12)

                                       (60 marks)

Solution

(a) Profit and Loss Account of Ross Plc for Year Ended 31/12/05		(48)
	€	€
Turnover		1,221,000 (3)
Cost of sales		(706,000) (6)
Gross profit		515,000
Distribution costs		(51,000) (2)
Administrative expenses		(314,700) (5)
		149,300
Other operating income		6,260 (1)
Operating profit		155,560
Profit on sale of land		80,000 (2)
Investment income		18,000 (3)
		253,560
Interest payable		(13,300) (3)
Profit on ordinary activities before taxation		240,260 (1)
Taxation		(40,000) (1)
Profit after taxation		200,260
Dividends paid	29,000 (2)	
Dividends proposed	32,000 (2)	(61,000)
Profit retained for year		139,260
Profit brought forward at 1/1/2005		78,000 (1)
Profit carried forward at 31/12/2005		217,260 (3)

Workings

		€	€
1	Cost of sales		
	Stock 1/1/2005	70,000	
	Purchases	700,000	
	Patents written off	8,000	
	Stock 31/12/2005	(72,000)	706,000
2	Distribution costs		
	Advertising	23,000	
	Depreciation – delivery vans	28,000	51,000
3	Administrative expenses		
	Directors' fees	89,000	
	Salaries and general expenses	175,000	
	Rent	30,000	
	Auditors' fees	8,400	
	Depreciation – buildings	12,300	314,700

Notes to the accounts

1 Tangible fixed assets (5)

	Land €	Buildings €	Vehicles €	Total €
Cost or valuation 1/1/2005	150,000	530,000	140,000	820,000
Disposal	(100,000)	–	–	(100,000)
Revaluation surplus	110,000	170,000	–	280,000
Value at 31/12/2005	160,000	700,000	140,000	1,000,000
Depreciation at 1/1/2005	–	–	64,000	64,000
Depreciation charge for year	–	12,300	28,000	40,300
		12,300	92,000	104,300
Net book value 1/1/2005	150,000	530,000	76,000	756,000
Net book value 31/12/2005	160,000	687,700	48,000	895,700

2 Stock (1)

Stocks are valued on a first-in-first-out basis at the lower of cost and net realisable value.

3 Dividends (3)

	€	€
Ordinary dividends		
Interim paid 7.0c per share	21,000	
Final proposed 8.0c per share	24,000	45,000
Preference dividends		
Interim paid 5.0c per share	8,000	
Final proposed 5.0c per share	8,000	16,000

4 Operating profit

The operating profit is arrived at after charging:

	€
Depreciation on tangible fixed assets	40,300
Patent amortised	8,000
Directors' remuneration	89,000
Auditors' fees	8,400

5 Profit on sale of property

(2)

The company sold land for €80,000 more than it cost. Cost was €100,000.

(b)

(12)

Audit

(4)

Refer to the theory section below.

Regulatory Framework of Accounting

The following is **essential** knowledge in relation to the theory required for this section.

AN AUDIT

An audit is an **independent examination** of and **expression of opinion** on the **financial statements** of an enterprise by an appointed auditor.

Role/purpose

An auditor examines the financial statements of a company and expresses an opinion on whether or not they are a **true and fair view** of the business and whether the financial statements **comply with the Companies Acts**.

The financial statements give a true and fair view of the state of affairs of the business if:

- They contain all the information required by the Companies Acts and Accounting Standards
- In preparing the accounts, accounting concepts have been followed
- The accounts are prepared in a way that is consistent with the previous year's accounts

The Companies Acts do not require the auditor to certify that the company's records are correct or accurate – only that the accounts give a true and fair view of the financial position of the firm. The auditor is appointed by the shareholders and must prepare a report for the shareholders on the accounts examined.

Unqualified auditor's report

An unqualified auditor's report is often referred to as a **clean report**. The auditor's report is unqualified when the auditor states that he/she **is satisfied** that the following apply:

Point to note

An unqualified auditor's report is a good report.

- The financial statements give a true and fair view of the state of affairs of the company at the end of the year and of its profit and loss account for the year
- The financial statements are prepared in accordance with the Companies Acts
- All the information necessary for the audit was available
- The information given by the directors is consistent with the financial statements
- The net assets are more than 50% of the called-up capital

Qualified auditor's report

The auditor's report is qualified when the auditor states that he/she is **not satisfied** or unable to conclude that all of the following apply:

- The financial statements give a true and fair view of the state of affairs of the company at the end of the year and of its profit and loss account for the year
- The financial statements are prepared in accordance with the Companies Acts
- All the information necessary for the audit was available
- The information given by the directors is consistent with the financial statements
- The net assets are more than 50% of the called-up capital

The report will state the elements of the accounts or of the directors' report that are unsatisfactory.

AGENCIES THAT REGULATE THE PRODUCTION, CONTENT AND PRESENTATION OF COMPANY FINANCIAL STATEMENTS

- The **government**, through legislation – the Companies Act
- The **European Union**, through directives to standardise accounting practice for all member states
- The **Accounting Standards Board**, through FRSs (Financial Reporting Standards) and SSAPs (Statements of Standard Accounting Practice)
- The **stock exchange**, through listing rules and extra disclosures that need to be made

Accountants must observe the regulations laid down by these agencies when preparing financial statements for publication.

Accounting Standards Board

The Accounting Standards Board issues new accounting standards and amends or withdraws old standards. An example of an accounting standard is FRS 1, which requires large companies to prepare cash-flow statements using specific headings and supply two separate reconciliation notes.

CRITERIA THAT DETERMINE THE SIZE OF A SMALL PRIVATE COMPANY, A MEDIUM PRIVATE COMPANY AND A LARGE PRIVATE OR PUBLIC COMPANY

The size of a company (small, medium or large) is determined by 3 criteria:

- The annual turnover
- The balance sheet
- The number of employees

To Classify as	Small	Medium	Large
Balance sheet	≤ €4.4m	≤ €7.62m	> €7.62m
Annual turnover	≤ €8.8m	≤ €15.24m	> €15.24m
Employees	≤ 50	≤ 250	> 250

Companies must meet two out of three criteria in two consecutive years.

RESPONSIBILITIES OF DIRECTORS

Directors must:

- Comply with the Companies Acts
- Keep proper accounting records, enabling financial statements to be prepared
- Prepare **annual** financial statements in accordance with the Companies Acts
- Sign financial statements
- Select suitable accounting policies (e.g. method of depreciation)
- Look after the assets of the company

- Present an annual report to shareholders at AGM, to include:
  - Directors' report
  - Auditor's report
  - Financial statements

A directors' report must contain the following:

- The amount to be transferred to reserves
- The principal activities of the company; a fair review of the development of the business of the company during the year and of its end-of-year position; a report of any changes in the nature of the company's business during the year
- Details of important events that have affected the company since the end of the financial year; any likely future developments in the business; details of activities undertaken in the area of research and development
- Details of significant changes in fixed assets
- Details of shares purchased
- A list of the company's subsidiaries and affiliates
- Details of directors' share holdings and dealings in company shares during the year
- An evaluation of the company's compliance with its safety statement

Previous Theory Exam Questions

2013, Q6, Part (b) (15 marks)

(i) Name the bodies/institutions that regulate the production, content and presentation of company financial statements.

(ii) What is an audit? Explain a qualified auditor's report.

2012, Q7, Part (b)

(ii) Outline two responsibilities of the directors of a PLC.

2011, Q3, Part (b) (12 marks)

(i) State how a company should deal with a contingent liability which is probable.

(ii) Explain the difference between an auditor's qualified and unqualified report.

2009, Q6, Part (b) (15 marks); 2005, Q6, Parts (b) and (c) (16 marks)

(i) State three items of information that must be included in a director's report.

(ii) Explain the term 'exceptional item' and give an example.

2008, Q4, Part (b) (10 marks)

(i) State how a company would deal with a contingent liability which is possible but unlikely.

(ii) What regulations must accountants observe when preparing financial statements for publication?

2008, Q6, Part (b) (5 marks)

(ii) Write a note on the Accounting Standards Board.

2006, Q4, Part (b) (12 marks)

What is an audit? Describe an auditor's report that is qualified.

2003, Q2, Part (b) (10 marks)

Name the agencies that regulate the production, content and presentation of company financial statements.

2002, Q6, Part (b) (15 marks)

State the difference between an auditor's qualified and unqualified report.

2000, Q3, Part (b) (15 marks)

What is an audit? What is the purpose of an audit?

1999, Q6, Part (b) (15 marks)

State the criteria that determine the size of a public and large private company.

Cash-Flow Statements

11

The cash-flow statement can explain the difference between the cash balances at the beginning of the year and the cash balances at the end of the year.

FRS 1 (Financial Reporting Standard 1) details how the actual cash-flow statement and the two accompanying reconciliation notes are to be prepared. The layouts given must be strictly followed.

There are three steps involved.

Point to note

Cash balances are amounts held in cash or on deposit in the bank **minus** any bank overdraft.

Step 1 Reconciliation of Operating Profit to Net Cash Flow from Operating Activities

The purpose of this step is to find out the cash flow generated from the operating activities of the business. Operating profit is adjusted for changes in:

- Stock
- Debtors
- Creditors
- Non-cash items

Reconciliation of Operating Profit to Net Cash Flow from Operating Activities	€
Operating profit	X
Add Depreciation charges	X
Less Profit on disposal of fixed assets	(X)
Add Loss on disposal of fixed assets	X
Add Decrease in stock (*Less* Increase in stock)	X
Add Decrease in debtors (*Less* Increase in debtors)	X
Less Decrease in creditors (*Add* Increase in creditors)	(X)
Add Increase in bad debt provision (*Less* Decrease in BDP)	X
Add Patents written off	X
Net cash flow from operating activities	X

Point to note

Non-cash item: an item that affects net profit but does not cause an inflow/outflow of cash, e.g. depreciation; profit/loss on disposal of assets; changes in the provision for bad debts/writing-off of patents.

Outflows of cash	Purchase of stock; increase in debtors and payments to creditors	Subtracted
Inflows of cash	Sale of stock; payments made by debtors and increase in creditors	Added
Non-cash expense	Depreciation; loss on disposal; reduction in bad debt provision	Added
Non-cash gain	Profit on disposal; increase in bad debt provision	Subtracted

Actual bad debts have the effect of reducing the debtors figure and would be accounted for in the change in debtors; it is changes in the **provision for bad debts** that is treated as a non-cash item.

Step 2 Cash-Flow Statement

Begin with the net cash flow from operating activities and detail all inflows/outflows of cash under **very specific** headings.

Top Tip!

Learn the following layout; know the inflows/outflows that appear under each heading. Using the layout as your guide, check the question for all the necessary information and enter it appropriately.

Cash-Flow Forecast of Company Z for Year Ended 31/12/09	€	€
Operating activities		
Net cash flow from operating activities		X
Return on investment and servicing of finance		
Interest received	X	
Interest paid	(X)	
Preference dividend paid	(X)	
Dividends received	X	(X)
Taxation		
Tax paid	(X)	(X)
Capital expenditure and financial investment		
Payments to acquire fixed assets	(X)	
Receipts from sale of fixed assets	X	
Payments to acquire investments	(X)	
Receipts from sale of investments	X	(X)
Equity dividend paid		
Ordinary dividends paid		(X)
Net cash inflow before liquid resources and financing		X

contd →

Cash-Flow Forecast of Company Z for Year Ended 31/12/09 (continued)		
Management of liquid resources		
Purchases of government securities of <1 year	(X)	
Sale of government securities of <1 year	X	
Payments into current asset investments/short-term deposits	(X)	
Withdrawal from current asset investments/short-term deposits	X	X
Financing		
Receipts from the issue of shares	X	
Receipts from share premium	X	
Repayment of debentures/loan	(X)	
Receipts from issue of debentures/loans	X	X
Increase/decrease of cash		X

Top Tips!

- Be clear that liquid resources refer to any type of short-term investments such as government securities/short-term deposits; liquid resources are listed as current assets in the balance sheet.
- Check the increase or decrease in cash against the difference in actual cash/bank and bank overdraft figures to ensure that the answer is correct.

Step 3 Reconciliation of Operating Profit to Net Cash Flow from Operating Activities

Two items affect this reconciliation:

- Payments into/withdrawals from liquid resources
- Repayment of debentures/receipt of new debentures/loans

Positive effect on the amount of debt **ADDED**	Payments into liquid resources Repayment of debentures
Negative effect on the amount of debt **SUBTRACTED**	Withdrawals from liquid resources Receipts from issue of new debentures

Point to note

Net debt is calculated as follows:

Borrowings (Debentures + Overdraft + Other loans) — Cash + Liquid resources (current asset investments). If the net debt turns out to be a positive figure, it is then called net funds.

Begin with the increase/decrease in cash and follow this layout:

Reconciliation of Movement in Cash to Movement in Net Debt	
Increase/decrease in cash	X
Cash used to increase liquid resources (withdrawals from liquid resources)	X
Cash used to repay debentures (receipt from issue of new debentures/loans)	X
Change in net debt	X
Net debt at 1/1/2009	(X)
Net debt at 31/12/2009	(X)

Abridged Profit and Loss Account

It may be necessary to prepare an abridged profit and loss account. The layout is the same as any profit and loss account (shown below). It will be necessary to work back from the profit and loss balance figures given in the balance sheet to find the retained profit. Insert the figures for dividends, taxation and interest, then work back to the operating profit. Proceed as normal with the reconciliation of operating profit to net cash flow from operating activities.

Abridged Profit and Loss Account for Year Ended 31/12/09		
Operating profit		X
Interest for the year		(X)
Profit before taxation		X
Taxation for the year		(X)
Profit after taxation		X
Dividends – interim	X	
– proposed	X	(X)
Retained profits for the year		X
Retained profits on 1/1/2009		X
Retained profits on 31/12/2009		X

Profit does not equal cash because:

Items affect cash but not profit, such as:	*Items affect profit but not cash, such as:*
• Amounts paid for fixed assets or amounts received from the sale of fixed assets	• Non-cash expenses/gains such as depreciation, profit on disposal of fixed assets, reduction in bad debt provision
• Amounts paid into the business by the owners or amounts withdrawn from the business by the owners	• Credit sales and credit purchases
• Loans received by the business or loans repaid by the business	

Question 1

The following are the balance sheets of Brink PLC as at 31/12/2008 and 31/12/2009, together with an abridged profit and loss account for the year ended 31/12/2009.

Abridged Profit and Loss Account for Year Ended 31/12/09	€	€
Operating profit		368,000
Interest for the year		(8,800)
Profit before taxation		359,200
Taxation for the year		(46,000)
Profit after taxation		313,200
Dividends – interim	38,400	
– proposed	44,000	(82,400)
Retained profits for the year		230,800
Retained profits on 1/1/2009		103,000
Retained profits on 31/12/2009		333,800

Balance Sheet as on	31/12/09 €	31/12/09 €	31/12/08 €	31/12/08 €
Fixed assets				
Land and buildings at cost	980,000		850,000	
Less Accumulated depreciation	(90,000)	890,000	(70,000)	780,000
Machinery at cost	170,000		230,000	
Less Accumulated depreciation	(125,000)	45,000	(104,000)	126,000
		935,000		906,000
Financial assets				
Quoted investments		100,000		50,000
Current assets				
Stock	190,000		120,000	
Debtors	187,000		150,000	
Government securities	24,000			
Bank	4,000			
Cash	7,000		5,000	
	412,000		275,000	
Less **Creditors: amounts falling due within 1 year**				
Trade creditors	115,000		145,000	
Interest due	2,200		3,300	
Taxation	42,000		38,000	
Dividends	44,000		29,700	
Bank			12,000	
	(203,200)		(228,000)	
Net current assets		208,800		47,000
		1,243,800		1,003,000
Financed by				
Creditors: amounts falling due after 1 year				
11% debentures		80,000		150,000
Capital and reserves				
€1 ordinary shares	810,000		750,000	
Share premium	20,000			
Profit and loss account	333,800	1,163,800	103,000	853,000
		1,243,800		1,003,000

The following information is also available:
  (i) There were no disposals of buildings during the year but new buildings were acquired.
  (ii) There were no purchases of machinery during the year. Machinery was disposed of for €30,000.
  (iii) Depreciation charged for the year on machinery in arriving at the operating profit was €50,000.

You are required to:
  (a) Prepare the cash-flow statement of Brink PLC for the year ended 31/12/2009, including reconciliation statement(s)   (48)
  (b) Explain why cash-flow statements are prepared   (8)
  (c) Identify a non-cash expense and a non-cash gain   (4)

          (60 marks)

Solution

Part (a)

Note 1

Land and Buildings Account			
Balance b/d	850,000		
Bank C/F	**130,000**	Balance c/d	980,000
	980,000		980,000

Provision for Depreciation Account			
		Balance b/d	70,000
Balance c/d	90,000	**P+L R**	**20,000**
	90,000		90,000

Note 2

Machinery Account			
Balance b/d	230,000	**Disposal**	**60,000**
		Balance c/d	170,000
	230,000		230,000

Provision for Depreciation Account			
Disposal	**29,000**	Balance b/d	104,000
Balance c/d	125,000	**P+L R**	**50,000**
	154,000		154,000

Disposal Account			
Machinery	60,000	Depreciation	29,000
		Bank C/F	**30,000**
		Loss R	**1,000**
	60,000		60,000

Note 3

Interest Account			
Bank C/F	**9,900**	Balance b/d	3,300
Balance c/d	2,200	P+L	8,800
	12,100		12,100

Note 4

Taxation Account			
Bank C/F	**42,000**	Balance b/d	38,000
Balance c/d	42,000	P+L	46,000
	84,000		84,000

Note 5

Dividends Account			
Bank C/F (29,700 + 38,400)	**68,100**	Balance b/d	29,700
Balance c/d	44,000	P+L (38,400 + 44,000)	82,400
	112,100		112,100

Note 6

Increase in stock	70,000 (190,000 − 120,000)	Outflow = Subtract
Increase in debtors	37,000 (187,000 − 150,000)	Outflow = Subtract
Decrease in creditors	30,000 (115,000 − 145,000)	Outflow = Subtract

Note 7 Investments
Purchases of investments of €50,000 **C/F**

Note 8 Debentures
Repayment of debentures €70,000 **C/F**

Note 9 Share capital
Receipt from issue of shares €60,000 **C/F**
Receipt form share premium €20,000 **C/F**

Reconciliation of Operating Profit to Net Cash Flow from Operating Activities	
	€
Operating profit	368,000
Add Depreciation charges	70,000
Add Loss on disposal of fixed assets	1,000
Less Increase in stock	(70,000)
Less Increase in debtors	(37,000)
Less Decrease in creditors	(30,000)
Net cash flow from operating activities	302,000

Cash-Flow Forecast of Brink Ltd for Year Ended 31/12/09	€	€
Operating activities		
Net cash flow from operating activities		302,000
Return on investment and servicing of finance		
Interest paid	(9,900)	(9,900)
Taxation		
Tax paid	(42,000)	(42,000)
Capital expenditure and financial investment		
Payments to acquire fixed assets	(130,000)	
Receipts from sale of fixed assets	30,000	
Payments to acquire investments	(50,000)	(150,000)
Equity dividend paid		
Ordinary dividends paid		(68,100)
Net cash inflow before liquid resources and financing		32,000
Management of liquid resources		
Purchases of government securities of <1 year	(24,000)	(24,000)
Financing		
Receipts from the issue of shares	60,000	
Receipts from share premium	20,000	
Repayment of debentures	(70,000)	10,000
Increase of cash		18,000

Check

2008	€	2009	€
Cash	5,000	Cash and bank	11,000
Bank overdraft 2008	(12,000)	Bank overdraft 2008	0
Balance	(7,000)	Balance	11,000
Net increase in cash of 18,000			

Reconciliation of Movement in Cash to Movement in Net Debt	
	€
Increase in cash	18,000
Cash used to increase liquid resources	24,000
Cash used to repay debentures	70,000
Change in net debt	112,000
Net debt at 1/1/2009 ([150,000 + 12,000] − 5,000)	(157,000)
Net debt at 31/12/2009 (80,000 − [24,000 + 4,000 + 7,000])	(45,000)

Part (b)
Reasons for the preparation of cash-flow statement:
- To show the cash inflows and outflows during the past year
- To help predict future cash flows
- To help financial planning
- To provide information to enable the assessment of the liquidity of the business
- To comply with legal requirements
- To show that profits do not equal cash

Part (c)

Non-cash expenses Depreciation; loss on sale of fixed asset; increase in bad debt provision
Non-cash gains Profit on sale of fixed asset; decrease in bad debt provision

Question 2

The following are the balance sheets of Carey PLC as at 31/12/2009 and 31/12/2010.

Balance Sheet as on	31/12/10		31/12/09	
	€	€	€	€
Fixed assets				
Land and buildings	750,000		650,000	
Less Accumulated depreciation	(120,000)	630,000	(110,000)	540,000
Machinery	370,000		430,000	
Less Accumulated depreciation	(180,000)	190,000	(150,000)	280,000
Financial assets				
Quoted investments		100,000		
Current assets				
Stock	508,000		390,000	
Debtors	368,000		242,000	
	876,000		632,000	
Less **Creditors: amounts falling due within 1 year**				
Trade creditors	380,000		420,000	
Taxation	84,000		66,000	
Dividends	116,000		142,000	
Bank	26,000		74,000	
	606,000		702,000	
Net current assets		270,000		(70,000)
		1,190,000		750,000
Financed by				
Creditors: amounts falling due after 1 year				
10% debentures		360,000		240,000
Capital and reserves				
€1 ordinary shares	740,000		500,000	
Share premium	36,000			
Profit and loss account		54,000		10,000
		1,190,000		750,000

The following information is also available:

(i) 240,000 shares were issued at €1.15 per share.
(ii) Buildings costing €50,000 were sold during the year for €55,000.
(iii) Machinery costing €110,000, with a book value of €65,000, was sold during the year for €35,000.
(iv) Depreciation on tangible fixed assets charged for the year in arriving at the operating profit was €100,000.
(v) €120,000 of debentures were issued on 1/1/2010.
(vi) Dividends due and taxation due on 31/12/2009 were paid. Interim dividends amounting to €37,000 were paid during 2010.

You are required to:

(a) Prepare an abridged profit and loss account for the year ended 31/12/2010   (25)

(b) Prepare the cash-flow statement of Carey PLC for the year ended 31/12/2010 including reconciliation statement(s)   (65)

(c) Explain why cash-flow statements are prepared   (10)

(100 marks)

Solution

Note 1

Buildings Account			
Balance b/d	650,000	Disposal	50,000
Bank C/F	**150,000**	Balance c/d	750,000
	800,000		800,000

Provision for Depreciation Account			
Disposal	15,000	Balance b/d	110,000
Balance c/d	120,000	**P+L R**	**25,000**
	135,000		135,000

Disposal of Buildings Account			
Buildings	50,000	Depr.	15,000
Profit R	**20,000**	**Bank C/F**	**55,000**
	70,000		70,000

Machinery Account			
Balance b/d	430,000	Disposal	110,000
Bank C/F	**50,000**	Balance c/d	370,000
	480,000		480,000

Provision for Depreciation Account			
Disposal	45,000	Balance b/d	150,000
Balance c/d	180,000	**P+L R**	**75,000**
	225,000		225,000

Disposal of Machinery Account			
Machinery	110,000	Depr.	45,000
		Bank C/F	**35,000**
		Loss R	**30,000**
	110,000		110,000

Note 2   Interest

10% of 360,000 = 36,000 Profit and loss account and cash-flow statement

> **Point to note**
>
> The debentures were issued on 1/1/2010; therefore the interest is payable on the full amount for a full year. There is no interest due at the end of 2010; therefore the full amount must have been paid.

Note 3   Dividends

Dividends Account			
Bank C/F (142,000 + 37,000)	**179,000**	Balance b/d	142,000
Balance c/d	116,000	**P+L (37,000 + 116,000)**	**153,000**
	295,000		295,000

> **Point to note**
>
> The dividends due on 31/12/2009 were paid along with the interim dividends for 2010; the profit and loss figure will include the interim dividends of €37,000 and the dividends due on 31/12/2010 of €116,000.

Note 4

Taxation Account			
Bank C/F	**66,000**	Balance b/d	66,000
Balance c/d	84,000	**P+L**	**84,000**
	150,000		150,000

Point to note

The tax due on 31/12/2009 was paid and needs to be entered in the cash-flow statement; the amount due on 31/12/2010 is the amount to be charged to the profit and loss account.

Note 5   Investments
Purchases of investments of €100,000 **C/F**

Note 6   Debentures
Receipt of a further loan of €120,000 **C/F**

Note 7   Share capital
Receipt from issue of shares €240,000 **C/F**
Receipt from share premium €36,000 **C/F**

Part (a)

Abridged Profit and Loss Account for Year Ended 31/12/09		€	€
Operating profit			317,000
Interest for the year	N2		(36,000)
Profit before taxation			677,000
Taxation for the year	N4		(84,000)
Profit after taxation			593,000
Dividends – interim	N3	37,000	
– proposed	N3	116,000	
			(153,000)
Retained profits for the year			44,000
Retained profits on 1/1/2009			10,000
Retained profits on 31/12/2009			54,000

Top Tip!

Be sure to use the P+L **balance** figures in the abridged P+L account.

Part (b)

Reconciliation of Operating Profit to Net Cash Flow from Operating Activities		€
Operating profit		317,000
Add Depreciation charges	N1	100,000
Add Loss on disposal of machinery	N1	30,000
Less Profit on disposal of buildings	N1	(20,000)
Less Increase in stock		(118,000)
Less Increase in debtors		(126,000)
Less Decrease in creditors		(40,000)
Net cash flow from operating activities		143,000

Cash-Flow Forecast of Carey PLC for Year Ended 31/12/10

		€	€
Operating activities			
Net cash flow from operating activities			143,000
Return on investment and servicing of finance			
Interest paid	N2	36,000	(36,000)
Taxation			
Tax paid	N4	66,000	(66,000)
Capital expenditure and financial investment			
Payments to acquire fixed assets	N1	(200,000)	
Receipts from sale of fixed assets	N1	90,000	
Payments to acquire investments	N5	(100,000)	(210,000)
Equity dividend paid			
Ordinary dividends paid	N3		(179,000)
Net cash inflow before liquid resources and financing			(348,000)
Management of liquid resources			
Financing			
Receipts from the issue of shares	N7	240,000	
Receipts from share premium	N7	36,000	
Receipts from issue of debentures	N6	120,000	396,000
Increase of cash			48,000

Check

Bank overdraft 2009	(74,000)
Bank overdraft 2010	(26,000)
Increase in cash of	48,000

Reconciliation of Movement in Cash to Movement in Net Debt

	€
Increase in cash	48,000
Cash used to increase liquid resources	0
Cash from issue of debentures	(120,000)
Change in net debt	(72,000)
Net debt at 1/1/2010 (240,000 + 74,000 − 0)	(314,000)
Net debt at 31/12/2010 (360,000 + 26,000 − 0)	(386,000)

Part (c)

See solution to **part (c)** in sample Question 1 part (b) (p.184).

Tabular Statements

12

Learning objectives

In this chapter you will learn about:

1 The preparation of a tabular statement

The balance sheet is a list of the assets and liabilities of a company on a particular day. A tabular statement shows the effect that transactions have on the balance sheet.

Points to note

- Assets = liabilities (the balance sheet should always balance)
- Increase an asset = decrease another asset **or** increase a liability
- Decrease an asset = increase another asset **or** decrease a liability

Exam procedure

1 List all assets vertically; allow three extra rows for new assets that may arise, and total.

2 List all liabilities vertically; allow three extra rows for new liabilities that may arise, and total.

3 Record the effect of **each** transaction on the appropriate assets and liabilities, making sure that in each case total assets = total liabilities.

4 When all transactions have been included, total the assets and liabilities vertically, then cross check that horizontal totals = vertical totals.

Top Tip!

The **yearly amount of an expense/gain** should **only** be **charged to the profit and loss account on the last day** of the trading period.

Point to note

Tabular statements will test your knowledge of how the following affect the balance sheet:

- Goodwill
- Disposal of fixed assets
- Accruals
- Bad debts/bad debts recovered
- Dividends
- Depreciation

- Revaluation
- Issue of shares; share premium
- Prepayments
- Sales/purchases/sales returns/purchases returns
- Discounts

- A tabular statement question can arise in **Section 2** for **100 marks** or **Section 1** for **60 marks**.

- Assets must always equal liabilities; thus, when the effect of each transaction is totalled, it will either have an equal effect on the assets and liabilities **or** the total will be zero.

- Remember that gains and expenses are often prepaid but that they are **only charged** to the profit and loss account at the end of the year.

- Tabular statement questions simply bring together knowledge of adjustments previously dealt with. Use this knowledge, follow the procedure and read the question carefully.

Sample questions and solutions

Question 1

The financial position of Johnstown Ltd on 1/1/2009 is shown in the following balance sheet.

Balance Sheet as on 1/1/09	Cost €	Depr. to date €	Net €
Fixed assets			
Land and buildings	320,000	30,000	290,000
Vehicles	40,000	15,000	25,000
	360,000	45,000	315,000
Current assets			
Stock		80,000	
Debtors		84,000	
Insurance prepaid		1,000	
		165,000	
Less **Creditors: amounts falling due within 1 year**			
Creditors	90,000		
Bank	12,000		
Wages due	2,500	104,500	
Net current assets			60,500
			375,500
Financed by			
Capital and reserves			
Authorised – 450,000 ordinary shares @ €1			
Issued – 320,000 ordinary shares @ €1			320,000
Share premium			22,500
Profit and loss balance			33,000
			375,500

The following transactions took place during 2009:

Jan   On 1/1/2009 Johnstown Ltd decided to revalue land and buildings at €500,000. This valuation included land now valued at €100,000.

Feb   On 1/2/2009 Johnstown Ltd bought an adjoining business which included buildings €80,000, equipment €24,000, debtors €15,000 and creditors €38,000. The purchase price was discharged by granting the seller 85,000 shares in Johnstown Ltd at a premium of 20 cent per share.

March A payment of €800 was received from a debtor whose debt had been previously written off and who now wishes to trade with Johnstown Ltd again. This represents 40% of the original debt and the debtor undertook to pay the remainder of the debt by December 2009.

April Goods previously sold for €6,000 were returned. The selling price of these goods was cost plus 20%. A credit note was issued, showing a deduction of 12% of the selling price as a restocking charge.

May Johnstown Ltd received a bank statement on 31 May showing a credit transfer received of €2,750 to cover 11 months' rent in advance from 1 May and a direct debit of €3,600 to cover insurance for the year ended 30/4/2010.

June Johnstown Ltd settled by cheque a creditors' account of €820, receiving a discount of €50.

July Goods previously bought for €2,000 were returned. The credit note received showed an 8% deduction due to a restocking charge.

Aug An interim dividend of 3c per share was paid on all paid-up shares.

Sept A van which cost €16,000 was traded in against a new van costing €30,000. An allowance of €3,500 was made for the old van. Depreciation to date on the old van was €11,000.

Oct Johnstown Ltd received the balance of a previously written-off bad debt as agreed in March.

Nov Johnstown Ltd received €58,500 from the issue of the remaining shares.

Dec The buildings are to be depreciated at the rate of 2% of cost and equipment is to be depreciated at a rate of 20% of cost. The total depreciation charge on vehicles for the year was €12,200.

You are required to:

Record on a tabular statement the effect each of the above transactions had on the relevant asset, liability and capital accounts and ascertain the total assets and liabilities on 31/12/2009

(100 marks)

Solution

Jan Increase land and buildings by €180,000; decrease depreciation by the full amount of €30,000; total revaluation reserve (new liability) of €210,000

Point to note

Goodwill is often a missing figure when a new business is purchased.

Feb Total paid €102,000

€85,000 × 1 = €85,000 and €85,000 × 0.20 = €17,000

Net tangible assets €81,000; missing figure of €21,000 is goodwill (new asset)

March 40% = €800; 100% = €2,000 bad debt recovered; record the full amount as a gain in the profit and loss account

€800 received into the bank and a further €1,200 to be received, so add to debtors

Point to note

Sales returns affect stock, debtors and the profit and loss account.

April 120% = €6,000; 100% (cost price) = €5,000; add on to stock as goods were returned

12% of €6,000 = €720; €6,000 − €720 = €5,280; deduct from debtors for the returns

Profit decreased by €280 (€1,000 − €720; the firm did not lose out on all of the profit due to the fact that the debtor incurred a delivery charge for returning the goods)

Point to note

Yearly amounts of expenses/gains are only charged to the profit and loss account on the last day of the trading period.

May Firstly work out the bank figure and enter it correctly:

Credit transfer = money lodged into the bank; direct debit = money withdrawn from the bank:

+ €2,750 − €3,600 = − €850; net effect of €850 withdrawn from the bank

Only entry other than bank should be €3,600 insurance prepaid and €2,750 rent receivable prepaid (new liability)

June Paid €770 from bank; reduce creditors by €820

€50 as a gain in the profit and loss account (discount received)

Point to note

Purchases returned affect creditors and stock; any charges incurred in the return are charged as an expense to the profit and loss account.

July Returned goods which cost €2,000; as the company no longer has these goods, deduct €2,000 from stock:

8% of €2,000 = €160

Reduce creditors by €1,840 and the charge of €160 goes into the profit and loss account

Aug Interim dividend on €405,000 × 0.03 = €12,150; paid out of bank and charged to the profit and loss account

Sept Vehicles increase by €14,000 (€30,000 – €16,000)

Depreciation decreases value by €11,000

Cost €16,000 – Depr. €11,000 = €5,000 = Worth

Allowance of €3,500 received; therefore a loss of €1,500 is charged to profit and loss account

Top Tip!

Include the shares issued in February when calculating the dividend.

Oct Increase bank and decrease debtors with the remainder of the bad debt recovered: €1,200

Nov Received €58,500 from the issue of the 45,000 remaining shares (€450,000 – €405,000); therefore shares were issued at a premium of €13,500

Dec

Point to note

Two columns are used here – one for **depreciation** and one for **rent receivable/insurance**.

Depreciation	Buildings	2% of €480,000 (€580,000 – €100,000 land) = €9,600
	Equipment	20% of €24,000 ÷ 12 × 11 = €4,400
	Vehicles	€12,200
	Total	€26,200

Rent receivable: €2,750 = 11 months

Paid in May; therefore 8 months for this year and 3 months prepaid

€2,750 ÷ 11 × 8 = **€2,000 P+L**; €2,750 ÷ 11 × 3 = **€750 Balance**

Insurance: €3,600 = 12 months

Paid in May; therefore 8 months for this year and 4 months prepaid

€3,600 ÷ 12 × 8 = €2,400 P+L; prepaid beginning €1,000 = **€3,400 P+L**; €3,600 ÷ 12 × 4 = **€1,200 Balance**

Gain of €2,000 and expense of €3,400 leaves a net effect of −€1,400 in the profit and loss account

Point to note

Depreciation is recorded as a minus as it is making the liability larger; it is an expense in the profit and loss account and thus reduces profit, so it is also a minus in the profit and loss account.

Point to note

The business is no longer overdrawn. The bank balance can still be shown with the liabilities but as a minus figure (i.e. the money in the bank reduces the liabilities).

	1/1/2009 €	Jan €	Feb €	Mar €	Apr €	May €	Jun €	Jul €	Aug €	Sept €	Oct €	Nov €	Dec €	Dec €	Total €
Land and buildings	320,000	180,000	80,000												580,000
Depreciation	(30,000)	30,000												(9,600)	(9,600)
Vehicles	40,000									14,000					54,000
Depreciation	(15,000)									11,000				(12,200)	(16,200)
Stock	80,000				5,000			(2,000)							83,000
Debtors	84,000		15,000	1,200	(5,280)										93,720
Insurance prepaid	1,000					3,600					(1,200)		(3,400)		1,200
Equipment			24,000												24,000
Depreciation														(4,400)	(4,400)
Goodwill			21,000												21,000
TOTAL	480,000	210,000	140,000	1,200	(280)	3,600	–	(2,000)	–	25,000	(1,200)	–	(3,400)	(26,200)	826,720
Creditors	90,000		38,000				(820)	(1,840)							125,340
Bank	12,000			(800)		850	770		12,150	26,500	(1,200)	(58,500)			(8,230)
Wages due	2,500														2,500
Ordinary shares	320,000		85,000									45,000			450,000
Share premium	22,500		17,000									13,500			53,000
P+L balance	33,000			2,000	(280)		50	(160)	(12,150)	(1,500)			(1,400)	(26,200)	(6,640)
Revaluation reserve		210,000													210,000
Rent receivable						2,750							(2,000)		750
TOTAL	480,000	210,000	140,000	1,200	(280)	3,600	–	(2,000)	–	25,000	(1,200)	–	(3,400)	(26,200)	826,720

Question 2 (2004, HL, Section 1, Q2)

The financial position of Casey Ltd on 1/1/2003 is shown in the following balance sheet.

Balance Sheet as at 1/1/03	Cost €	Depr. to date €	Net €
Fixed assets			
Land and buildings	460,000	13,800	446,200
Delivery vans	76,000	33,000	43,000
	536,000	46,800	489,200
Current assets			
Stock	59,800		
Insurance prepaid	1,500		
Debtors	61,700	123,000	
Less **Creditors: amount falling due within 1 year**			
Creditors	62,500		
Bank	10,100		
Wages due	2,400	75,000	
Net current assets			48,000
			537,200
Financed by			
Capital and reserves			
Authorised – 850,000 ordinary shares @ €1 each			
Issued – 430,000 ordinary shares @ €1 each			430,000
Share premium			40,000
Profit and loss balance			67,200
			537,200

The following transactions took place during 2003:

Jan   Casey Ltd decided to revalue the land and buildings at €580,000 on 1/1/2003, which includes land now valued at €100,000.

Feb   On 1/2/2003 Casey Ltd bought an adjoining business which included buildings €360,000, delivery vans €58,000, stock €25,000 and creditors €33,000. The purchase price was discharged by granting the seller 400,000 shares in Casey Ltd at a premium of 20p per share.

March   Goods, previously sold by Casey Ltd for £1,800, were returned. The selling price of these goods was cost plus 20%. Owing to the delay in returning these goods, a credit note was issued showing a deduction of 10% of the invoice price as a restocking charge.

April   A delivery van which cost €20,000 was traded in against a new van costing €36,000. An allowance of €12,500 was made for the old van. Depreciation to date on the old van was €6,600.

May   Casey Ltd received a bank statement on 31 May showing a direct debit of €4,800 to cover fire insurance for the year ended 31/5/2004.

July   A payment of €720 was received from a debtor whose debt had been previously written off and who now wished to trade with Casey Ltd again. This represents 60% of the original debt and the debtor had undertaken to pay the remainder of the debt in January 2004.

Dec   The buildings depreciation charge for the year was to be 2% of book value. The depreciation charge was to be calculated from date of valuation and date of purchase. The total depreciation charge on delivery vans for the year was €22,000.

You are required to:

Record on a tabular statement the effect each of the above transactions had on the relevant asset and liability and ascertain the total assets and liabilities on 31/12/2003 **(60 marks)**

Solution

	1/1/2003 €	Jan €	Feb €	March €	Apr €	May €	July €	Dec €	Total €
Assets									
Land and buildings	460,000	120,000 (2)	360,000 (2)						940,000
Accumulated depreciation	(13,800)	13,800 (2)						(16,200) (2)	(16,200)
Delivery vans	76,000		58,000		16,000 (2)				150,000
Accumulated depreciation	(33,000)				6,600 (2)			(22,000) (1)	(48,400)
Stock	59,800		25,000 (2)	1,500 (3)					86,300
Debtors	61,700			(1,620) (2)			480 (3)		60,560
Insurance a/c (prepaid)	1,500					4,800 (3)		(4,300) (1)	2,000 (1)
Goodwill			70,000 (3)						70,000
TOTAL	612,200	133,800	513,000	(120)	22,600	4,800	480	(42,500)	1,244,260 (1)
Liabilities									
Share capital	430,000		400,000 (2)						830,000
Share premium	40,000		80,000 (2)						120,000
Revaluation reserve		133,800 (3)							133,800
Profit and loss	67,200			(120) (1)	(900) (3)		1,200 (2)	(42,500) (3)	24,880 (2)
Creditors	62,500		33,000 (2)						95,500
Wages due	2,400								2,400
Bank	10,100				23,500 (1)	4,800 (2)	(720) (1)		37,680 (1)
TOTAL	612,200	133,800	513,000	(120)	22,600	4,800	480	(42,500)	1,244,260 (1)

13 Product Costing

Learning objectives

In this chapter you will learn about:

1 Cost classification
2 Controllable and uncontrollable costs
3 Stock valuation using FIFO
4 Absorption costing

5 Overhead absorption rates
6 Over-/under-absorption of costs
7 Reasons for product costing

> **Top Tip!**
>
> **Cost classification** and **controllable/uncontrollable costs** are part of the management accounting sections of **costing and budgeting** and could be **examined in either section**.

Cost Classification

Firstly, costs can be classified into manufacturing and non-manufacturing costs. Remember the **manufacturing account** prepared previously, which had three main parts: raw materials, direct costs and factory overheads. These **manufacturing costs** can be classified as:

- **Direct costs**, e.g. raw materials, direct labour and other direct costs such as the hire of special equipment used in the manufacturing process.
- **Indirect costs** (factory overheads), e.g. supervisor's salary, depreciation of plant and machinery.

Non-manufacturing costs were shown in the **profit and loss account** as administration expenses, e.g. light and heat, depreciation of office equipment and selling and distribution expenses such as advertising and depreciation of delivery vans.

Costs can also be divided into fixed costs, variable costs, mixed costs and step-fixed costs:

- **Fixed costs:** Costs that remain constant regardless of the level of production; these costs are incurred even if no product is produced, e.g. rent, rates, insurance
- **Variable costs:** Costs that vary with the production level; these costs increase or decrease directly as output increases or decreases, e.g. direct materials, direct labour
- **Mixed costs:** Costs that have a fixed element and a variable element, e.g. a telephone bill contains a charge for line rental (fixed) and a charge for the number of calls made (variable)
- **Step-fixed costs:** Costs that remain fixed up to a certain level of activity, e.g. once capacity has been reached bigger premises will be needed to increase production; this will cause an increase in fixed costs

> **Top Tip!**
>
> You must be able to separate mixed costs into fixed and variable costs using the **high/low method**. See Chapter 15, Budgeting, p.233 for an example.

Controllable Costs Versus Uncontrollable Costs

Controllable costs

These are costs that can be controlled by the manager of the department/section. The manager can decide whether or not to incur the cost and how much to incur, e.g. the sales manager can decide on the commission paid to the sales team. The manager is responsible for variances in these costs. All variable costs are controllable.

Uncontrollable costs

These are costs over which the manager of a department/section has no control and therefore he/she cannot be held responsible for the variances in these costs, e.g. the sales manager cannot control the amount of rates to be paid; this is set by the local authority.

Stock Valuation

Stock is always valued at the **lower** of cost or net realisable value. As cost is usually lower, stock is usually valued at cost.

FIFO (First In First Out)

This method means the stock that is received first is the first to be issued out for sale or production. A simple method for calculating the value of closing stock when stock has been purchased on different dates at different prices is illustrated in sample Question 1 on p.210.

Absorption Costing

Absorption costing includes direct costs and indirect costs (overheads) in the cost of a product; it is sometimes referred to as **full costing**.

- **Direct costs** are costs that are easily identifiable as belonging to a particular product/department, e.g. direct labour, direct materials.
- **Indirect costs** are overheads/expenses that are not directly related to a single product/department but that must be divided out in a fair manner between all departments/products, e.g. light and heat, depreciation, rent, etc.

The procedure for absorption costing is as follows:

1	Allocation	Direct costs are allocated to the correct department or job
2	Apportionment	Indirect costs/overheads are divided out to the various departments using a suitable basis of apportionment
3	Reapportionment	Service departments need to be redivided out (reapportioned) to the production departments because costs can only be absorbed by being included in the cost of production
4	Absorption	An absorption rate for each department is calculated using a suitable basis such as machine *or* labour hours

Top Tip!

It is vital to choose the correct basis when apportioning the overheads; choose carefully, using the information given. Commonly used bases include:

Basis	Overhead
Floor area	Rent, rates, cleaning, depreciation of buildings
Book value/cost of plant/equipment	Depreciation of plant/equipment
Volume of space	Light and heat
Number of employees	Canteen costs, administration costs
Machine hours	Machine maintenance

Overhead Absorption Rates

Absorption rates can be **per labour hour, per machine hour or per unit**; the rate used will be determined by the dominant activity of the department.

Example: A labour-intensive department such as finishing will use labour hours to calculate its absorption rate as follows:

$$\frac{\text{Total department overhead}}{\text{Total department labour hours}} = \text{Rate per labour hour}$$

The absorption rates are then used to absorb budgeted overheads into specific jobs based on the number of labour hours/machine hours used in the actual job, thus allowing for calculation of the selling price.

Over-/Under-Absorption of Costs

Overhead absorption rates are always **based on budgeted rather than actual costs** because actual costs may not be known until the end of the year. The selling price needs to be calculated in order to be able to sell products, so the business simply cannot wait until the actual costs are known.

Over-absorption of costs

This occurs when **too much** cost has been charged to the product/department; actual costs turn out to be less than budgeted costs. This means profits will be **greater** than expected. This can occur for a number of reasons, e.g. reduction in rent or rates, fall in the cost of heating, lighting, insurance or canteen costs, etc.

Under-absorption of costs

This occurs when **too little** cost has been charged to the product/department; actual costs turn out to be greater than budgeted costs. This means profits will be **less** than expected. This can occur for a number of reasons, e.g. increase in rent or rates, increase in the cost of heating, lighting, insurance or canteen costs, etc.

Reasons for Product Costing

- To calculate selling price; the business will not know how much to charge if they do not know how much the product cost them to produce
- To determine the value of closing stock for the trading account and balance sheet at the year end
- To help control costs by comparing budgeted costs to actual costs
- To help in planning and decision-making

Study Tips

- A product costing question will arise in **Section 3** for **80 marks**.
- Be familiar with **all** parts of this section:
  - Valuation of closing stock using FIFO
  - Apportioning overhead to different departments
  - Reapportioning service departments to production departments
  - Calculating absorption rates
  - Calculating the cost of a product/job
  - Calculating the selling price of a product/job
  - Calculating whether under-/over-absorption has taken place and commenting on the subsequent effect on profit
- When apportioning overheads, the **correct basis** must be used; always choose the most suitable basis using the information given.
- **Learn the theory:** controllable and uncontrollable costs, reasons for product costing, over-absorption and under-absorption of overheads.

Question 1 – Stock valuation

White Ltd is a retail store that buys and sells one commodity. The following information relates to the purchases and sales of the firm for the year 2009.

Period	Purchases on credit	Credit sales	Cash sales
01/1/2009 to 31/3/2009	2,900 @ €6 each	600 @ €12 each	1,000 @ €10 each
01/4/2009 to 30/6/2009	1,900 @ €8 each	1,100 @ €13 each	1,300 @ €11 each
01/7/2009 to 30/9/2009	2,200 @ €9 each	1,200 @ €14 each	1,000 @ €12 each
01/10/2009 to 31/12/2009	1,500 @ €10 each	1,300 @ €15 each	1,100 @ €13 each

On 1/1/2009 there was opening stock of 2,400 units @ €6 each.

You are required to:

(i) Calculate the value of closing stock using the 'first in first out' (FIFO) method

(ii) Prepare a trading account for the year ended 31/12/2009

Solution

> **Top Tip!**
>
> In this question the opening stock is 2,400 units/€14,400 (2,400 × €6). These figures are required to enable you to determine closing stock on hand and for inclusion in the trading account.

Purchases		
Quantity	Price	Amount
	€	€
2,900	6	17,400
1,900	8	15,200
2,200	9	19,800
1,500	10	15,000
8,500		67,400

Sales		
Quantity	Price	Amount
	€	€
600	12	7,200
1,000	10	10,000
1,100	13	14,300
1,300	11	14,300
1,200	14	16,800
1,000	12	12,000
1,300	15	19,500
1,100	13	14,300
8,600		108,400

Now that you know the number of units purchased and sold for the period, you can calculate the number of units of closing stock you have on hand and value the stock using FIFO.

	Units
Opening stock	2,400
Add Purchases	8,500
	10,900
Less Sales	8,600
Closing stock	2,300

Valuation of Closing Stock			
Units		€	€
1,500	@	10	15,000
800	@	9	7,200
2,300			22,200

Trading Account of White Ltd for Year Ended 31/12/2009		
	€	€
Sales		108,400
Less Cost of sales		
Opening stock	**14,400**	
Purchases	67,400	
	81,800	
Less Closing stock	**22,200**	
Cost of sales		59,600
Gross profit		57,800

Top Tip!

Include opening and closing stock and total purchases and sales in the trading account.

Question 2 – Apportionment of overheads, reapportionment of service departments, calculation of the cost of a job and explanation of over-absorption

Thompson Ltd has 2 production departments, machining and assembly, and 2 service departments, A and B.

The following are the expected overhead costs for the next period.

Overhead Total	€
Rent and rates	40,000
Factory light and heat	19,200
Factory cleaning	4,000
Factory canteen	28,800
Depreciation of equipment	32,000

The following information relates to the production and service departments of the factory.

	Production		Service	
	Machining	Assembly	Dept. A	Dept. B
Volume in cubic metres	3,000	6,000	2,000	1,000
Floor area in square metres	1,200	1,600	800	400
Number of employees	120	120	60	60
Book value of equipment	€30,000	€20,000	€10,000	€20,000
Machine hours	6,000	2,000		

Job no. 204 has just been completed. The details are:

	Direct Materials	Direct Labour	Machine Hours	Labour Hours
	€	€		
Machining	12,000	2,000	60	20
Assembly	2,200	8,400	20	10

The company budgets for a profit margin of 20%.

You are required to:

(i) Calculate the overhead to be absorbed by each department, stating clearly the basis of apportionment used

(ii) Transfer the service department costs to production departments machining and assembly on the basis of machine hours

(iii) Calculate machine-hour overhead absorption rates for the machining and assembly departments.

(iv) Compute the selling price of job no. 204

(v) Explain what is meant by 'reapportionment' of overheads

(vi) Explain what is meant by 'under-absorption' of overheads, using an example to illustrate your answer

(80 marks)

Solution

Parts (i) and (ii)

Choose a suitable basis and then divide the overhead between the different departments using this basis. **These calculations can be done quickly using a calculator and should be entered directly into the table.**

> Worked example (for illustration purposes only)
>
> Rent and rates of 40,000 apportioned using floor space; total floor space is 4,000
>
> | Machining | 1,200 | $1,200 \div 4,000 = 0.3$ of $40,000 = €12,000$ |
> | Assembly | 1,600 | $1,600 \div 4,000 = 0.4$ of $40,000 = €16,000$ |
> | Dept A | 800 | $800 \div 4,000 = 0.2$ of $40,000 = €8,000$ |
> | Dept B | 400 | $400 \div 4,000 = 0.1$ of $40,000 = €4,000$ |

| | | | | Production | | Service | |
	Basis	Overhead €	Machining €	Assembly €	Dept A €	Dept B €
Rent and rates	Floor area	40,000	12,000	16,000	8,000	4,000
Light and heat	Volume	19,200	4,800	9,600	3,200	1,600
Factory cleaning	Floor area	4,000	1,200	1,600	800	400
Factory canteen	Employees	28,800	9,600	9,600	4,800	4,800
Depr. of equipment	Book value	32,000	12,000	8,000	4,000	8,000
Costs before apportionment		124,000	39,600	44,800	20,800	18,800
Apportion Dept A	Machine hours		15,600	5,200	(20,800)	
Apportion Dept B	Machine hours		14,100	4,700		(18,800)
Total costs		124,000	69,300	54,700	0	0

> **Top Tip!**
>
> Reapportion using machine hours: divide the service departments between the machinery and assembly departments on the basis of machine hours.
>
> Example: Dept A = 20,800 ÷ 8,000 (machine hours) × 6,000 (machining) = €15,600
>
> 20,800 ÷ 8,000 (machine hours) × 2,000 (assembly) = €5,200

Part (iii)

Calculate the absorption rate using machine hours:

Machine-hour absorption rate: $\dfrac{\text{Total department overhead}}{\text{Total department machine hours}}$

Machining Dept $\dfrac{69,300}{6,000} = €11.55$ per machine hour

Assembly Dept $\dfrac{54,700}{2,000} = €27.35$ per machine hour

Part (iv)

Cost of Job No. 204		€
Direct materials	12,000 + 2,200	14,200
Direct labour	2,000 + 8,400	10,400
Overheads		
Machining	€11.55 × 60	693
Assembly	€27.35 × 20	547
Cost of job (80%)		**25,840**
Margin (20%)		**6,460**
Selling price (100%)		**32,300**

Part (v)

Reapportionment involves service departments being redivided out (reapportioned) to the production departments because costs can only be absorbed by being included in the cost of production.

Part (vi)

Too little cost has been charged to a department, i.e. budgeted costs are less than actual costs. Examples include increase in rent, increase in light and heat, etc.

Question 3 – Product costing of a particular job and explanation of the reasons for product costing

Armstrong Ltd is a small company with 3 departments. The following are the company's budgeted costs for the coming year.

Department	Variable Costs	Fixed Costs	Wage Rate Per Hour
A	€49,400	€13,000	€6
B	€57,600	€9,600	€7
C	€25,200	€7,000	€5

Budgeted hours for each department for the year are:

Department	Hours
A	1,300
B	2,400
C	1,400

General administration overheads are expected to be €30,600 for the year.

The following are the specifications for a quotation for job no. 112:

Material costs 250 metres @ €20 per metre

Labour hours required in each department are:

Department	Hours
A	55
B	90
C	35

You are required to:

(i)   Calculate the selling price of job no. 112 if the profit is set at 20% of selling price

(ii) State two reasons for product costing and explain each

Solution

Part (i)

Variable Overhead Absorption Rates		
Dept A	$\dfrac{49,400}{1,300}$	= €38 per labour hour
Dept B	$\dfrac{57,600}{2,400}$	= €24 per labour hour
Dept C	$\dfrac{25,200}{1,400}$	= €18 per labour hour

Fixed Overhead Absorption Rates		
Dept A	$\dfrac{13,000}{1,300}$	= €10 per labour hour
Dept B	$\dfrac{9,600}{2,400}$	= €4 per labour hour
Dept C	$\dfrac{7,000}{1,400}$	= €5 per labour hour

General overhead absorption rate

$$\dfrac{30,600}{5,100} = €6 \text{ per labour hour}$$

Cost of Job No. 211		
		€
Direct materials	250 × €20	5,000
Direct wages		
Department A	55 hours × €6	330
Department B	90 hours × €7	630
Department C	35 hours × €5	175
Variable overheads		
Department A	55 hours × €38	2,090
Department B	90 hours × €24	2,160
Department C	35 hours × €18	630
Fixed overheads		
Department A	55 hours × €10	550
Department B	90 hours × €4	360
Department C	35 hours × €5	175
General admin overhead	180 hours × €6	1,080
Total cost (80%)		13,180
Profit (20%)		3,295
Selling price (100%)		16,475

Part (ii)

Reasons for product costing:

- To calculate selling price; the business will not know how much to charge if they don't know how much the product cost them to produce
- To determine the value of closing stock for the trading account and balance sheet at the year end

Top Tip!

Overhead absorption rates are always based on budgeted rather than actual overhead costs. To determine whether an overhead has been under-absorbed (too little absorbed; actual greater than budgeted) or over-absorbed (too much absorbed; actual less than budgeted), it is essential that the **actual overhead incurred** is compared with the **budgeted overhead rate x actual hours incurred**. You must state clearly whether under-absorption or over-absorption has taken place and the effect that this has had on profits.

Question 4 – Under- and over-absorption (2013, HL, Section 3, Q8(c))

The information set out below refers to the budgeted and actual costs of Hake Manufacturing Ltd.

Budgeted	Direct Labour Hours	Machine Hours	Total Overhead
Department A	7,000	32,000	€160,000
Department B	48,000	7,000	€33,600
Department C	22,000	—	€46,200
Actual	**Direct Labour Hours**	**Machine Hours**	**Total Overhead**
Department A	9,000	37,000	€175,000
Department B	40,000	12,000	€29,000
Department C	27,000	—	€50,000

You are required to:

(i) Calculate departmental overhead absorption rates for Departments A, B and C

(ii) Show the under-/over-absorption by department and in total for the period and explain what these figures mean

(80 marks)

Solution

Part (i)

Under-and over-absorption of costs

Dept A	Dept B	Dept C
€160,000	€33,600	€46,200
32,000	48,000	22,000
= €5 per M.H. (2)	= €0.70 per L.H. (2)	= €2.10 per L.H. (2)

Part (ii)

	Dept A €	Dept B €	Dept C €	Total €
Actual overhead incurred	175,000 (1)	29,000 (1)	50,000 (1)	254,000
Absorbed overhead	185,000 (1)	28,000 (1)	56,700 (1)	269,700
Over-/under-absorption	10,000	(1,000)	6,700	15,700

Actual absorbed overheads

Dept A	Actual machine hours × Machine hour rate	=	37,000 x €5.00	=	€185,000
Dept B	Actual labour hours × Labour hour rate	=	40,000 x €0.70	=	€28,000
Dept C	Actual labour hours × Labour hour rate	=	27,000 x €2.10	=	€56,700

In Department A, the costs incurred were €10,000 less than expected/budgeted and therefore profits are €10,000 greater than expected.

In Department B, the costs incurred were €1,000 more than expected/budgeted and therefore profits are €1,000 less than expected.

In Department C, the costs incurred were €6,700 less than expected/budgeted and therefore profits are €6,700 greater than expected.

Overall, the costs incurred were €15,700 less than expected/budgeted and therefore profits are €15,700 greater than expected.

Marginal Costing and Cost Volume Profit (CVP) Analysis

14

Cost volume profit analysis is a tool used by management in decision-making. It studies the relationship between costs and volume and the subsequent effect on profits. Both absorption and marginal costing are used in CVP.

Marginal Costing

Marginal costing is an alternative to absorption costing. The principles of marginal costing are:

- All costs can be divided into fixed and variable elements.
- Fixed costs remain constant regardless of production levels.
- Variable costs vary in line with production; as production levels increase, so too do variable costs.
- The selling price per unit (SP) minus the variable cost per unit (VC) is known as contribution; this is the amount available to cover fixed costs and any remainder is profit.
- Thus SP − VC = Contribution; and Contribution = Fixed costs + Profit.

This relationship between sales, variable costs, fixed costs and profit can be illustrated as follows:

Marginal Costing Statement	
Sales (SP × Number of units)	X
Less Variable costs (VC × Number of units)	X
Contribution	X
Less Fixed costs	X
Profit	X

Or alternatively by the formula:

Sales (SP × Number of units) − Variable costs (VC × Number of units) − Fixed costs = Profit

Limitations of marginal costing

Marginal costing has limitations due to the fact that it is based on the following assumptions:

- Fixed costs are constant; however, most fixed costs are in fact step-fixed costs.
- Variable costs vary consistently with level of output; however, as greater amounts are produced, economies of scale can mean that costs decrease.
- Mixed costs can be divided into fixed and variable elements; however, it may not be possible to separate some costs.
- Selling price is constant; however, prices vary, for example due to discounts offered to increase sales.
- Firms sell only one product or a constant mix of products; this is rarely the case, as the majority of firms sell a variety of products.
- Production usually equals sales; any closing stock is valued using variable costs only; fixed costs are applied in full to the period in question and are not carried forward as part of closing stock.

Marginal costing compared to absorption costing

Absorption costing must be used to value closing stock as it agrees with accounting concepts and regulations. Closing stock is valued higher under absorption costing than marginal costing, as fixed costs are included in the valuation; therefore profits are higher. Marginal costing can help firms make decisions, as the effect on profit of changes in production, costs and selling price can be analysed.

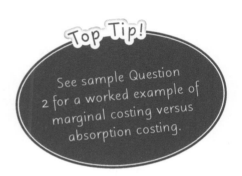

Top Tip!

See sample Question 2 for a worked example of marginal costing versus absorption costing.

Break-Even Point (BEP)

The break-even point is the level of sales at which the firm is neither making a profit or a loss; Sales = Total costs.

$$\text{Break-even point (BEP)} = \frac{\text{Fixed costs}}{\text{SP} - \text{VC}} = \text{Answer in units}$$

If you wish to calculate BEP in sales revenue, multiply the break-even point by the selling price.

Margin of Safety

This is the amount by which sales can fall before the break-even point is reached.

Margin of safety = Sales − Break-even point

If you wish to calculate the margin of safety in sales revenue, multiply your answer by the selling price.

Level of Sales Required to Reach a Target Profit

It is possible to find out what level of sales is necessary to reach a fixed profit:

$$\frac{\text{Fixed costs} + \text{Target profit}}{\text{SP} - \text{VC}} = \text{Answer in units}$$

If you wish to calculate the level in sales revenue, multiply your answer by the selling price.

Contribution/Sales Ratio

This shows contribution per unit expressed as a percentage of sales.

$$\frac{\text{Contribution (SP – VC)}}{\text{Sales}} \times 100 = \text{Answer in \%}$$

The C/S ratio can be used to calculate:

BEP in sales revenue $= \dfrac{\text{Fixed costs}}{\text{C/S ratio}}$ **Level of sales required for a target profit** $= \dfrac{\text{Fixed costs + Target profit}}{\text{C/S ratio}}$

Break-even chart

To draw a break-even chart:

1 The *x*-axis shows the number of units produced.
2 The *y*-axis shows costs and revenue in euro.
3 The fixed-cost line is a horizontal line at a specific cost level.
4 Total costs = Fixed costs + Variable costs × No. of units
5 The total-cost line begins at the fixed-cost line rather than at zero; even if no products are produced fixed costs are still incurred.
6 Total revenue = Selling price × No. of units
7 Total costs = Total revenue; this point of intersection is the break-even point.

Study Tips

- Past exam questions are based on discovering the effect that changes to any of the elements of sales volume, selling price, variable costs and fixed costs have on the original figures; this is known as sensitivity analysis.

- A marginal costing question will arise in **Section 3** for **80 marks**.

- Remember: Sales – Variable costs – Fixed costs = Profit; be able to represent this information using a marginal costing statement.

- Learn the formulae for the break-even point and the margin of safety.

- Be familiar with the theory: the principles, the limitations and how marginal costing compares to product costing.

Question 1 – Marginal costing

White Ltd produces a single product. The company's profit and loss account for the year ended 31/12/2008, during which 40,000 units were produced and sold, was as follows:

	€	€
Sales (40,000 units)		560,000
Materials	193,500	
Direct labour	126,500	
Factory overheads	35,000	
Administration expenses	54,500	
Selling expenses	49,000	458,500
Net profit		101,500

The materials, direct labour and 40% of the factory overheads are variable costs. Apart from sales commission of 5% of sales, selling and administration expenses are fixed.

You are required to calculate:
(a) The company's break-even point and margin of safety
(b) The number of units that must be sold in 2009 if the company is to increase its net profit by 15% over the 2008 figure, assuming the selling price and cost levels and percentages remain unchanged
(c) The profit the company would make in 2009 if it decreased its selling price to €13, increased fixed costs by €16,000 and thereby increased the number of units sold to 55,000, with all other cost levels and percentages remaining unchanged
(d) The selling price the company must charge per unit in 2009 if fixed costs are increased by 5% but the volume of sales and the profit remain the same
(e) The number of units that must be sold at €14 per unit to provide a profit of 20% of the sales revenue received from the sale of these same units   **(80 marks)**

Solution

Cost Classification and Preparation of Marginal Costing Statement						
Cost Classification				**Marginal Costing Statement at 40,000 Units**		
	Fixed **€**	**Variable** **€**			**€**	**Per unit** **€**
Materials		193,500				
Direct labour		126,500	Sales		560,000	14
Factory overheads (variable = 40%)	21,000	14,000	*Less* Variable costs		362,000	9.05
Administration	54,500		Contribution		198,000	4.95
Selling (variable = 5% of 560,000)	21,000	28,000	*Less* Fixed costs		96,500	
	96,500	362,000	Profit		101,500	

Part (a)

Break-even point and margin of safety:

$$\text{BEP} = \frac{\text{Fixed costs}}{\text{SP} - \text{VC}} \quad \frac{96,500}{4.95} = 19,495 \text{ units}$$

$$
\begin{aligned}
\text{Margin of safety} &= \text{Budgeted sales} - \text{Break-even point} \\
&= 40,000 - 19,495 \\
&= 20,505 \text{ units}
\end{aligned}
$$

Part (b)

Increase profit by 15%; cost levels remain constant

15% of the 2008 profit = 15% of €101,500 = €15,225

New profit = €101,500 + €15,225 = €116,725

$$\frac{\text{Fixed costs} + \text{Target profit}}{\text{SP} - \text{VC}} = \frac{96,500 + 116,725}{4.95} = 43,076 \text{ units}$$

Part (c)

Find profit, taking into account a number of changes:

Fixed costs increase by €16,000   €96,500 + €16,000 = €112,500

Selling price = €13

Number of units sold = 55,000

5% of new selling price = 0.65; new variable cost per unit €8.35 + €0.65 = €9.00

Formula

Sales – Variable costs – Fixed costs = Profit

(13 × 55,000) – (9 × 55,000) – (112,500) = Profit

€715,000 – €495,000 – €112,500 = €107,500

Profit = €107,500

Part (d)

Find new selling price:

Fixed costs increase by 5%; 5% of €96,500 = €4,825; €96,500 + €4,825 = €101,325

Profit = €101,500

Volume of sales = 40,000 units

Selling price is the unknown; let selling price be **S**; sales = 40,000 × **S** = 40,000**S**

Selling price affects variable cost, so part of variable cost is also unknown

Variable costs = (40,000 × 8.35) + (40,000 × 0.05**S**) = 334,000 + 2,000**S**

Formula
> Sales – Variable costs – Fixed costs = Profit
>
> (40,000**S**) – (334,000 + 2,000**S**) – 101,325 = 101,500
>
> 40,000**S** – 2,000**S** = 101,500 + 334,000 + 101,325
>
> 38,000**S** = 536,825
>
> **S** = €13.27

Part (e)

Number of units to provide a percentage profit of those units:

Selling price = €14

Variable cost = €9.05

Fixed costs = €96,500

Volume of sales is unknown; let the number of sales be **N**

Profit = 20% of the sales of **N** amount of units at €14 = 0.2(14 × **N**)

Formula
> Sales – Variable costs – Fixed costs = Profit
>
> 14**N** – 9.05**N** – 96,500 = 0.2(14**N**)
>
> 14**N** – 9.05**N** – 2.8**N** = 96,500
>
> 2.15**N** = 96,500
>
> **N** = 44,884 units

Question 2 – Marginal and absorption costing (2006, HL, Section 3, Q8)

A. Harrington Ltd produces a single product. The company's profit and loss account for the year ended 31/12/2005, during which 60,000 units were produced and sold, was as follows:

	€	€
Sales		720,000
Materials	288,000	
Direct labour	144,000	
Factory overheads	51,000	
Administration expenses	96,000	
Selling expenses	68,000	647,000
Net profit		73,000

The materials, direct labour and 40% of the factory overheads are variable costs. Apart from sales commission of 5% of sales, selling and administration expenses are fixed.

You are required to calculate:
  (a) The company's break-even point and margin of safety
  (b) The number of units that must be sold at €13 per unit to provide a profit of 10% of the sales revenue received from these same units
  (c) The profit the company would make in 2006 if it reduced its selling price to €11, increased fixed costs by €10,000 and thereby increased the number of units sold to 80,000, with all other cost levels and percentages remaining unchanged

B. Cloud Ltd produced 8,000 units of product Z during the year ended 31/12/2005. 6,000 of these units were sold at €6 per unit. The production costs were as follows:

Direct materials	€0.50 per unit
Direct labour	€0.80 per unit
Variable overheads	€0.50 per unit
Fixed overhead cost for the year	€3,000

You are required to:
  (a) Prepare profit and loss statements under marginal and absorption costing principles
  (b) Outline the differences between marginal and absorption costing; indicate which method should be used for financial accounting purposes and why **(80 marks)**

Solution

PART A

Cost Classification and Preparation of Marginal Costing Statement					
Cost Classification			**Marginal Costing Statement at 60,000 Units**		
	Fixed €	**Variable €**		**€**	**Per unit €**
Materials		288,000	Sales	720,000	12
Direct labour		144,000	Less Variable costs	488,400	8.14
Factory overheads (variable = 40%)	30,600	20,400	Contribution	231,600	3.86
Administration	96,000		Less Fixed costs	158,600	
Selling (variable = 5% of 720,000)	32,000	36,000	Profit	73,000	
	158,600	488,400			

5% of €12 = €0.60; €8.14 − 0.60 = €7.54

Part (a)

Break-even point and margin of safety:

$$\text{BEP} = \frac{\text{Fixed costs}}{\text{SP} - \text{VC}} \quad \frac{158,600}{3.86} = 41,089 \text{ units}$$

Margin of safety = Budgeted sales − Break-even point
  = 60,000 − 41,089
  = 18,911 units

Part (b)

Number of units to provide a percentage profit of those units:

Selling price = €13
5% of new selling price = €0.65
New variable cost per unit: €7.54 + €0.65 = €8.19
Fixed costs = €158,600
Volume of sales is unknown; let the number of sales be **N**

Profit = 10% of the sales of **N** units at €13 = 0.1(13 × **N**)

Formula	Sales − Variable costs − Fixed costs = Profit
	13**N** − 8.19**N** − 158,600 = 0.1(13**N**)
	13**N** − 8.19**N** − 1.3**N** = 158,600
	3.51**N** = 158,600
	N = 45,186 units

Part (c)

Find profit, taking into account a number of changes:

Fixed costs increase by €10,000 = €158,600 + €10,000 = €168,600

Selling price = €11

Number of units sold = 80,000

5% of new selling price = €0.55

New variable cost per unit: €7.54 + €0.55 = €8.09

Formula	Sales − Variable costs − Fixed costs = Profit
	(11 × 80,000) − (8.09 × 80,000) − (168,600) = Profit
	€880,000 − €647,200 − €168,600 = €64,200

PART B
Part (a)

Absorption Costing	€	€
Sales (6,000 × €6)		36,000 (1)
Less Production cost of 8,000 units		
Direct materials (8,000 × 0.50)	4,000 (1)	
Direct labour (8,000 × 0.80)	6,400 (1)	
Variable overheads (8,000 × 0.50)	4,000 (1)	
Fixed overheads	3,000 (1)	
	17,400	
Less Closing stock (¼ of 17,400)	(4,350) (1)	(13,050)
Profit		22,950

Marginal Costing	€	€
Sales		36,000 (1)
Less Production costs		
Direct materials	4,000 (1)	
Direct labour	6,400 (1)	
Variable overheads	4,000 (1)	
	14,400	
Less Closing stock (¼ of 14,400)	(3,600)	(10,800)
Contribution (1)		25,200
Less Fixed cost		(3,000) (1)
Profit		22,200

Part (b)

(5)

- There is a different profit figure because closing stock is valued differently.
- Marginal costing does **not** include fixed costs when costing a product, whereas absorption costing does include the fixed costs.
- Therefore closing stock under marginal costing is valued lower than under absorption costing because a share of fixed costs is included in the value of stock under absorption costing but not included under marginal costing.
- Under absorption costing, closing stock is valued at ¼ of the production cost of €17,400.
- Under marginal costing, closing stock is valued at ¼ of the production cost of €14,400.

	€
Closing stock – Absorption costing	4,350
Closing stock – Marginal costing	(3,600)
Difference	750

The profit difference is 22,950 − 22,200 = 750

Absorption costing should be used as it agrees with standard accounting practice and concepts and matches costs with revenues.

(5)

Question 3

The following is a summary budgeted profit statement for the next financial year of Whitethorn Ltd, a manufacturing company. The company is expecting to be operating at 80% of capacity.

	€	€
Sales: 20,000 units @ €25 each		500,000
Less Direct materials	90,000	
Direct wages	120,000	
Production overheads: fixed	52,000	
variable	20,000	282,000
Gross profit		218,000
Less Administration, selling and distribution costs		
Fixed	44,000	
Varying with sales volume	30,000	74,000
Net profit		144,000

Based on the above figures, Whitethorn Ltd has decided to examine 3 possible alternatives.

1. It is estimated that if selling price was reduced to €24 and an additional €4,000 was spent on advertising, demand would increase to 90% of capacity.
2. It is estimated that if the selling price was reduced by 10%, demand would increase to 95% of capacity without any increase in fixed costs.
3. Research shows that by spending €15,000 on advertising the company could operate at full capacity without any change to the selling price of €25 per unit.

You are required to:

(a) Calculate the variable cost and contribution per unit
(b) Calculate the company's break-even point and margin of safety
(c) Draw a break-even chart, showing the break-even point and the margin of safety at 20,000 units
(d) Present a marginal costing statement showing the effect of the 3 alternatives compared to the original budget and advise management which of the 3 possible plans ought to be adopted

(80 marks)

Solution

Part (a)

Cost Classification	Fixed €	Variable €
Materials		90,000
Direct wages		120,000
Production overheads	52,000	20,000
Administration, selling, distribution costs	44,000	30,000
	96,000	260,000

Marginal Costing Statement at 20,000 Units, 80% Capacity	€	Per unit €
Sales	500,000	25
Less Variable costs	260,000	13
Contribution	240,000	12
Less Fixed costs	96,000	
Profit	144,000	

Part (b)

Break-even point and margin of safety:

$$\text{BEP} = \frac{\text{Fixed costs}}{\text{SP} - \text{VC}} \qquad \frac{96,000}{12} = 8,000 \text{ units}$$

Break-even sales value = 8,000 units × €25 (selling price) = €200,000

Margin of safety = Budgeted sales − Break-even point

= 20,000 − 8,000

= 12,000 units

Part (c)

> **Top Tips!**
> - To draw any line you need 2 points; you have calculated the break-even point, so mark it on the diagram; at **8,000** the **costs** and the **revenue** both equal **€200,000**.
> - Begin the total cost line at the point 0 units and €96,000 and ensure it goes through the break-even point of 8,000 units and €200,000.
> - Begin the total revenue line at 0, and ensure it also goes through the break-even point.
> - Label your diagram clearly.

Fixed costs = 96,000 — Horizontal line

Total cost line at 8,000 = 96,000 + (8,000 × 13) = 200,000 — Draw from the fixed cost line

Total revenue at 8,000 = 200,000 — Draw from zero

> **Top Tips!**
> - The accuracy of your graph can be improved by taking a point of production both **below** and **above** the BEP and calculating the total costs and total revenue at these points, e.g.
>   Total cost at 4,000 = 96,000 + (4,000 × 13) = 148,000
>   Total revenue at 4,000 = 4,000 × 25 = 100,000
>   Total cost at 12,000 = 96,000 + (12,000 × 13) = 252,000
>   Total revenue at 12,000 = 12,000 × 25 = 300,000
> - Mark these points on the graph and ensure that when you are drawing the total cost and total revenue line it passes through not only the BEP but these points as well.

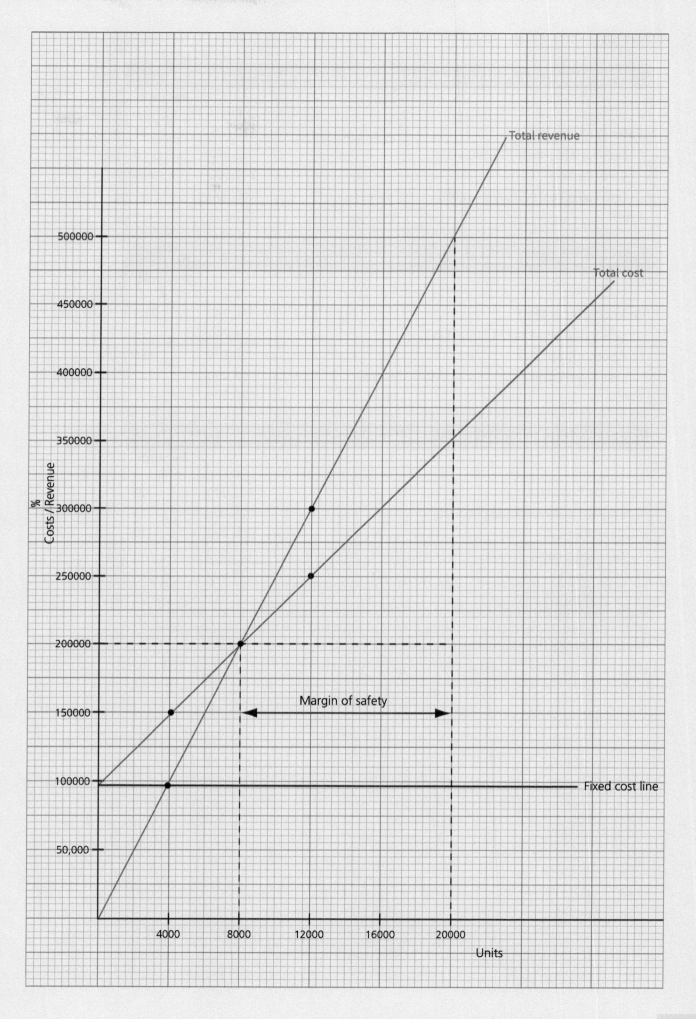

Part (d)

Option 1 Marginal Costing Statement at 22,500 Units, 90% Capacity		Per unit
	€	€
Sales (22,500 × 24)	540,000	24
Less Variable costs (22,500 × 13)	292,500	13
Contribution	247,500	11
Less Fixed costs (96,000 + 4,000)	100,000	
Profit	147,500	

Option 2 Marginal Costing Statement at 23,750 Units, 95% Capacity		Per unit
	€	€
Sales (23,750 × 22.5)	534,375	22.5
Less Variable costs (23,750 × 13)	308,750	13.0
Contribution	225,625	9.5
Less Fixed costs	96,000	
Profit	129,625	

Option 3 Marginal Costing Statement at 25,000 Units, 100% Capacity		Per unit
	€	€
Sales (25,000 × 25)	625,000	25
Less Variable costs (25,000 × 13)	325,000	13
Contribution	300,000	12
Less Fixed costs	121,000	
Profit	179,000	

Option 3 would generate a profit of €179,000, which is better than either option 1 or 2. Options 1 and 2 would only generate profits of €147,500 and €129,625 respectively. Option 3 should be adopted by management.

Budgeting 15

Learning objectives

In this chapter you will learn about:

1 Budgeting and its advantages
2 Principal budget factor
3 Production and cash budgets
4 Flexible budgeting: what it is and what it shows
5 Variances: adverse and favourable

A budget is a financial plan for a specific period of time **in the future**; it is part of the overall long-term plan of the company.

Budgetary Control

Budgetary control involves comparing actual outcomes with budgeted outcomes; any differences that arise are identified, analysed and corrected. Correcting differences could involve improving performance or resetting targets.

Advantages of Budgeting

1 The activities of management are coordinated; all staff members work towards a common goal.
2 Targets are set and act as a motivator for management and staff.
3 It ensures that management is engaged in planning its departments' activities.
4 It makes it possible to control costs by comparing budgeted to actual costs.

Principal Budget Factor

This is the factor that limits output and therefore limits expansion. It is **usually sales demand** but could be any other limiting factor, such as the availability of raw materials, the availability of skilled workers, the capacity of the factory or the availability of capital.

Production and Cash Budgets

Budgets to be prepared:

1 Sales budget

It is essential that the sales budget is accurate and reliable, as all other budgets are based on it. It shows budgeted sales revenue by multiplying expected sales by expected selling price.

Sales Budget	Product 1	Product 2
Expected sales (units)	X	X
× Expected selling price per unit (€)	X	X
Budgeted sales revenue (€)	X	X

Sales can be forecast through study of:

- Market research
- Projections of managers/sales team
- Market trends
- Past sales records
- Economic conditions
- Competitors' performance

2 Production budget (in units)

This budget shows the quantity of product that needs to be produced using expected sales and accounting for opening and closing stock.

Production Budget	Product 1	Product 2
Required sales (units)	X	X
Add Closing stock (units)	X	X
Less Opening stock (units)	(X)	(X)
Budgeted production (units)	X	X

Point to note

The production budget tells the firm how many units they are going to make; **opening stock** is already made and so **is subtracted**; **closing stock** needs to be produced so it **is added on**. This is the opposite of how we usually treat stock.

3 Raw materials purchases budget

Firstly calculate how much raw material is needed for the actual products (raw material usage). Account for the need for opening stock and closing stock to find the amount of material required and multiply this amount by the price of the raw material to calculate cost of purchases.

Point to note

As in the production budget, **opening stock** is **subtracted** (already purchased) and **closing stock** is **added on** (needs to be purchased).

Raw Material Purchases Budget (kg)	Material 1	Material 2
Materials required for production: Product 1 (kg)	X	X
Product 2 (kg)	X	X
Total materials required (kg)	X	X
Add Closing stock of raw materials (kg)	X	X
Less Opening stock of raw materials (kg)	(X)	(X)
Required purchases (kg)	X	X
× Purchases price (€)	X	X
Purchases cost (€)	X	X

4 Direct labour budget

This shows the number of hours required for production and the cost of this labour.

Direct Labour Budget	Product 1	Product 2
Budgeted production (units)	X	X
× Labour hours per unit	X	X
Budgeted labour hours	X	X
× Labour rate per hour (€)	X	X
Direct labour costs (€)	X	X

5 Factory overhead budget

This shows the indirect materials, indirect labour and other indirect costs, i.e. the variable and fixed overheads such as light and heat, maintenance, depreciation, rent and rates, etc.

Budgeted variable and fixed overheads are totalled and an appropriate absorption rate is calculated (usually based on direct labour hours).

6 Administration budget

This lists budgeted administration costs, e.g. directors' fees, stationery.

7 Selling and distribution budget

This lists budgeted costs associated with selling and distribution, e.g. advertising, commission.

8 Capital budget

This shows planned capital expenditure, e.g. purchase of fixed assets and planned capital receipts, e.g. issue of shares.

9 Cash budget

This is a plan showing expected future cash inflows and outflows for a period of time. Also included are the opening cash figure and the expected closing cash figures for the period.

Importance of a cash budget:

- It highlights whether there will be enough cash to meet the day-to-day needs of the company.
- Deficits can be anticipated and action taken, e.g. suitable finance can be arranged, expenditure can be postponed.
- Surpluses can be anticipated and the best use possible made of the funds available, e.g. short-term investment that would generate a good return.

10 Master budget

A master budget is a summary of all other budgets and provides an overview of the operations for the planned period. It is prepared after all other budgets and consists of:

- Budgeted manufacturing account (if the company is a manufacturing firm)
- Budgeted trading, profit and loss account
- Budgeted balance sheet

Flexible Budgeting

Flexible budgeting allows for an original fixed budget to be adapted to take account of changes in the level of production. Thus **budgeted costs can be compared to actual costs at the same level of activity, i.e. on a like-for-like basis**. This will help in controlling costs and in planning the company's activities, e.g. production levels.

Flexible budgeting involves:

- Classifying costs into fixed, variable or mixed costs
- Separating mixed costs into fixed and variable costs using the high/low method
- Preparing a budget at a particular level of activity
- Restating the budget using marginal costing principles, thus showing costs and profit at this level of production.

Variances

A variance is the difference between actual costs and budgeted costs.

Adverse variance occurs when **actual costs are greater than budgeted costs**.

Favourable variance occurs when **actual costs are less than budgeted costs**.

Variances can arise due to a **price variance** or a **usage variance**. Adverse variance in direct materials may arise due to an increase in the price of raw materials (price variance) or an increase in the amount of raw materials needed for production (usage variance). Similarly, favourable variance in direct labour costs may arise due to a reduction in the number of hours required for production (usage variance) or a reduction in the wage rate (price variance).

Variances need to be analysed and responsibility for the differences attributed to the correct department, e.g. an increase in the amount of raw materials used would be attributable to the production department, whereas an increase in the price of the raw materials would be the responsibility of the purchasing department.

Flexible budgeting shows:

- Variances: whether actual costs were greater or less than budgeted costs
- Costs at different levels of production
- Profit at different levels of production
- The best level of production to maximise profit

Study Tips

- A budgeting question will arise in **Section 3** for **80 marks**. A budget is a plan for a period in the future.
- There are **3** main types of budgets: production budgets, cash budgets (two types as shown in this chapter) and flexible budgets.
- **Production budgeting** involves a **budgeted manufacturing account** and a **budgeted trading account** as well as a number of production budgets.
- **Cash budget** questions can include **a budgeted profit and loss account** and a **budgeted balance sheet**.
- **Flexible budgeting** involves classifying costs into fixed, variable and mixed. It also involves the **separation of mixed costs** using the high/low method and an **understanding of marginal costing**.
- Learn the theory, in particular reasons for all types of budgeting, the principal budgeting factor, variances (adverse and favourable) and controllable and uncontrollable costs.

Question 1 – Budgeting

Bosco Ltd has recently completed its annual sales forecast to December 2009. It expects to sell 2 products – Basic at €155 and Luxury at €185.

All stocks are to be increased by 20% from their opening levels by the end of 2009 and are valued using the FIFO method.

	Basic	Luxury
Sales are expected to be	9,000 units	4,800 units

Stocks of finished goods on 1/1/2009 are expected to be:

Basic	600 units @ €130 each
Luxury	450 units @ €150 each

Both products use the same raw materials and skilled labour but in different quantities per unit as follows:

	Basic	Luxury
Material A	8 kgs	6 kgs
Material B	7 kgs	9 kgs
Skilled labour	6 hours	7 hours

Stocks of raw materials on 1/1/2009 are expected to be:

Material A	4,600 kgs @ €1.90 per kg
Material B	3,500 kgs @ €3.80 per kg

The expected prices for raw materials during 2009 are:

Material A	€3 per kg
Material B	€5 per kg

The skilled labour rate is expected to be €9 per hour.

Production overhead costs are expected to be:

Variable	€3.50 per skilled labour hour
Fixed	€133,425 per annum

You are required to:
  (a) Prepare a production budget (in units)
  (b) Prepare a raw materials purchases budget (in units and €)
  (c) Prepare a production cost/manufacturing budget
  (d) Prepare a budgeted trading account
  (e) Explain why budgeting is important

(80 marks)

Solution

Note 1

Sales Budget	Basic	Luxury
	€	€
Expected sales (units)	9,000	4,800
× Expected selling price per unit	155	185
Budgeted sales revenue (€)	1,395,000	888,000

(a) Production Budget (Units)	Basic	Luxury
Required sales	9,000	4,800
Add Closing stock (120% of opening stock)	720	540
Less Opening stock	(600)	(450)
Budgeted production	9,120	4,890

(b) Raw Materials Purchases Budget	Material A	Material B
Materials for production: Basic (9,120 × 8) and (9,120 × 7)	72,960	63,840
Luxury (4,890 × 6) and (4,890 × 9)	29,340	44,010
Total materials required	102,300	107,850
Add Closing stock of raw materials (120% of opening stock)	5,520	4,200
Less Opening stock of raw materials	(4,600)	(3,500)
Required purchases (kg)	103,220	108,550
Purchases price (€)	3	5
Purchases cost (€)	309,660	542,750

Note 2

Direct Labour Budget	Basic	Luxury	
Budgeted production (units)	9,120	4,890	
× Labour hours per unit	6	7	
Budgeted labour hours	54,720	34,230	€88,950
× Labour rate per hour (€)	9	9	
Direct labour costs	492,480	308,070	

Note 3

Costing of Closing Stock (Per Unit) for Inclusion in Budgeted Trading Account			
Basic	€	**Luxury**	€
Material A 8 kg × 3	24.00	Material A 6 kg × 3	18.00
Material B 6 kg × 5	30.00	Material B 9 kg × 5	45.00
Labour 6 × 9	54.00	Labour 7 × 9	63.00
Variable O/H 6 × 3.50	21.00	Variable O/H 7 × 3.50	24.50
Fixed O/H 6 × 1.50	9.00	Fixed O/H 7 × 1.50	10.50
	138.00		161.00

Note 4

$$\text{Fixed overhead per direct labour hour} = \frac{\text{Total fixed overhead}}{\text{Total direct labour hours}} = \frac{133{,}425}{88{,}950} = \text{€}1.50$$

(c) Budgeted Manufacturing Account

	€	€
Direct materials		
Opening stock of raw materials Basic (4,600 × 1.90)	8,740	
Luxury (3,500 × 3.80)	13,300	22,040
Purchases of raw materials (309,660 + 542,750)		852,410
		874,450
Less Closing stock of raw materials Basic (5,520 × 3)	16,560	
Luxury (4,200 × 5)	21,000	(37,560)
Cost of raw materials used		836,890
Add **Direct costs**		
Direct labour (492,480 + 308,070)		800,550
		1,637,440
Add **Factory overheads**		
Variable overheads (88,950 × 3.50)	311,325	
Fixed overheads	133,425	444,750
Cost of manufacture		2,082,190

(d) Budgeted Trading Account

		€	€	€
Sales	1,395,000 + 888,000			2,283,000
Less Cost of sales				
Opening stock of finished goods	Basic (600 × 130)	78,000		
	Luxury (450 × 150)	67,500	145,500	
Cost of manufacture			2,082,190	
			2,227,690	
Less Closing stock of finished goods	Basic (720 × 138)	99,360		
	Luxury (540 × 161)	86,940	(186,300)	
Cost of sales				(2,041,390)
Gross profit				241,610

Part (e)

Budgeting is important because:

1 The activities of management are coordinated; all staff members work towards a common goal.
2 Targets are set and act as a motivator for management and staff.
3 It ensures that management is engaged in planning its departments' activities.
4 It makes it possible to control costs by comparing budgeted to actual costs.

Question 2 – Cash budget

Smith Ltd had the following assets and liabilities at 1/1/09.

	€	€
Assets		
Stock	50,400	
Debtors	9,000	
Cash	2,500	
Rates prepaid (2 months)	600	62,500
Liabilities		
Capital		62,500

Smith expects the sales for the next 7 months to be as follows:

Jan	Feb	March	April	May	June	July
€72,000	€85,000	€98,000	€83,000	€95,000	€84,000	€102,000

(i) 80% of sales are for cash and 20% are on credit, collected 1 month after sale.

(ii) Gross profit as percentage of sales is 30%.

(iii) Smith wishes to keep a minimum cash balance of €8,000 at the end of each month.

(iv) All borrowings are in multiples of €1,000 and interest is at the rate of 12% per annum.

(v) Purchases each month should be sufficient to cover the following month's sales.

(vi) Purchases are paid for by the end of the month.

(vii) Smith purchased a new computer system on 1 January for €11,000 (depreciation 20% per annum on cost).

(viii) Smith rents the premises for €42,000 per annum, payable each month.

(ix) Wages amounting to €16,500 are paid each month.

(x) Smith purchased for cash on 1 April equipment for €15,000 (depreciation of 10% per annum on cost).

(xi) Annual rates paid from 1 March were €4,800 (paid in March).

(xii) One quarter of the money borrowed on 31/1/2008 is to be repaid at the end of June, together with interest to date on the repaid amount.

You are required to prepare a:

(a) Cash budget for the 6-month period from January to June

(b) Budgeted profit and loss (pro-forma income statement) for the 6 months ending 30/6/2009

(c) Pro-forma balance sheet at 30/06/2009 **(80 marks)**

Solution

Top Tip!

Workings should be entered into the budget as completed; the cash balance must not fall below €8,000, so each month you must determine whether it is necessary to borrow and if so how much. **Note that Smith can only borrow in multiples of €1,000.**

Note 1 Sales
80% received in the month of sale and 20% in the following month
NB: Debtors at 1/1/2009 will be paid in January (20% of December sales payable in arrears).
Calculations can be entered directly into the cash budget.
NB: Debtors at the end of June are 20% of June sales = €16,800 (include in balance sheet).

Note 2 Purchases
Sales – Profit = Purchases
100% – 30% = 70%
Purchases should be sufficient to cover the following month's sales: January purchases will be 70% of February sales and so on for the 6 months. Enter calculations directly. **Purchases made in June will be used for July sales; these are the closing stock at the end of the period.**

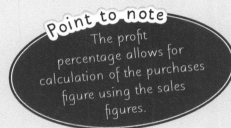

Point to note

The profit percentage allows for calculation of the purchases figure using the sales figures.

Note 3 Loan

Jan	€	Feb	€	April	€
Outflow in Jan	(23,900)	Outflow in Feb	(6,200)	Outflow in April	(15,500)
Opening cash	+2,500	Opening cash	8,600	Opening cash	20,900
	(21,400)		2,400		5,400
Need to have	8,000	Need to have	8,000	Need to have	8,000
Borrow	30,000	Borrow	6,000	Borrow	3,000

Note 4 Interest
Repaid ¼ of amount borrowed in Jan with interest:
$30,000 \div 4 = 7,500$; $7,500 \times 12\% = 900 \div 12 \times 5 = 375$; Total repaid = €7,875

> **Top Tip!**
>
> When calculating the interest, note carefully how much was borrowed and in what month, e.g. borrowing €30,000 at the end of January incurs **5 months'** interest; though ¼ of this interest is paid, the **full amount** is charged to the profit and loss account.

	€
$30,000 \times 12\% = 3,600 \div 12 \times 5$	1,500
$6,000 \times 12\% = 720 \div 12 = 60 \times 4$	240
$3,000 \times 12\% = 360 \div 12 = 30 \times 2$	60
P+L account	1,800
Paid	375
Due (BS)	1,425

Note 5 Depreciation
Computer 20% of 11,000 = 2,200 for 6 months = €1,100
Equipment 10% of 15,000 = 1,500 for 3 months = €375

Note 6 Rates
Annual rates paid on 1 March = €4,800
$4,800 \div 12 = 400 \times 4 = 1,600 + 600$ (2 months prepaid) = €2,200

(a) Cash Budget January to June

	Jan €	Feb €	March €	April €	May €	June €
Receipts						
Cash sales	57,600	68,000	78,400	66,400	76,000	67,200
Credit sales	9,000	14,400	17,000	19,600	16,600	19,000
	66,600	82,400	95,400	86,000	92,600	86,200
Payments						
Purchases	59,500	68,600	58,100	66,500	58,800	71,400
Computer system	11,000					
Rent	3,500	3,500	3,500	3,500	3,500	3,500
Wages	16,500	16,500	16,500	16,500	16,500	16,500
Equipment				15,000		
Rates			4,800			
Loan repayment with interest						7,875
	90,500	88,600	82,900	101,500	78,800	99,275
Net monthly cash flow	(23,900)	(6,200)	12,500	(15,500)	13,800	(13,075)
Loan (**N3**)	30,000	6,000		3,000		
Opening cash	2,500	8,600	8,400	20,900	8,400	22,200
Closing balance	8,600	8,400	20,900	8,400	22,200	9,125

(b) Budgeted Trading, Profit and Loss Account for 6 Months Ending 30/6/09

	€	€
Sales		517,000
Less Cost of sales		
Opening stock	50,400	
Purchases	382,900	
	433,300	
Less Closing stock (**N2**)	71,400	
Cost of sales		361,900
Gross profit		155,100
Less Expenses		
Wages	99,000	
Rent	21,000	
Rates (**N6**)	2,200	
Interest (**N4**)	1,800	
Depreciation: Computer (**N5**)	1,100	
Machinery (**N5**)	375	125,475
Net profit		29,625

(c) Budgeted Balance Sheet at 30/6/09

	Cost €	Depr. €	NBV €
Fixed assets			
Computer	11,000	1,100	9,900
Equipment	15,000	375	14,625
	26,000	1,475	24,525
Current assets			
Cash		9,125	
Debtors (**N1**)		16,800	
Closing stock		71,400	
Rates prepaid		3,200	
		100,525	
Less **Current liabilities**			
Interest due (**N4**)		1,425	99,100
			123,625
Financed by			
Loan			31,500
Capital		62,500	
Net profit		29,625	92,125
			123,625

Question 3 – Cash budgeting (2007, HL, Section 3, Q9)

Aisling Ltd is preparing to set up business on 1/7/2007 and has made the following forecast for the first 6 months of trading:

	July €	August €	September €	October €	November €	December €	Total €
Sales	425,000	440,000	580,000	590,000	600,000	652,000	3,287,000
Purchases	200,000	215,000	252,000	260,000	350,000	356,000	1,633,000

(i) The expected selling price is €50 per unit.

(ii) The cash collection pattern from sales is expected to be:

Cash customers 30% of sales revenue will be for immediate cash and cash discount of 5% will be allowed.

Credit customers 70% of sales revenue will be from credit customers. These debtors will pay their bills 50% in the month after sale and the remainder in the second month after sale.

(iii) The cash payments pattern for purchases is expected to be:

Credit suppliers 50% of the purchases will be paid for in the month after purchase, when 2% cash discount will be received.

The remaining purchases will be paid for in the second month after purchase.

(iv) Expenses of the business will be settled as follows:

Expected costs	Wages, €35,000 per month will be payable as incurred.	
	Variable overheads, €10 per unit, will be payable as incurred.	
	Fixed overheads (including depreciation), €42,000 per month, will be payable as incurred.	
Capital costs	Equipment will be purchased in July, costing €45,000, which will have a useful life of 5 years. To finance this purchase a loan of €40,000 will be secured at 10% per annum.	
	Interest will be paid monthly, but capital loan repayments will not commence until January 2007.	

You are required to:

(a) Prepare a cash budget for the 6 months July to December 2007   (58)

(b) Prepare a budgeted profit and loss account for the 6 months ended 31/12/2007   (14)

(c) Define 'cash budget' and describe two of its advantages   (8)

(80 marks)

Solution

Top Tips!

Sales

Figures can be worked out directly into the budget; take care that the description matches the figure, i.e. cash sales received; credit sales 1 month; credit sales 2 months.

An immediate cash discount is allowed on the portion of sales paid for straight off;

Discount allowed = Expense; $3,287,000 \times 30\% \times 5\% = €49,305$

Purchases

Again figures can be worked out directly into the budget.

Cash discount is received in the month after purchase; Discount received = Gain

Cash discount for December purchases is not earned until January; it is not included in the profit and loss account.

		€
Jul	$200,000 \times 50\% \times 2\%$	2,000
Aug	$215,000 \times 50\% \times 2\%$	2,150
Sept	$252,000 \times 50\% \times 2\%$	2,520
Oct	$260,000 \times 50\% \times 2\%$	2,600
Nov	$350,000 \times 50\% \times 2\%$	3,500
Discount received		12,770

Variable costs

Sales ÷ Selling price = Number of units sold

Work out variable cost per unit, e.g. July $425,000 \div 50 = 8,500$ units

Variable cost $8,500 \times €10 = €85,000$

Fixed costs

Depreciation is a **non-cash expense**; it needs to be removed from fixed costs.

Equipment cost €45,000; useful life of 5 years

$45,000 \div 5 = 9,000 \div 12 = €750$ per month; $42,000 - 750 = €41,250$

750×6 months $= 4,500$ P+L

Interest

10% of $40,000 = 4,000 \div 12$ months $\times 6$ months $= €2,000$

$4,000 \div 12 = €333$ per month

(a) Cash Budget – July to December

Receipts	Jul €	Aug €	Sept €	Oct €	Nov €	Dec €	Total €
Cash sales	121,125 (1)	125,400 (1)	165,300 (1)	168,150 (1)	171,000 (1)	185,820 (1)	936,795
Credit sales (1 mth)		148,750 (1)	154,000 (1)	203,000 (1)	206,500 (1)	210,000 (1)	922,250
Credit sales (1 mth)			148,750 (1)	154,000 (1)	203,000 (1)	206,500 (1)	712,250
	121,125	274,150	468,050	525,150	580,500	602,320	2,571,295
Payments							
Purchases	(1)	98,000 (1)	105,350 (1)	123,480 (1)	127,400 (1)	171,500 (1)	625,730
Purchases			100,000 (1)	107,500 (1)	126,000 (1)	130,000 (1)	463,500
Wages	35,000 (3)	35,000	35,000	35,000	35,000	35,000	210,000
Variable overheads	85,000 (1)	88,000 (1)	116,000 (1)	118,000 (1)	120,000 (1)	130,400 (1)	657,400
Fixed overheads	41,250 (2)	41,250 (1)	41,250 (1)	41,250 (1)	41,250 (1)	41,250 (1)	247,500
Equipment	45,000 (1)						45,000
Interest	333 (2)	333 (1)	333 (1)	333 (1)	333 (1)	333 (1)	1,998
	206,583	262,583	397,933	425,563	449,983	508,483	2,251,128
Net cash flow	(85,458) (1)	11,567 (1)	70,117 (1)	99,587 (1)	130,517 (1)	93,837 (1)	320,167
Bank loan	40,000 (1)						40,000
Opening balance		(45,458) (1)	(33,891)	36,226	135,813	266,330	
Closing balance	(45,458)	(33,891)	36,226	135,813	266,330	360,167 (2)	360,167

(b) Budgeted Profit and Loss Account for 6 months Ending 31/12/07

	€	€
Sales (65,740 @ 50)		3,287,000 (2)
Less Cost of sales		
Material	1,633,000 (1)	
Labour (6 × 35,000)	210,000 (1)	
Variable overheads	657,400 (1)	
Fixed overheads (6 × €41,250)	247,500 (1)	(2,747,900)
Gross profit		539,100
Depreciation – equipment	4,500 (1)	
Discount allowed (€3,287,000 × 30% × 5%)	49,305 (2)	(53,805)
		485,295
Add Discount received		12,770 (2)
		498,065
Less Interest		(2,000) (1)
Net profit		496,065 (2)

(c) Definition and advantages of cash budget

A cash budget is a forecast or plan of cash inflow and cash outflow over a period.

Advantages

- It highlights whether or not enough cash will be available to meet future needs.
- It helps to give advance knowledge so that overdraft can be arranged if shortfall occurs.
- It helps to predict future surpluses so that short-term investment can be made.

Question 4

Bling Ltd is planning to set up business on 1/1/2014 to manufacture a single product. Below is the sales budget for the company for the first 6 months of 2014.

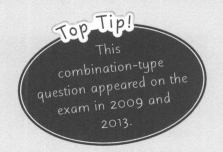

Sales Budget						
	January	**February**	**March**	**April**	**May**	**June**
Sales units	9,000	11,000	13,000	15,000	17,000	19,000
Sales revenue	€225,000	€275,000	€325,000	€375,000	€425,000	€475,000

(i) Each product unit requires 4 kg of material A, which costs €3.00 per kg.

(ii) Stocks of finished goods are maintained at 50% of the following month's sales requirement.

(iii) Stocks of raw materials, sufficient for 10% of the following month's requirements in kg, are held at the end of each month.

(iv) The cash collection pattern from sales is expected to be:

Cash customers   50% of sales revenue will be for immediate cash.

Credit customers   50% of sales revenue will be from credit customers. These debtors will pay 50% of their bills in the month after sale and the remainder in the second month after sale.

(v) One month's credit is received from suppliers.

(vi) Expenses of the business will be settled as follows:

Expected costs   Wages will be €22,000 per month, payable as incurred.

Variable overheads will be €4 per unit, payable as incurred.

Fixed overheads (including depreciation) will be €20,000 per month, payable as incurred.

Capital costs   Equipment costing €24,000 will be purchased in January and will have a useful life of 8 years. To finance this purchase a loan of €20,000 will be secured at 6% per annum interest, to be paid monthly at the end of each month. The loan will be repaid in 10 equal quarter-yearly instalments. The first will become due on 31/3/2014.

You are required to:

(a) Prepare a production budget for the 4 months from January to April 2014

(b) Prepare a raw materials purchases budget (in units and euro) for the 4 months from January to April 2014

(c) Prepare a cash budget for the 4 months from January to April 2014

(d) Prepare a budgeted trading and profit and loss account for the 4 months ending 30/4/2014 (if the budgeted cost of a unit of finished goods is €12)

(e) (i) Explain the term 'master budget'

(ii) List the components of a master budget for a manufacturing firm

Solution

Note 1   Depreciation 24,000 ÷ 8 = €3,000 per year; included in fixed costs which are payable monthly 3000 ÷ 12 = 250 per month; fixed costs 20,000 − 250 = €19,750

Note 2   **Loan**

Instalments   20,000 ÷ 10 = €2,000; instalment due on 31/3/2013

Interest   first 3 months   20,000 × 6% = 1,200 ÷ 12 = €100

remaining 1 month   18,000 × 6% = 1,080 ÷ 12 = €90

(a) Production Budget (Units)

	Jan	Feb	March	April	May
Sales	9,000	11,000	13,000	15,000	17,000
Add Closing stock	5,500	6,500	7,500	8,500	9,500
	14,500	17,500	20,500	23,500	26,500
Less Opening stock	0	5,500	6,500	7,500	8,500
Production units required	14,500	12,000	14,000	16,000	18,000

(b) Raw Materials Purchases Budget

	Jan	Feb	March	April	May
Units of production	14,500	12,000	14,000	16,000	18,000
Material required per unit	× 4	× 4	× 4	× 4	× 4
Material required for producion	58,000	48,000	56,000	64,000	72,000
Add Closing stock	4,800	5,600	6,400	7,200	
	62,800	53,600	62,400	71,200	
Less Opening stock	0	4,800	5,600	6,400	
Material required for purchases (kg)	62,800	48,800	56,800	64,800	
Price per kg (€)	× 3	× 3	× 3	× 3	
Cost of raw materials (€)	188,400	146,400	170,400	194,400	

(c) Cash Budget

	Jan €	Feb €	March €	April €	Total €
Receipts					
Cash sales received	112,500	137,500	162,500	187,500	
Credit sales – 1 month		56,250	68,750	81,250	
Credit sales – 2 months			56,250	68,750	
	112,500	193,750	287,500	337,500	
Payments					
Purchases		188,400	146,400	170,400	
Wages	22,000	22,000	22,000	22,000	88,000
Variable overheads	58,000	48,000	56,000	64,000	226,000
Fixed overheads (**N1**)	19,750	19,750	19,750	19,750	79,000
Equipment	24,000				
Loan instalment			2,000		
Interest	100	100	100	90	390
	123,850	278,250	246,250	276,240	
Net monthly cashflow	(11,350)	(84,500)	41,250	61,260	
Bank loan	20,000				
Opening balance	0	8,650	(75,850)	(34,600)	
Closing balance	8,650	(75,850)	(34,600)	26,660	

> **Point to note**
>
> The trading, profit and loss account is for a given period and it must include **all sales and purchases** that have taken place **in that period**, regardless of whether the goods have been paid for or not.

(d) Budgeted Trading, Profit and Loss Account for 4 Months Ending 30/4/2014

Sales			1,200,000
Less Cost of sales			
Opening stock		0	
Purchases		699,600	
		699,600	
Less Closing stock			
Raw materials (7,200 x 3)	21,600		
Finished goods (8,500 x 12)	102,000	123,600	
Cost of sales			576,000
Gross profit			624,000
Less Expenses			
Wages		88,000	
Variable overheads		226,000	
Fixed overheads		79,000	
Interest (**N2**)		390	
Depreciation – equipment (**N1**)		1,000	394,390
Net profit			229,610

Part (e)

See p.219.

Question 5 – Flexible budgeting

McFadden Ltd manufactures a component for the computer industry. The following flexible budgets have already been prepared for 60%, 75% and 85% of the plant's capacity.

Output levels	60%	75%	85%
Units	24,000	30,000	34,000
Costs	€	€	€
Direct materials	168,000	210,000	238,000
Direct wages	288,000	360,000	408,000
Production overheads	130,000	157,000	175,000
Other overhead costs	90,000	108,000	120,000
Administration expenses	33,000	33,000	33,000
	709,000	868,000	974,000

Profit is budgeted to be 20% of sales.

You are required to:

(a) (i) Classify the above costs into fixed, variable and mixed costs

(ii) Separate production overheads into fixed and variable elements

(iii) Separate other overhead costs into fixed and variable elements

(iv) Prepare a flexible budget for 95% activity level

(v) Restate the budget, using marginal costing principles, and show the contribution

(b) Define a favourable variance and state why favourable variances may arise in direct material costs

(c) Explain, with examples, 'controllable' and 'uncontrollable' costs   **(80 marks)**

Solution

> **Point to note**
>
> Fixed costs remain constant regardless of output; variable costs vary directly with the level of output; mixed costs are part fixed and part variable.

(a)(i) Cost Classification	
Direct materials	Variable (168,000 ÷ 24,000 = 7; 210,000 ÷ 30,000 = 7; 238,000 ÷ 34,000 = 7)
Direct wages	Variable (288,000 ÷ 24,000 = 12; 360,000 ÷ 30,000 = 12; 408,000 ÷ 34,000 =12)
Production overheads	Mixed (130,000 ÷ 24,000 = 5.42; 157,000 ÷ 30,000 = 5.23; 175,000 ÷ 34,000 = 5.15)
Other overheads	Mixed (90,000 ÷ 24,000 = 3.75; 108,000 ÷ 30,000 = 3.60; 120,000 ÷ 34,000 =3.53)
Administration	Fixed (33,000; 33,000; 33,000)

Part (a)(ii) Separate production overheads into fixed and variable using the high/low method.

Production Overheads	Units	Total Costs €
High	34,000	175,000
Low	24,000	130,000
Difference	10,000	45,000

The variable cost of €10,000 is €45,000; therefore the variable cost of 1 unit is €4.50 (45,000 ÷ 10,000).

	€ 24,000	€ 30,000	€ 34,000
Total production overhead costs	130,000	157,000	175,000
Less Variable costs (24,000 × 4.50; 30,000 × 4.50; 34,000 × 4.50)	108,000	135,000	153,000
Fixed costs	22,000	22,000	22,000

Part (a)(iii) Separate other overhead costs into fixed and variable using the high/low method.

Other Overhead Costs	Units	Total Costs €
High	34,000	120,000
Low	24,000	90,000
Difference	10,000	30,000

The variable cost of 10,000 is €30,000; therefore the variable cost of 1 unit is €3 (30,000 ÷ 10,000).

	€ 24,000	€ 30,000	€ 34,000
Total other overhead costs	90,000	108,000	120,000
Less Variable costs (24,000 × 3; 30,000 × 3; 34,000 × 3)	72,000	90,000	102,000
Fixed costs	18,000	18,000	18,000

Part (a)(iv) Prepare a flexible budget for a 95% activity level.

Activity level	95%
Units	38,000
Direct materials 38,000 × 7	€266,000
Direct wages 38,00 × 12	€456,000
Production overheads (22,000 + 38,000 × 4.50)	€193,000
Other overhead costs (18,000 + 38,000 × 3)	€132,000
Administration expenses	€33,000
Total costs (80% of sales)	€1,080,000

Part (a)(v)

Costs are 80% of sales; therefore **Sales = 1,080,000 ÷ 80 × 100 = €1,350,000**

Profit 20% of 1,350,000 = €270,000

Flexible Budget in Marginal Costing Format	€	€
Sales		1,350,000
Less **Variable costs**		
Direct materials	266,000	
Direct wages	456,000	
Variable production overheads	171,000	
Other overhead costs	114,000	1,007,000
Contribution		343,000
Less **Fixed costs**		
Production costs	22,000	
Other overhead costs	18,000	
Administration costs	33,000	73,000
Profit		270,000

Part (b) Favourable variance in direct materials

Favourable variance occurs when **actual costs are less than budgeted costs**. Variances can arise due to a price or a usage change. Favourable variance in direct materials may arise due to a decrease in the price of raw materials (price variance) or a decrease in the amount of raw materials needed for production (usage variance).

Part (c) Controllable and uncontrollable costs

Controllable costs are costs that can be controlled by the manager of the department/section. The manager can make a decision whether or not to incur the cost and how much to incur, e.g. the sales manager can decide on the commission paid to the sales team. The manager is responsible for variances in these costs. All variable costs are controllable.

Uncontrollable costs are costs over which the manager of a department/section has no control and therefore he/she cannot be held responsible for the variances in these costs. For example, the sales manager cannot control the amount of rates to be paid; this is set by the local authority.

Conceptual Framework of Accounting

16

Learning objectives

In this chapter you will learn about:
1 The fundamental accounting concepts
2 Additional concepts
3 The qualities of financial information

Accounting Concepts

Accounting concepts are rules that are followed when preparing accounts to ensure that the accounts show a 'true and fair' view of the business.

There are **4** fundamental accounting concepts:
1 Going concern
2 Accruals
3 Prudence
4 Consistency

Going concern

It is assumed that the business will continue in existence in the future, i.e. it is not going bankrupt.

Accruals

If expenses or income relate to a particular period, they are charged to that period regardless of whether or not they have been paid or received yet, e.g. the total amount incurred for light and heat must be included in the accounts for the year, even if the electricity bill will not be paid until January.

Prudence

Profits/income are not recorded in the accounts until they have been realised. However, provisions are made for any expected losses or expenses, e.g. provision for bad debts provides for the fact that some debtors may not be able to pay their debts.

Consistency

Accounts are prepared using the same accounting systems from period to period so that meaningful comparisons can be made, e.g. calculating depreciation using the same method from year to year.

Additional Concepts

Other important concepts are:

Entity concept: The business is seen as separate to the owner.

Money measurement: Accounts show only what can be measured in monetary terms.

Realisation: Profit is earned at the time of the sale rather than when the goods are paid for.

Double entry: For every debit there is a credit; when an asset increases, either a liability will increase or another asset will decrease, hence Assets = Liabilities.

Objectivity: Accounts are prepared on a factual basis and are free from the personal bias of the accountant.

Materiality: Some items purchased by the firm may be too small to be regarded as materially significant. In this case, they are not included in the balance sheet, but instead recorded as expenses in the profit and loss account. Each item should be considered relative to the size of profits. If the item is greater than 5% of profits, it should be considered material.

For financial information to be useful it must be:

Understandable: The information should be clearly presented so that those for whom it is prepared can easily understand it.

Reliable: The accounts should be true, fair and complete and should be verified by an appropriate authority e.g. auditor or director.

Relevant: The information should meet the needs of those for whom it is intended.

Comparable: Accounts should be prepared in a consistent way so that it will be possible to compare the information year on year.

Accounting bases

These are methods used to apply the accounting concepts to the accounts, e.g. to depreciate assets, the straight-line or reducing-balance method may be used.

Accounting policies

These are the specific methods chosen for use by the firm, e.g. the first-in-first-out (FIFO) method for stock valuation.

Study Tips

- The regulatory framework of accounting has been included in Chapter 10 (Published Accounts); it is necessary to be familiar with the theory in this chapter **and** the theory in Chapter 10.
- See Chapter 7 (Incomplete Records, Question 4, p.128) for a question on the accounting concepts.

STUDY GUIDE

Date:				
Time:				
Section to be revised:				

Date:				
Time:				
Section to be revised:				

Date:				
Time:				
Section to be revised:				

Date:				
Time:				
Section to be revised:				

Date:				
Time:				
Section to be revised:				

Date:				
Time:				
Section to be revised:				

Night before exam:

Sections to be revised:

STUDY GUIDE

Date:				
Time:				
Section to be revised:				

Date:				
Time:				
Section to be revised:				

Date:				
Time:				
Section to be revised:				

Date:				
Time:				
Section to be revised:				

Date:				
Time:				
Section to be revised:				

Date:				
Time:				
Section to be revised:				

Night before exam:

Sections to be revised:

STUDY GUIDE

Date:				
Time:				
Section to be revised:				
Date:				
Time:				
Section to be revised:				
Date:				
Time:				
Section to be revised:				
Date:				
Time:				
Section to be revised:				
Date:				
Time:				
Section to be revised:				
Date:				
Time:				
Section to be revised:				

Night before exam:

Sections to be revised:

S T U D Y   G U I D E

Date:				
Time:				
Section to be revised:				
Date:				
Time:				
Section to be revised:				
Date:				
Time:				
Section to be revised:				
Date:				
Time:				
Section to be revised:				
Date:				
Time:				
Section to be revised:				
Date:				
Time:				
Section to be revised:				

Night before exam:

Sections to be revised: